CHARLESTON FANCY

WITOLD RYBCZYNSKI

CHARLESTON FANCY

Little Houses & Big Dreams
in the Holy City

Yale University Press
New Haven and London

yalebooks.com/art

Set in Minion type by BW&A Books, Inc.
Printed in the United States of America by Sheridan Books

Library of Congress Control Number: 2018946045
ISBN 978-0-300-22907-3

A catalogue record for this book is available
from the British Library.

This paper meets the requirements of ANSI/NISO Z 39.48-1992
(Permanence of Paper).

10 9 8 7 6 5 4 3 2 1

Jacket illustration: (front) Charleston single house, 100 Queen
Street, built c. 1870. Drawing by Ralph Muldrow;
(back) Mary Turner House, Charleston, built 2012. Image
courtesy New World Byzantine.

To Historic Renovations of Charleston,
New World Byzantine, Urban Ergonomics,
and little builders everywhere

Fancy noun (pl. fancies)
1 a feeling of liking or attraction.
2 the faculty of imagination.
3 (in sixteenth and seventeenth cent. music) a composition
for keyboard or strings in free or variation form.

—*New Oxford American Dictionary*

Contents

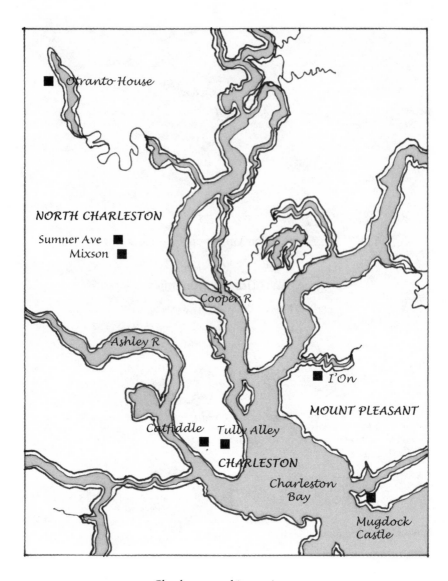

Charleston and its environs

Introduction

Cities endure. Nine out of ten seventeenth-century Londoners lost their homes in the Great Fire, yet they rebuilt and the city pulled through; Berlin was devastated by the Second World War and divided during the Cold War, yet it stubbornly persevered; New Orleans was decimated by Hurricane Katrina, there was talk of moving the city, yet it stayed put and emerged smaller but unbowed. "Men did not love Rome because she was great," observed the British essayist G. K. Chesterton. "She was great because they had loved her." He meant that great cities are the result of deeply felt attachments, not merely practicalities. "Go back to the darkest roots of civilization and you will find them knotted round some sacred stone or encircling some sacred well," he wrote. "People first paid honor to a spot and afterwards gained glory for it."

Picking the right spot is important. When a group of British colonists arrived on the Carolina coast in April 1670, they first occupied an inland site on the western bank of a broad river. It proved an unhealthy location, and ten years later, they moved to a breezy peninsula at the river's mouth. "The cituation of this Town is so convenient for public Commerce that it rather seems to be the design of some skilfull Artist than the accidentall position of nature," wrote one of the settlers. "There is a clean landing the whole length of the Town and also a most plesant prospect out to the Sea." The settlement grew, the landing was turned into a handsome esplanade, and Charles Town evolved into Charleston.

Many consider Charleston to be one of the most beautiful small cities in the United States. Its charm is elusive. There are no memorable public squares and few parks; the most prominent memorial is a column with a controversial statue of a dour John C. Calhoun, that ardent defender of slavery. There are some interesting old buildings, especially churches, but this is not a city of iconic monuments. Yet as you walk around—and this is a walker's paradise—the place grows on you. It is, above all, the everyday buildings that impress, less a matter of style than of human scale. Shaded verandas, or piazzas, as they are called locally, abound. Repetitive row houses, characteristic of northern cities, are absent. Instead, the typical Charleston house, the so-called single house, stands free with space around it, creating a lively streetscape and providing passersby with glimpses of green gardens and the ever-present palmettos.

The builders who create—and preserve—a city's everyday fabric are as important as the founders and city fathers, for it is *continuity* that is the key to effective city building: the efforts of successive generations, using different means, pursuing different goals, perhaps even different dreams, but sharing an affection for the place—and for what has gone before. Everyday builders tend to stay in the background. "The early history of architects in Charleston and its neighborhood consists largely of blanks, most of which can be filled only with question marks," wryly observed Beatrice St. Julien Ravenel, an early local historian. The origins of the ubiquitous single house, for example, remain murky. Questions such as who built the first one and when, whether it was a local invention or a Caribbean import, and why this useful model was not repeated elsewhere remain unanswered.

"Art is a result, not a product," wrote Ralph Adams Cram, a leading American architect of the early 1900s, who makes more than one appearance in these pages. Buildings are the result of many things: of time and place, of regional culture, and even, to use a word no longer fashionable, of civilization. And of people. My Charleston story involves a group of present-day builders: a self-taught lover of Byzantine architecture, an Air Force pilot, a trained architect who is also an accomplished craftsman, a developer who calls himself a civic artist, and a bluegrass mandolin player who dreams of Palladio. A motley crew, brought together by circumstance, curiosity, friendship, and love of their adopted city. And by love of building—all sorts of building: a bedecked Moorish house, an onion-domed Orthodox church, a spooky Victorian castle, and a latter-day medieval compound. My protagonists' quirky approach to architecture and urbanism exhibits a kind of amateur mastery that runs against our cultural obsession with globe-trotting architect-for-hire expertise. Call it locatecture.

I remember the iconic closing line of a 1960s television police drama: "There are eight million stories in the naked city." My narrative leans on vignettes rather than the big picture, on anecdotes rather than statistics, and on journalism rather than history. Yet it touches on several important questions: the challenges of renewing old neighborhoods, the art of creating brand-new places, the craft of building in an industrial age, the pros and cons of historic preservation, and the thorny question of architectural style. The answers demonstrate how living in a place affects people and how they in turn alter their surroundings; how an old city remakes itself by invention as well as replication; and how successful urban places are produced—intricately, slowly, and lovingly, by individuals, one piece at a time.

All cities suffer periodic calamities, and Charleston has had more than its share: a naval bombardment during the Revolutionary War, a two-year Civil War siege, a disastrous conflagration, a catastrophic earthquake, regular floods, and periodic hurricanes that have left thousands homeless. So, it's fitting that my story begins with a fire.

Part I

George's House

The education of a master builder,
or how I learned to love Byzantine

Ten days before Christmas 2015, George Holt's house burned down. A mutual friend e-mailed me a photograph: charred walls, scorched window frames, puddles of water on the floor. A pile of rubble filled the doorway of what had been the living room—it appeared that the roof had collapsed. I recognized a desk among the debris. The last time I had seen it, the surface had been covered with books and architectural drawings. Now it lay atop the pile with its cabriole legs sticking straight up into the air like a dead animal.

The painted surfaces of the wooden columns supporting an arcade in the atrium were blistered from the heat. Shafts of daylight streaked across the blackened walls. A marble bust that had stood on the windowsill lay in pieces on the flagstone floor, which was littered with broken glass. The sad scene had a curious poetry. "It probably sounds strange," George e-mailed to me, "but when emotions are set aside I find the remains of the principal rooms to be rather attractive." The great French architect Auguste Perret once observed, *"L'architecture, c'est ce qui fait les belles ruines"*—Architecture is what makes beautiful ruins. He meant that a good building's structural bones should be evident even—perhaps especially—in a ruined state. George's house, with its domed ceilings and arched colonnades, had reminded me of a film set for *The Thief of*

George Holt's house: an ancient atrium in old Charleston.

Baghdad; now it could convincingly serve for *The Last Days of Pompeii.*
Neither analogy was quite right, yet the distinct feeling of a place from
long ago had been heightened by the corrosive effects of the fire. The
house had always looked old—now it looked ancient.

George's house is in downtown Charleston, South Carolina. The
first time I approached it I wasn't impressed. The building stood at
the end of a back lane, and its undecorated plastered exterior, stained
and unkempt, resembled a down-at-heel body shop. The entrance was

through a pair of blank wooden doors, flanked by columns supporting a protective canopy in the form of a planter containing spiky cactuses— a Daliesque hint that all was not what it appeared to be. Inside, I was brought up short . . . to avoid stepping into the swimming pool that occupied most of the entrance hall. (Two firemen rushing into the burning building were less fortunate and fell into the water.) The pool was surrounded by an arched colonnade, the gilded wooden columns topped by chunky masonry imposts decorated with intricate filigree. Murky daylight filtered in from a skylight and heightened the effect of an archaic atrium. A pair of Venetian gondola lanterns provided additional illumination.

Beyond the atrium, a set of doors led to the main living quarters, an extremely tall room covered by a large dome. Four smaller domes in the corners completed the quincunx arrangement. The central dome was supported on triangular curved surfaces that architects call pendentives, a way of covering a square plan with a round dome. The pendentives rested on arches supported by tall wooden columns with chunky carved imposts, similar to the ones in the atrium. One side of the room was dominated by a massive fireplace, above which hung a gilt-framed mirror. Narrow arched windows on the other two walls overlooked tiny courtyards, light-wells really, one of which contained a carp pond. I could hear the trickling sound of a fountain. A couch, a velvet-covered chaise longue, and a cabriole-legged desk completed the furnishings. A ponderous bowl-shaped chandelier with candles was suspended from the domed ceiling and reminded me of a sanctuary lamp. Was this a living room or a converted chapel?

The room was a jumble of books, architectural drawings, and models; a small drafting table stood in the corner. A kitchenette and a small bedroom stood off to one side. Messy and unkempt and at the same time theatrical, the atmosphere reminded me of the Palazzo Fortuny in Campo San Beneto in Venice, the preserved home and studio of Mariano Fortuny, which I visited in the 1980s, before its current renovation. There, a rickety stair in an aged courtyard led to a dark interior cluttered with paintings, photographs, and models of stage sets. The multitalented Spanish-born artist was one of the early twentieth century's great fashion designers; his hand-pleated, body-clinging, jewel-toned gowns, made of materials manufactured in his own Venetian workshop, are at once simple and seductive, modern and ancient. To Marcel Proust the gowns suggested "Venice loaded with the gorgeous East from which they had been taken."

George built his house from scratch in 1996, but he told me that visitors often assumed that it was a converted old building. This mistaken impression was due to the general air of neglect, the rough plastering, and here and there a makeshift detail, a column out of plumb, a door not quite centered on a wall. George had worked hard to create this effect. "I like a sense of crudeness," he told me. "I noticed that when people come into the house they seem to unwind, slouching, taking it easy. The atmosphere makes them relax." He described it as a young person's architecture. "People react differently to my house," he said, "but the people who really, really like it are the college students." I'm not sure how my Penn students would react. Ivy League architecture schools are wedded to the avant-garde, and George's romantic exploration of historical themes and temporal decay would probably strike them as idiosyncratic, if not downright bizarre. More's the pity.

George Holt was born in Madrid. His mother was Spanish, and his father, who had served in the merchant marine in the Second World War, was in the U.S. Navy, posted to Spain. For the next fifteen years, young George lived on a succession of naval bases in Spain, Turkey, Scotland, and Colombia, as well as Key West, Norfolk, and Newport. His father's last posting was Charleston, and when he retired as a master chief petty officer, that is where the family settled—by now George had two younger brothers and a sister. They lived in the suburbs, where his parents started a business selling real estate.

George adjusted to life in the United States. After finishing high school, he attended the College of Charleston, majoring in Spanish, an undemanding choice since he already spoke the language. He moved downtown. This was the late 1970s. "Downtown Charleston was dangerous then, but was also filled with penniless artists and every other variety of alternative lifestyle–type person one could imagine," he remembers. "The numerous crumbling and many unsafe, but still fine buildings provided very cheap shelter and attracted the sort of people I was able to learn much from. My parents being horrified only added to the cachet." He rented a room in a restored carriage house owned by Randolph Martz, a young architect who specialized in restoration work. "He would let me use his library, and I'd hang out and watch him work," George said. "He was the first architect I had ever met, and he started me thinking about buildings, especially old buildings." It didn't occur to George to enroll in an architecture program, however. "I was interested in history and old buildings. What would I have learned in architecture school?"

George was not academically inclined, and he dropped out of his final college year. He applied for a job in a bookstore, which is where he met Cheryl Roberts, who was the manager. "Though she was six years older than me, we became pretty good friends," George says. Cheryl had been born in Birmingham, Alabama, where her father managed canteen services in a Veterans Administration hospital. In 1966, he was transferred to a new VA hospital in Charleston, where the family lived for three years, until her father, who had health problems, retired and moved the family to Boca Raton. Cheryl was in her last year of high school. "She hated high school and was extremely bored," her sister told me, "and truly believed that it was holding her back from life." Cheryl agreed to her parents' demand that she get a GED, left school, and got a job managing a local convenience store. This not only provided her the experience of dealing with customers and employees: the store was totally computerized—an early experiment. When her father passed away, her mother decided to move back to Charleston, and Cheryl accompanied her. She quickly got a job managing a chain of local bookstores, an attractive position since she was an avid reader. George was a reader, too. He and Cheryl were both dropouts, and were both uncomfortable with formal education. In that regard, they were throwbacks to an earlier American type: the self-made original.

The pair discovered a shared desire to experience life in a big city. Cheryl knew a high school classmate living in Chicago. "I really wanted to go to New York, but my mother would have had a fit," says George. "Chicago seemed a less threatening choice." In Chicago, Cheryl got a job as assistant manager of a giant bookstore on Michigan Avenue. On the strength of a previous summer job in a Charleston hotel, George worked behind the front desk of the nearby Drake Hotel. They shared an apartment in the Loop, near the Chicago Theatre. "I liked Chicago, but I couldn't stand the weather," George recalls. "By October it was already colder than it ever got in Charleston. In winter there were ropes on the sidewalks to keep you from falling on the ice." The following year, George moved back to Charleston; Cheryl wasn't happy about his departure, but stayed on.

In Charleston, George got another hotel job. "This was my starving artist period. I wanted to be a painter. I did sell some paintings, but basically I was really poor." After two years of the bohemian life, he gave in to his parents' demands and joined them in their real estate business. He describes the experiment as "a miserable failure." He got his realtor's license, but in one year made only three sales. He disliked the suburbs, the houses, and the work. By now, he was twenty-five. "What do you really want to do?" his patient father asked. George said that he wanted to buy an old house in downtown Charleston, fix it up, and sell it. "But you've never done this kind of work," his father objected." "I'll learn," said George. His father generously lent him $10,000 to get started.

It was at this time that George met Jerry Moran, a young Air Force captain stationed in Charleston. Jerry had been a flier since adolescence. As a teenager growing up on Long Island, he had worked after school in a grocery store to save up enough money to take flying lessons at a nearby airport. "I actually started flying before driving," he recalls. "I could only afford one lesson a month, but that convinced me that I wanted to fly for a living." Since most pilot jobs required a four-year college degree, Jerry enrolled at Hawthorne College, a small liberal arts college in New Hampshire that not only had courses in aviation, but also its own air strip and a collection of light planes as well as two DC-3s. Jerry, who majored in psychology, became a talented flier; he was awarded a scholarship and earned extra money as a flight instructor. When he graduated in 1980, the economy was in deep recession, and the commercial airlines were laying off pilots, so he enlisted in the Air Force. Jerry attended officer training school, graduated with distinction, and was given his pick of plane and base. "I wanted to fly heavy jets, C-141s, and there were only

A typical small Charleston single house: what looks from the street like a front door actually opens onto a veranda.

five bases to choose from. The 437th Military Airlift Wing in Charleston flew the most interesting missions, all over the world. I had never been to the city but I knew about it. One summer at Hawthorne I lived in a house that belonged to a retired Wellesley professor who had a winter home in Charleston. She was a sweet old lady and she told me stories about the city, so I knew it was an interesting place."

George and Jerry met in a downtown bar. It was later that they discovered a shared interest in building. "I was thirteen when my family moved from the Bronx to an old house in Garden City on Long Island," says Jerry. "The basement was unfinished and I spent hours there examining the construction, the ducts, and the plumbing; I was fascinated by how it all worked. That led to high school classes in architectural drafting." At home, Jerry worked with his father, a New York police captain, on home improvement projects; his best friend's father had a cottage in the Catskills, and Jerry spent a summer helping to build an addition. He also had a summer job as a carpenter's assistant. "I hadn't really thought about construction since that time, but George's plan to start a renovation business brought it all back," says Jerry, who became increasingly involved in the new venture. In due course, he sold his suburban house near the air base and moved into the city. "Downtown Charleston looked like the Civil War ended twenty years ago, but I liked the old buildings. It was more interesting than the suburbs."

George introduced Jerry to Cheryl, who had returned to Charleston from Chicago and was now managing a large toy store. Dissatisfied with her job, she decided to join George and Jerry. The trio had complementary skills: George was the artist; Cheryl had the management background (she also got her realtor's license); and Jerry not only had experience in building and a pilot's attention to detail but also, thanks to the sale of his suburban home, an actual credit rating. But that may be hindsight. According to George, "There was no big plan; it just sort of happened."

In 1985, George came across a listing for an old house for sale that had been repossessed by the Veterans Administration. It was on Perry Street in a rundown neighborhood on the edge of downtown. Jerry submitted a successful bid for $37,000. "I think as an active-duty officer I got preferential treatment," he says. Jerry, George, and Cheryl shared the investment and improvement costs. The renovation involved putting in new services, upgrading the kitchen and bathrooms, and plastering and painting. "I remember installing wainscoting on the staircase and laying tile in the bathroom with Cheryl," says Jerry. To save money, they lived in the house while doing the work.

The Perry Street house was a so-called single house, a type unique to Charleston that emerged in the early eighteenth century, though exactly how and why remains obscure. Single houses are narrow two-story buildings—a single room wide, hence the name—with the gable end facing the street, and a side yard overlooked by piazzas, or verandas, on both floors. This arrangement allows cross ventilation, which suits the hot climate, and is adaptable to a variety of sizes, ranging from grand mansions with tall ceilings and deep piazzas to modest homes such as the house on Perry Street. The piazzas face south or west, depending on the street orientation. Single houses are usually built in rows, and "North side manners" proscribe peeking out of windows into your neighbor's adjacent side yard. Single houses share an unusual feature: what looks like the front door from the street actually opens onto the piazza—the real front door is farther on, out of sight, a polite illusion that seems to characterize this courteous but private city.

Renovating old houses was hardly an original idea in Charleston in the 1980s. Thanks to a dynamic new mayor, a world-famous music festival, and an increase in tourism, Charleston was experiencing a small real estate boom. The city had a long history of historic preservation, but Mayor Joseph P. Riley, Jr., had brought new energy to the conservation of Charleston's architectural heritage. The historic center of the city, unlike most southern cities, had escaped the ravages of 1950s urban renewal, and its beautiful antebellum houses had become a major cultural attraction, not only for tourists but for wealthy second-home buyers. The main building activity was in the old historic district, but a few adventurous souls were buying old houses in rundown neighborhoods farther north on the peninsula. One of these people was George's younger brother, Bob. Bob was a successful businessman who had sold his book-scanning start-up to Amazon, and was now investing in local real estate. His contractor was a talented craftsman who turned out to be a poor manager, and so Bob hired Cheryl to put things in order. "She was so effective that after the job was done, my brother, who had decided to get out of the construction business, fired all the employees and gave her the company," George recounts. "That's how Cheryl, Jerry, and I became Historic Renovations of Charleston."

Their next project was more ambitious: a large, derelict house on President Street, not far from Perry Street. The two-story house had an apartment on each floor and a carriage house in the rear. In 1988, George bought the property, and Jerry financed the construction with a veteran's loan; he had completed his seven-year active-duty obligation and, faced with promotion to a desk job, had retired from the Air Force and was now flying jumbo jets for Delta. Cheryl moved in to the carriage house, which was finished first, while George and Jerry, who remained on Perry Street, worked on the wood-frame clapboard house in the front.

It was a complicated project. The house had been built in the 1850s and needed a new foundation, so they raised the entire building up in the air and built a walk-out basement underneath. When the house was finished, George and Jerry moved in, Jerry upstairs and George down. They kept the Perry Street house as a rental.*

The following fall, South Carolina was threatened by Hurricane Hugo. Much of the city was evacuated, but because of reports that the storm had weakened, George, Cheryl, and Jerry decided to stay. Unexpectedly, the storm increased to a Category 4—aimed directly at the city—but by then it was too late to leave. The trio spent a harrowing night fighting the elements. Hugo turned out to be the most intense tropical cyclone to strike the East Coast north of Florida since 1900, and the high winds tore the roof off the Perry Street house and flooded the carriage house. After the storm, as Charlestonians had done innumerable times before, the trio picked up the pieces and repaired the damage. "We stayed in that house for five years," George says. "That way we weren't under pressure to find a buyer." He had an unconventional theory of economics: "I've learned that if you need money you don't get it, but if you don't need it, you find it, or it finds you."

George taught himself construction. Like all small builders, he relied on subcontractors for specialized work such as electricity, plumbing, and cabinetry, but used his own crew of about half a dozen laborers for the main construction work. "They were mostly young boys in their twenties, former college students, dropouts, skateboarders. They were artistically motivated, but nobody had any real skills." It was an unconventional building site. George was a night owl and slept late, so work started in mid-morning. Jerry helped out when he was not flying, and it was left to Cheryl to oversee the day-to-day operations. "She was a very strong presence," remembers Jerry. "Her special qualification for running the crew was brute spunk. She quaked to nobody and prevailed over everyone. She was at once the loving den mother and the chief disciplinary officer and paymaster."

---

* When Jerry refinanced the Perry Street house he paid George and Cheryl their share and kept it as a rental, eventually selling the house to a tenant.

In addition to restoring old houses for resale, Historic Renovations of Charleston took on small construction jobs for individual homeowners. George learned from the experience. "Expectations are always the biggest area of misunderstanding and contention on a building project, particularly when the descriptions of particular work are subjective," he explained. "We found that some clients expected paté when they were only paying for cat food." To avoid such misunderstandings, George came up with an original solution. He offered clients three options in selected items for materials and workmanship: good, better, and best. For example, "good" plastering meant two minor imperfections per hundred square feet, "better" meant one, and "best" meant none—perfection. "Most clients selected the 'better' category, some chose 'good,' but very few chose 'best,'" he said. "Cheryl and I intentionally set the price of the last high to allow for hiring the most expensive craftsmen—or doing the job twice."

George combined the roles of designer and builder. Most architects are constrained by having to fully document their ideas on paper before construction begins, so making subsequent changes is time-consuming and expensive. By contrast, George was able to make changes on the spot. Young architects are also hindered by their frequently adversarial relationship with the contractor, who is generally more experienced in practical matters, and is often loath to implement unfamiliar details. George, on the other hand, worked with his own hand-picked crew. "My guys knew what I liked. If I asked for a certain historical detail, for example, they understood what I was talking about." Thus he was able to do unconventional things such as casting special column capitals, reusing decorative moldings that he found in the trash, and finishing the floor of a living room with fragments of marble wainscoting that he retrieved from a nearby demolition site. He could also realize the kind of rough details that he liked. "I didn't discuss the roughness at length with our clients, but I did describe it in the contract, otherwise they might think I'd made a mistake."

George's use of recycled materials reminds me of another self-taught master builder, Addison Mizner, who built seaside villas for wealthy winter residents in Palm Beach, Florida, in the 1920s. His designs are a picturesque hybrid of Mediterranean motifs loosely based on medieval Moorish Spain. Mizner was not interested in historical verisimilitude, as he explained:

> Most modern architects have spent their lives in carrying out a period to the last letter and producing a characterless copybook effect. My ambition has been to take the reverse stand—to make a building look traditional and as though it had fought its way from a small unimportant structure to a great rambling house that took centuries of different needs and ups and downs of wealth to accomplish. I sometimes start a house with a Romanesque corner, pretend that it has fallen into disrepair and been added to in the Gothic spirit, when suddenly the great wealth of the New World has poured in and the owner has added a very rich Renaissance addition.

To achieve this layered effect, Mizner made frequent shopping trips to Europe, particularly Spain, and brought back antique architectural fragments that he incorporated into his projects; he had a warehouse full of old terra-cotta tiles and wrought-iron railings, reused paneling, reclaimed limestone mantelpieces, and carved ceilings. Mizner favored a weathered look, which he achieved by smudging freshly painted walls with burning tar paper, and by having his workers tramp up and down newly poured concrete steps in hobnailed boots to create the effect of age. George's house, though hardly as expansive as Mizner's mansions, had a similar well-worn character. Not architecture as frozen music, in Goethe's oft-repeated phrase, but as frozen time.

George described the style of his own house as tenth-century Byzantine. He mentioned this matter-of-factly, the way someone else might say Victorian or American Colonial. What attracted him to Byzantine? As a boy, he had spent several happy years in Istanbul ("My mother tells me that I was fluent in Turkish"). The Byzantine mosaics of medieval churches he later saw in Rome resonated with him. Perhaps he was just bored with the polite American version of Georgian that was de rigueur in Charleston. Or perhaps, as a cultural misfit, he was drawn to what was an outsider's style.

The Byzantine Empire began in the fourth century when the Roman emperor Constantine moved his capital to Byzantium, which he renamed Constantinople. That city, which became the largest and wealthiest in Europe, developed a distinctive style of architecture, a blend of classical Roman elements—columns and arches—with an Oriental sensibility that favored low-relief decoration and walls covered with gilded and colored-glass mosaic murals. Byzantine builders replaced the traditional Greek orders—Doric, Ionic, Corinthian—with a variety of abstract geometrical patterns and Christian symbols. Above all, they perfected dome construction. Hagia Sophia, begun in the sixth century, had the largest masonry dome in the world until Brunelleschi's dome in Florence was completed in 1436.

At its height, the Byzantine Empire encompassed Greece, Italy, and the Middle East, and stretched as far as North Africa and Spain. The Byzantine architectural style spread with it—San Vitale in Ravenna and the Basilica of San Marco in Venice are two famous examples. Although architecture in Europe evolved into Romanesque, Gothic, and ultimately Renaissance classicism, the Byzantine style was slow to change, and traditional Byzantine motifs remained popular in the Orthodox countries of eastern Europe and influenced early Islamic building. But Byzantine never entered the architectural mainstream. In the nineteenth century, there was a small revival in Europe and Russia. In the 1920s, Byzantine Revival buildings appeared in the United States: the Catholic Basilica of the National Shrine of the Immaculate Conception in Washington, D.C., and Temple Emanu-El in San Francisco are prominent examples. On the whole, however, revivalist American architects tended to ignore Byzantine in favor of more conventional historical styles such as Gothic and Renaissance classicism.

Ralph Adams Cram and Bertram Grosvenor Goodhue were two exceptions. Although they are popularly associated with Gothic Revival churches, notably Saint Thomas and Saint John the Divine in Manhattan, and Collegiate Gothic buildings at West Point and Princeton, they were responsible for several notable Byzantine buildings. Goodhue,

George modeled his domed living room on
an 11th-century Byzantine church.

always stylistically adventurous, incorporated Byzantine mosaics and
a gilded dome in the Church of Saint Bartholomew on Park Avenue,
and Cram used Byzantine motifs in the new Rice University campus in
Houston.

Neither Cram nor Goodhue had firsthand experience of Byzantine architecture, but in 1929, at the age of sixty-five, Cram was invited
by a wealthy friend to go on a yacht cruise of the eastern Mediterranean,

which included a visit to recently renamed Istanbul. Although he found the city "sordid and degraded, harsh with the tumult of trolley cars and dilapidated automobiles," he was overcome by Hagia Sophia, which he described as "the greatest architectural work of man." The deeply religious Cram even allowed that this eastern manifestation of Christianity might be superior to his beloved Gothic: "What sets Hagia Sophia apart and raises it to architectural supremacy, is the unique genius, the creative imagination that assembled these domes and vaults and arcades in perfect unity, with an integrity of form, a perfection of articulation, a majesty in point of dimensions, together with a triumphant religious and emotional quality beyond all comparison." Shortly after returning from his Mediterranean cruise, Cram designed Christ Church United Methodist on Park Avenue in a style that he described as "late Hellenic Byzantine." Although the exterior of the church is less flamboyant than Saint Bartholomew, the interior, with its gilded apsidal half-dome, is similarly finished in multicolored marbles and Venetian mosaic tiles.

Like Cram and Goodhue, George taught himself the rudiments of the style. "When I became interested in Byzantine architecture, I couldn't find any books in local bookstores," he told me. "This was before the Internet. A friend would borrow books from the Clemson library, and I spent hours at Kinko's photocopying." While he was designing his house, George thought he should see the real thing, so he, Cheryl, and Jerry went to Istanbul on vacation. It would be the first of many visits to the city, "to worship at the altar of Byzantine architecture," as George put it. He had not been in Istanbul since he was a child, and unlike Cram, he loved its seedy, dirty, slightly rundown quality, its state of disrepair. They visited many buildings, starting with the great church of Hagia Sophia— Holy Wisdom. "The first time Cheryl saw the building she burst into tears. It was so moving," he remembers. "For me, too, Byzantine architecture is always an emotional experience." But it was another building that would have a more immediate influence on George: the Church of the Holy Savior in Chora, a small eleventh-century building whose *naos*, or sanctuary, consisted of a square room surmounted by a round dome. "The main space was only about thirty feet square, and I thought to myself, this could easily be a living room."

George's domestic version of Byzantine was considerably less elaborate than Cram's or Goodhue's. Of course, a house is not a place of worship, but the difference ran deeper than simply function. George's use of columns that were slightly out of plumb, and of a barely perceptible asymmetry, were not efforts at artificial aging but rather an attempt to incorporate what he saw as an essential architectural quality. He recounted visiting the Basilica of Santa Prassede, a ninth-century church in Rome decorated with Byzantine mosaics. The work of the early Christian builders, who were rediscovering the lost art of classical architecture, forgotten after centuries of barbarian invasions, is often described as crude and lacking virtuosity. That wasn't the way that George saw it. "At first I was disappointed by what appeared to be a clumsy and ill-formed imitation of ancient Roman architecture," he said. "But I changed my mind after a second visit when I realized that the builders had put a lot of love into their work. It was as if they were trying to make something and weren't sure exactly how to do it. The architecture wasn't perfect, but it was that lack of finesse that made it endearing." His own house had a similar sense of human frailty.

Several months after the fire, I heard from George. I had e-mailed him, asking him how he intended to rebuild. "I plan on renovating the house with the main rooms unchanged," he answered. "I'm still amazed by how much survived the seven-hour-long fire; there is surprisingly much left to work with. The original construction drawings of the house seem to have perished in the fire, and I never had them digitized, so everything will have to be measured anew before I can work on the renovation." He added that his insurance company was dragging its feet, so it might be some time before he could start.

Several weeks later, this e-mail: "The clean-up is beginning this weekend because I can't continue to just sit by waiting for the insurance company. The renovation plans can't commence until all debris is removed from the building so that my engineer can conduct a thorough structural evaluation. Only a small portion of the cement block walls visibly failed, where the fire was hottest, but of course spalling has occurred in a much larger area. It's been very interesting to compare levels of damage in areas very close to one another. I expect to learn many things in this process."

That was the builder speaking. At the same time, the artist was looking over his shoulder. "I've decided to not conceal the visible effects of the fire in those areas that won't require complete replacement during the renovation work," George wrote. "The heat created some remarkable color changes in the interior stucco . . . and in areas where missing stucco can be patched there'll be no attempt made for the new work to match the old. It feels more honest to accept the visible results of the fire despite my wishing that it had never occurred." And a week later: "The rubble from the main rooms is gradually disappearing. The rooms are getting lovelier as more debris is removed."

I flew down to Charleston to see for myself. George was living in a tiny ground-floor apartment, across the lane from the ruin. He wasn't home when I arrived, and while I was waiting, I noticed several objects retrieved from the fire drying out on the stoop: a water-damaged sketchbook, a pair of brass candlesticks, a letter opener, and, most touching of all, a partial set of drafting instruments—inking pens, compasses, protractors—in a velvet-lined box with the lid missing. I have a similar set from my school days. These are the sort of architect's tools that last— or should last—a lifetime.

George walked me through the remains of his house. The exterior fig-covered walls were much as I remembered; the front door was still surmounted by a planter with spiky cactuses. It was now three months since the fire, and the debris had been removed from the main parts of the interior, although the pool was still half full of inky, blackened water, an ashy scum floating on the surface. As George had described, the damage was uneven. The worst destruction was in the kitchen of the rental apartment where the fire had started. "I was woken that night by a loud bang," he recounted. "I thought someone was breaking in, so I got up and checked the house. When I went into the apartment I found the kitchen wildly ablaze, and my tenant trying to put out the fire with a garden hose. I hustled him out of there and called 911." How did the fire start? There was a butane canister in the kitchen and the tenant told the fire marshal that he had been making crème brûlée. But the fire investigators, who found dozens of discarded canisters in a nearby dumpster, concluded that the blaze was caused by something else—hash oil manufacturing. Hash oil is a marijuana concentrate made by dissolving cannabis leaves in liquid butane, a risky procedure when performed indoors because butane fumes are highly flammable and can cause explosions, which is what woke George up. "It's incredible to me that someone was making drugs in my house," he said. "I don't use drugs—I'm even allergic to marijuana."

We went into George's living room, which at first glance looked largely intact. The six-foot-tall fireplace was still there, as were the arched windows and the columns that supported the dome. But a glance upward revealed that the dome itself had completely disappeared, surgically removed, leaving the room entirely open to the sky. The sand-colored walls were smudged with soot, as if Addison Mizner had given them a light going-over. George pointed out the built-in shelves, which were still crammed with books. The contents had been untouched by the flames, but after being soaked by water the books had swollen into place; an antiquarian friend of George had declared them beyond salvage. When I first met George, he had told me, "I don't need a lot of stuff." But, of course, he *had* accumulated a lot of possessions. Not only books, but also drawings, paintings, carpets, furniture, and the usual impedimenta of everyday life.

I read a newspaper report about the fire that quoted a spokesman for the fire department. He said that the three-alarm fire had been particularly challenging because of the close surroundings. "I will say, with the building tucked into the alley it can be more difficult to get back in there, but you know that's Charleston." The narrow brick-paved lane wasn't a relic of the colonial city, however; it was created only two decades earlier by George and his friends. How they did it is a story of foresight, ingenuity, and perseverance.

Tully and Charles

*Creating a sense of place in
a neglected neighborhood*

George had come upon the lot where he built his house in 1991, about six years after he, Cheryl, and Jerry started their renovation business. The location was Saint Philip Street in Elliotborough. At that time Elliotborough was a rough neighborhood, known mainly for open drug dealing and consisting of dilapidated houses and scores of vacant and boarded-up structures. "I thought it was a good deal, in spite of that," George remembers. The Medical University of South Carolina and the College of Charleston were nearby, and they were a potential source of tenants. King Street, Charleston's main shopping street, was only a block away, although this end of King was distinctly seedy, lined with pawnshops, thrift shops, and empty storefronts. It was only a matter of time, George reasoned, before the neighborhood revived. The lot cost $78,000, their largest investment to date. The L-shaped property included four houses, all vacant: a large house on Saint Philip Street, a tiny masonry house behind it, and two derelict houses around the corner facing Cannon Street. As was common in Charleston, the lot was very deep—two hundred feet—so there was plenty of room for additional buildings. But that was in the future. "We didn't have anything specific in mind," says George. "At that point our plan was to fix up the old houses and rent them out."

About two months after the sale, something unexpected happened: the large house on Saint Philip Street collapsed—it simply fell down. Fortunately, it was still unoccupied; George had been negotiating with a local theater company that wanted to rent it for rehearsal space. "It looked okay inside," he recalls, "but the foundations turned out to be really bad." As a replacement, George designed a three-story structure with a two-bedroom apartment on the first floor and a four-bedroom dwelling with a tall veranda above. While this was under construction, he renovated the little masonry house in the rear, and an acquaintance bought it for about $80,000, which covered their initial investment.

The two boarded-up houses facing Cannon Street had been empty for a long time. The smaller one in the rear dated back to the early nineteenth century, but since it had been renovated in the 1930s, it did not require much work to turn it into rental apartments. "The front house on Cannon Street had been unoccupied for years when we bought it, and we discovered that it was being used as a squat and a shooting gallery by crack and heroin addicts," George recalls. "We hired a hazard cleaning crew to clear out all the needles, waste, and debris, and converted it to a rental property." Despite the rundown neighborhood, both rentals were successful. "Our tenants were mostly young downtown restaurant and bar workers who didn't make the sort of money that's typical today. They couldn't even scrape together enough cash to make a security deposit, or pay a full month's rent in advance, so we screened carefully and rented by the week."

The back half of the lot on Saint Philip Street was empty. After a year George, Cheryl, and Jerry decided that they should do something with the vacant land. They had been renting out the house on President Street and living together in a rented row house on an alley in the historic district. It was time to build houses for themselves, one with apartments for George and Cheryl, and another one for Jerry. That was how the Byzantine House came about. George made the exterior nondescript so that it did not seem out of place in the neighborhood—the magic was all on the inside. Where did the swimming pool come from? "That was Cheryl's idea," says George. "She was overweight and she wanted a pool for exercise. I had designed an entrance atrium between our two apartments, so that seemed the best place to put it. She didn't want the bother of cleaning leaves and debris, so I put a roof over it." Jerry's house was more conventional, two stories with stepped gables and an attic with dormers; it was small, but with the luxury of a walled garden.

What was unusual about both houses was that the walls were built out of cement block rather than framed in wood. "Wood today is either poor quality fast-growth, or it's impregnated with chemicals, so I prefer to build in masonry," says George. Charleston is low-lying—not for nothing is the region called the Lowcountry—and this produces a damp environment in which wood tends to rot and require constant repainting, so masonry made sense. Of course, masonry was more expensive. "When we started, a well-intentioned friend of my parents who was a real estate banker told me that my construction methods and exorbitant building costs would eventually leave me penniless," said George. "Since Cheryl and I were essentially already penniless, it wasn't as dire a warning as presumably he intended."

George painted the exteriors of the stuccoed houses different colors: the house on Saint Philip Street was pink, Jerry's was adobe-colored, and his own was white. The colors and the walls and arched gateways enclosing the backyards recalled a Mediterranean village. The walls were not decorative—they were there for security. After they moved in, George and Jerry discovered that conditions in the neighborhood were much worse than anything they had experienced elsewhere. The vacant houses had attracted a flourishing drug trade, crime was widespread, and drive-by shootings were a regular occurrence. George and Jerry installed floodlights. When that didn't work, they took other measures. "We reckoned that if we could discourage the drug buyers, who were chiefly college students who lived elsewhere, that would disrupt the drug trade," George explains. At that time Charleston police officers were allowed to moonlight in their off-duty hours as security monitors in stores and bars. "We hired the officers for two or three late-night shifts a week at random times to ensure a lack of predictability, and asked them to park their squad cars out front, on the street. Things would get really quiet during those times." Eventually, the drug buyers stayed away, and the dealers, who were likewise not from the neighborhood, took their business elsewhere.

The house immediately behind Jerry and George's homes was

another source of aggravation. The broken-down duplex contained an illegal bar where drug dealing was rampant, and the parking lot was the site of nightly fights and occasional shootings. George and Jerry spoke to the absentee owner, who indicated that he was willing to sell. The problem was the price, almost twice as much as George and Jerry had paid for the first lot. They needed an outside investor, and so George approached his brother Bob, who was interested in building a house for himself. Pooling their resources, they bought the lot, evicted the tenants, and tore down the duplex. Bob reserved the back part of the lot for his own house. He wanted George to design it, but George was busy and suggested Randolph Martz, the architect who had been his landlord when he was a student. Martz designed a villa-like house facing a large garden. That left space on the property for four small houses. The first was for Jerry's newly married sister, Mary Turner, a tiny house with two stories and an attic, and a two-level piazza on the side. This was followed by a similar house next door, and two narrow houses facing Saint Philip Street. "We built the first of these for a friend of mine, and subsequently after a year he sold to another friend who still owns it," says George. "When we finished the second house, the market had softened, so we rented it for two years before selling it." The architectural style of the four houses— built in 1996–97—was unremarkable, with gable roofs, clapboard siding, traditional details. The exteriors were painted different colors—yellow, green, aquamarine, plum; Bob's house was white. To provide access for parking, George laid out a narrow lane down one side of the lot. Because Mary was the first resident, they asked her to name the lane, and being of Irish descent she settled on Tully Alley.

George and Jerry were turning into experienced developers. When a lot next door to Tully Alley came on the market in 1998, despite the high asking price, they made an offer. The property included a house in good condition that was rented to an elderly Army veteran. "We tried to sell him the house for eighty thousand, because what we really wanted was the land behind it and the money would have recouped the house value for us and made our financing of the new construction easier," George recalls. "The tenant had full military retirement benefits and he could have bought the house with no down payment. His mortgage payment, including taxes and insurance, would

The Moorish House on Tully Alley. The walls are
painted the color of marigolds.

have been a hundred dollars less than he was paying in rent. But he
explained that he didn't want the hassles of home ownership, so he
rented from us for another year and then moved in with a relative. It
was too bad for him, really. We spent twenty thousand renovating the
exterior and four months later sold the house for a hundred and fifty
thousand to a group of investors who still own it."

George's brother bought the back third of the new lot that adjoined
his property, which allowed him to enlarge his garden and add a guest-
house, also designed by Martz. There was space remaining on the lot to

build two additional houses. The first was rather conventional: a pretty pastel-pink cottage with shuttered windows and an airy second-floor veranda. The second house was different. "I wanted to have some fun," George says. He designed a striking Mizner-like entrance porch with Moorish pointed arches and square columns topped by low-relief capitals. The porch was cast in concrete in a single pour using elaborate sculpted molds; the balcony above included a balustrade with concrete grills and ornamental urns. The stucco walls of the house were painted with an orange wash the color of marigolds. The interior was similarly exotic. George worked with a team of cabinetmakers, who paneled the walls in black walnut. The vaulted living room had a massive fireplace decorated with a relief pattern of swirling acanthus leaves that George had seen in a Byzantine church. This was not the first Moorish building in Charleston. In 1854, local architects Edward C. Jones and Francis D. Lee had built the remarkable Farmers' and Exchange Bank on East Bay Street. The tiny building, which still stands, has horseshoe arches and striped brownstone modeled on the Islamic architecture of Spain; the elaborate ironwork of the door grills is copied from the Alhambra.

More than ten years had passed since George, Cheryl, and Jerry had bought the first lot on Saint Philip Street. As they anticipated, the neighborhood had slowly improved. Vacant houses were renovated, abandoned corner stores were turned into coffee shops, bakeries, and restaurants, boutiques popped up here and there. In the process, real estate values and rents went up. One of the small houses on Tully Alley that had sold for $220,000 in 1995 was resold six years later for more than twice as much. As for the Moorish House, it fetched the princely sum of $595,000. Their gamble was paying off.

"About five years ago I was showing a group of historic preservation students from the College of Charleston around Tully Alley," George recounted. "One of the students asked me if I felt uncomfortable knowing that I was gentrifying this part of Elliotborough. I don't like being asked questions in an accusatory manner, and anyway I wasn't interested in engaging somebody who had drawn conclusions without evidence." Gentrification is a controversial subject. When downtown living attracts middle-class residents, real estate values rise and property owners are able to undertake long-deferred maintenance. The place physically improves—often dramatically. At the same time, the improvements produce higher house prices and rents. These increases have different effects. Existing homeowners who are able to sell benefit, but low-income tenants may be forced to move, a pattern that has been repeated in many southern cities. Because the majority of the lower-income downtown population is African American, that group is disproportionately affected. This was the case in Charleston. In 1980, early in the real estate boom, the population of the peninsula was 65 percent black and 35 percent white; by 2010, those figures were reversed. Not because so many people were moving in—the overall population of the peninsula had actually dropped—but because more than a third of the black population had moved away.

It is true that the efforts of George and his friends had helped to drastically reshape the Elliotborough neighborhood, but he did not believe that this had come at the expense of displacing a vibrant existing community.

There seems to be an assumption, especially among younger people not from Charleston, that Elliotborough was a thriving black neighborhood before being bought out by others. That assumption is wildly off base. When we moved in, at least half the buildings in the immediate vicinity were boarded up and vacant, and according to older neighbors had been so for many years. Our side of the Saint Philip Street block had only one occupied house, other than the illegal bar and the bar owner's apartment. Down the street was a triplex owned by an elderly black couple. He earned the money to buy the house from tip money he saved carrying luggage for tourists at the Mills House Hotel. He told me that he raised five children in that home, but since the kids had all grown up and had their own families, it was just him and his wife. This gentleman was the first resident to welcome us to the neighborhood. He later enlisted our help in trying to get the city to close the three crack houses that were next door to him, and directly across the street from us.

Neighborhood change is sometimes described as if it were purely local, but it is generally part of a larger urban dynamic. That is why political writer Alan Ehrenhalt prefers the term "demographic inversion" to "gentrification." In *The Great Inversion and the Future of the American City,* he defines demographic inversion as "the rearrangement of living patterns across an entire metropolitan area, all taking place at roughly the same time." Charleston had experienced several such inversions. For its first two hundred years, the city occupied the lowest portion of the small peninsula between the Ashley and Cooper rivers—approximately eight square miles. The population peaked in 1940 at seventy thousand, which is when the first inversion began. The immediate cause was the wartime expansion of a naval base and shipyard on the Cooper River in North Charleston, which pulled people away from the old city. The postwar construction of highways, bridges, residential subdivisions, and shopping malls, which represented what local historian Robert Rosen calls the "Americanization of Charleston," further encouraged city dwellers to move from the peninsula to the suburbs. The population of the peninsula continued to shrink, even as the city annexed suburban communities—today the City of Charleston encompasses almost 130 square miles. By 1990, the time that George and his friends started developing Tully Alley, considerably less than a third of Charlestonians lived on the peninsula, whose population had fallen to about thirty-five thousand.

The fortunes of Elliotborough were directly affected by these changes. In the late nineteenth century, the neighborhood was a blue-collar immigrant enclave of Germans, Poles, and Jews, although it was not exclusively white. "In terms of housing patterns, Charleston was certainly not a segregated city from 1880 to the 1940s," writes Rosen. The black population "continued to live where they had lived for centuries—in the slave quarters behind the great houses, in houses of their own throughout the city, in villages on the edge of town." Vestiges of this pattern were still evident in Elliotborough when George moved in. The largest structures in the neighborhood were the churches—Baptist, Roman Catholic, African Methodist Episcopal—as well as a synagogue. "Segregation in Elliotborough was block by block and sometimes building by building," George said. "Our block had been Jewish while the next block to the west was occupied by black middle-class Roman Catholics. I learned this history from an elderly neighbor who is the last remaining black Catholic homeowner on that block. He told me that after the Second World War, when many of the original Jewish homeowners started to move to the suburbs, some of the houses became rental properties, while others were bought by middle-class black families. He said that the neighborhood didn't start to decline until the late 1970s, when the poorly maintained rental properties no longer attracted middle-class tenants." As these people moved out, rents fell, houses deteriorated further, and the number of abandoned buildings increased—a depressingly familiar cycle in American cities.

The second demographic inversion, which affected Elliotborough directly, began in 1970, when the College of Charleston, which had been founded by the city a hundred years earlier, was taken over by the state. An infusion of new funds was followed by a dramatic increase in student enrollment, from a mere five hundred to more than eleven thousand by 1998. Thus, just as the middle class—white as well as black—was moving out of downtown Charleston to the suburbs, large numbers of students were moving in. Renting to college students—as well as to students, staff, and faculty of the nearby medical university—enabled building owners in neighborhoods such as Elliotborough to invest in renovations and long-needed repairs. When George, Cheryl, and Jerry rebuilt their small portion of Saint Philip Street, they displaced the owners of an illegal bar and a single tenant—who left voluntarily. On the other hand, they added a dozen new homes to the city's housing stock, repaired four vacant houses, and put several new rental apartments on the market. This admittedly small operation stands in sharp contrast to many large-scale efforts at urban renewal that end up displacing more persons than they house.

In 2000, shortly after George finished the Moorish House, he was approached by the owners of the property immediately adjacent to the Pink House on Saint Philip Street. The Sunsetter Elks Lodge was a fraternal order that used the old house as a social club. George recalls the members well.

> The Sunsetters were a fun group of older black men who had boisterous weekly outdoor fish-fries with often more than a hundred people. I was invited to hang out and did so on a few occasions. There was a clubhouse-type bar and grill for members in a series of cobbled-together additions. They only used the ground floor of the house, due to years of a dilapidated roof letting water into the building. The place was in bad shape.

The lodge was interested in relocating, not only because of the poor condition of its building—and insufficient parking—but chiefly because most of its members had moved out of downtown Charleston. If the Sunsetters could sell the old house, they could buy a newer building in the suburbs of North Charleston, close to where the majority of their members now lived. The lodge had acquired the old house on Saint Philip Street in the early 1980s for $24,000; two decades later, thanks in large part to George and Jerry's efforts, the property was worth considerably more: their asking price was $280,000—they eventually settled for $240,000. "That was three times as much as we paid for our first property," George said, "but it was the last piece we could buy, and the deep lot had space for as many as three additional houses." The new lot was also wide enough to accommodate a narrow lane that would provide car access all the way back to George's house. Jerry bought the property and immediately resold the front house and one building lot to Bob Holt, and the rear lot to George.

Jerry kept the center lot for himself. He had decided to build a new house. "My first house was the equivalent of a starter home," he explained. "I wanted more space as well as income-generating apartments." George designed a U-shaped, two-story building around a second-floor terrace, sitting on top of three small guest apartments and

Giant Tuscan columns enclose the raised terrace of Jerry Moran's
Roman villa and frame his old house across the street.

a carport. A roof deck provided splendid views across the city. It was not
a shy building. The exterior was painted pink and ochre with green shutters. A giant order of Tuscan columns supported an architrave across
the face of the raised terrace. The architrave included a frieze with a
medieval quotation that George had come across in an old book on
Venetian architecture: "ANTIQUORUM YSTORIAS SCIRE DESIDERANS,
IPSARUM PRINCIPIUM OPORTET COGNOSCERE" (Should you desire to
know the affairs of the ancients, it is well to know their beginnings). It
seemed appropriate for this distinctly Roman villa.

The sort of inner-block development that George, Cheryl, and
Jerry were engaged in was not unusual in Charleston. Space on the peninsula had always been in short supply, and the city had a long tradition of small outbuildings—slave quarters, carriage houses, artisans'
dwellings. The modern zoning code encouraged what city planners call
infill development—adding dwelling units to the rear of lots to increase
neighborhood density. The zoning along Saint Philip Street, for example, allowed a maximum of 35 percent coverage—that is, buildings could

occupy up to 35 percent of the ground area. That meant that a typical deep lot could accommodate as many as three or four additional houses—as long as they were small. The exact number was dictated largely by the city's parking requirements: two car spots for each freestanding house, one-and-a-half for each rented apartment. Tully Alley had seven houses; Charles Street, which is what they named the new lane, had five houses, with space for two more. The lots were combined into a single property, which was owned in condominium. The advantage was that all the open space, whether it was a lane, a parking spot, or a private garden, was counted together. The nature of the private outdoor spaces varied; some houses had courtyards or walled gardens, others made do with a veranda or a porch.

Tully and Charles, which comprise almost an acre, did not develop according to a master plan. Like Topsy, they just "grow'd." This seemingly haphazard way of building contributed to the impression of an old, established place. Speculating about the beauty of old towns, the celebrated art historian E. H. Gombrich wrote: "The very conditions of slow and unplanned growth may sometimes be productive of qualities that are hard to imitate by deliberate planning." Gombrich called this quality organic. So does the architect and theorist Christopher Alexander.

> This feeling of "organicness," is not a vague feeling of relationship with biological forms. It is not an analogy. It is instead, an accurate vision of a specific structural quality which these old towns had . . . and have. Namely: Each of these towns grew as a whole, under its own laws of wholeness . . . and we can feel this wholeness, not only at the largest scale, but in every detail: in the restaurants, in the sidewalks, in the houses, shops, markets, roads, parks, gardens, and walls. Even in the balconies and ornaments.

Alexander describes the features of organic urban growth in *A New Theory of Urban Design*. First, such growth is piecemeal, occurring bit by bit. This is certainly the case with George, Cheryl, and Jerry's project, which was built over more than a decade. The parts are not uniform. George, Jerry, and Bob's houses are the largest, the old masonry house

Cannon Street

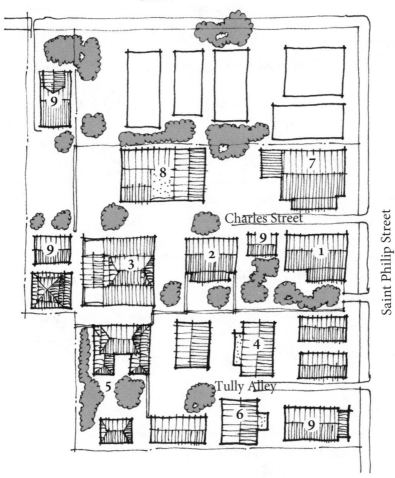

Saint Philip Street

1 Pink house
2 Jerry's first house
3 George's house
4 Mary's house
5 Bob Holt's house
6 Moorish house
7 Sunsetter Lodge
8 Jerry's second house
9 Existing house

The organic plan of Tully Alley and Charles Street:
seventeen houses occupy less than an acre.

on Charles Street is the smallest, and there are many sizes in-between. Since the houses were not all constructed at the same time—and some were built a long time ago—there is the same pleasant variety that we take for granted in old towns, but which is missing in brand-new developments, whether they are public housing projects or upscale planned communities.

Second, according to Alexander, organic growth is unpredictable —that is, the end result is not necessarily apparent at the beginning. The earliest houses on Tully Alley are straightforward, almost generic— pitched roofs, dormers, balconies—and the two unprepossessing houses that face Saint Philip Street are almost identical, except that one is painted plum and the other aquamarine. George's self-effacing house is almost invisible; on the other hand, the theatrical Moorish House and Jerry's Roman villa stand out like hothouse flowers. There is a similar variety in the nature of the private outdoor spaces: a mixture of porches, balconies, verandas, terraces, and walled gardens. The front doors are carefully located, generally—but not always—to create intimate semipublic spaces in front of the house. Houses that face the street line up with their neighbors, whereas houses inside the block face different directions. As in a medieval European town, you are never quite sure what you will find around the corner.

Alexander's third organic feature concerns coherence: piecemeal growth should not result in a jumbled free-for-all, but rather the fragments should adhere and form a harmonious whole. Coherence contributes to what architects call a sense of place. Not all coherence is the same, however. A conventional parking lot, for example, is coherent, but it is a mechanical sort of coherence: the entire surface covered in asphalt, the regular white lines of the parking stalls, the uniform lighting fixtures. One parking lot looks pretty much like another. The parking in Tully Alley and Charles Street is different: cars are sometimes parked in front of houses, sometimes alongside a lane, sometimes in an auto court, and sometimes under a covered carport. The lanes are paved with old bricks dug up on the site, and some of the parking spots are paved. The parking court outside Bob's house is paved with stone slabs, while the parking lot in front of the Pink House is gravel, the stalls demarcated by thin stone strips. While an asphalt parking lot appears orderly, the parking on Tully

Alley and Charles Street represents a richer order—of different textures, materials, and scales.

Tully Alley contains bollards to protect exposed building corners from being damaged by carelessly driven vehicles. Such devices are commonly steel pipes painted safety orange; in other words, they are eyesores. On Tully Alley they are square masonry piers topped by slightly projecting imposts made of flat tiles; at the corners of the Moorish House the imposts are pyramidal. Not much of a difference, just enough to signal that somebody cared. Which is Alexander's fourth and final feature: an organic place must be "full of feeling." He is referring to the impression that a place has been thoughtfully made, that it has a human imprint. That is something that Tully Alley—like so much of the old city of Charleston—most certainly demonstrates.

Tully and Charles developed without a plan, but they did not come about in a vacuum. Building projects in Elliotborough, as in all neighborhoods in the lower Charleston peninsula, were subject to the approval of the Board of Architectural Review, known locally as the BAR. The BAR is a city-appointed citizens' panel charged with "the preservation and protection of the old historic or architecturally worthy structures and quaint neighborhoods which impart a distinct aspect to the city and which serve as visible reminders of the historical and cultural heritage of the city, the state, and the nation." The five members represent the city zoning commission, the architectural and engineering professions, the real estate industry, and the arts community. Their job is to review proposed buildings and demolitions as well as any modifications to the exteriors of buildings. All cities review new construction to see that it meets zoning and building codes, but the BAR is different—it is concerned with how buildings look, that is, with aesthetics.

I asked George how the BAR had reacted to his unusual designs such as the Moorish House and Jerry's Roman villa. "I don't think we would have been allowed such architectural exuberance without the support and encouragement of the city architect, Charles Chase," he answered. "Charles explained to the individual board members what was going on architecturally and why he thought what we were proposing would work for its location. He was knowledgeable about different styles of architecture and, what's more, he reviewed applications on their own merit without trying to force his personal taste on the applicant. He helped us a lot, gave us advice, and warned us about what might not pass muster with the board." What did the neighbors think of Tully and Charles? "Our block was so depopulated and with so many boarded-up buildings, that wasn't an issue," George answered. "The main community complaints were about the high density, and these came from a neighborhood association well to the south of us. But after we completed Tully Alley, that group did a complete one-eighty and strongly supported our later work." Chase eventually left Charleston to join a conservation design firm in San Francisco; George and Jerry later named Charles Street in his honor.

THREE

The Unholy City

A *historical interlude*

What drew George, Cheryl, and Jerry to Charleston? Samuel Gaillard Stoney, a native and the author of several early books on the city's historic buildings, put it this way: "The difficulty that comes from being a Charlestonian is that the things and thoughts, the memory and the manners that make up the Charleston that count are too completely part of one's heart and one's soul to be realizable. . . . Charleston is largely a matter of feeling." George C. Rogers, Jr., South Carolina's preeminent historian, was less sentimental but also emphasized the sense of a special place: "This continuity in the city's life came as much from the physical setting as from the generations of Charlestonians. The people came and went, prospered and went bankrupt; the rivers, beaches, and islands, the marshes, trees, and buildings remained, creating the sights and sounds, the taste, feel, and smell which lingered on for generations to absorb, savor, and love."

This sounds a bit like Chesterton's "Rome was great because men had loved her." Yet Charleston's beginnings were hardly Romulus and Remus among the palmettos—the city was founded by the seventeenth-century equivalent of venture capitalists. The hardheaded Lords Proprietors, to whom Charles II granted the Province of Carolina as political payback, planned the colony on a feudal model, with aristocrats at the top of a social pyramid and freeholders at the bottom. Freeholders did have a vote in the colony's affairs, however, and to attract settlers the charter allowed that "any seven or more persons agreeing in any religion, shall constitute a church or profession." In an unusual aside, the charter also tolerated "Jews, heathens, and other dissenters from the purity of Christian religion."*

The province's capital was Charles Town, founded in 1670 and named in the king's honor. The settlement was located on the tip of a tongue of land between the mouths of the Ashley and Cooper rivers, which were named after the leading Proprietor, Anthony Ashley Cooper, Earl of Shaftesbury. Unlike Boston and New Amsterdam, which grew higgledy-piggledy over time, Charles Town developed in an orderly fashion because, as the Proprietors instructed, the streets were staked out in advance. These requirements were contained in a document called the Grand Modell, which stated that Carolina towns were "to be laid out into large, straight and regular streets, and sufficient room left for a wharf if it be on a navigable river," and specified block dimensions, street widths, and lot sizes. John Culpeper, the surveyor general, was responsible for the gridded plan of Charles Town, whose only memorable features were a central public square and unusually large blocks—six hundred feet a side (which produced the extremely deep lots that would later enable infill projects such as Tully Alley). "There is nothing particularly noteworthy about the scheme," observed the urban historian John Reps. "The Lords Proprietors were never known for particularly lavish expenditures on behalf of the well-being of the colony, and one is forced to conclude that they carried over this niggardly attitude when they decided on the plan of the capital city."

Culpeper's plan was not implemented all at once. The first phase, begun in 1680, divided roughly eighty acres into a grid of eight blocks. It was not thought necessary to name the streets: they were simply "a street running parallel to the Cooper River" and "the great street that runs north and south." Of the first wooden buildings, which were susceptible to fire and decay, none survives today. The little settlement was fortified by a stockade to protect against attack by Indians and marauding

---

* Roman Catholics were not included, and it was not until the end of the eighteenth century that the proscription against them in Charleston was lifted.

pirates, as well as by the Spanish, who were based on the Florida coast in Saint Augustine. Beyond the wall, the swampy peninsula was dotted with small farms. The Proprietors cheerfully instructed the first governor: "Be the buildings never so mean and thin at first, yet as the town increases in riches and people, the void places will be filled up and the buildings will grow more beautiful." The filling-up proved slow, however, and for the next fifty years the settlement remained little more than a walled village. It was hardly a propitious beginning.

If the Proprietors did not invest in the colony, that may have been because the expected riches of the New World were slow to materialize. The chief early exports were animal hides traded with the natives. In 1719, in what was effectively a revolt, the disgruntled Carolinians overthrew the rule of the Lords Proprietors and successfully petitioned the Crown to become a self-governing royal colony. This political change coincided with a rise in Charles Town's fortunes. The settlement became the main port for exporting rice grown on plantations in the Carolina backcountry. Provided with a protected harbor and fortuitously located on the Great Circle route for sailing ships returning to Europe from the West Indies, Charles Town developed into a mercantile center, and its population expanded accordingly. In time, the stockade was removed, the moat was filled in, and the street grid extended across the peninsula. It was the beginning of a century of prosperity.

A 1739 issue of *London Magazine* included an engraving titled "An Exact Prospect of Charles Town, the Metropolis of the Province of South Carolina." The foreground of the panoramic view is a harbor crowded with ships of every size. The buildings on the shore stretch along a wharf between two protective bastions, identified by giant Union flags. The street along the wharf is lined with buildings—residences above storehouses—whose two- and three-story facades form a continuous and varied street wall. Several larger structures stand out: the Council Chambers, the Exchange, and the Custom House. Not exactly a metropolis, perhaps, but an attractive maritime town, neat and businesslike and comfortably old-fashioned.

The tallest structure in the *London Magazine* engraving is the spire of Saint Philip's, the establishment Anglican church. A second spire, slightly lower, belongs to the "French Church," established by Hugue-

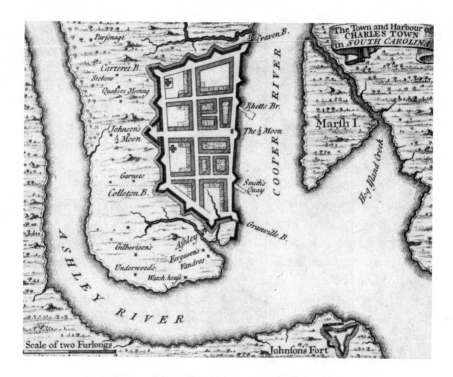

A 1733 plan of Charles Town shows a little walled settlement
between the Ashley and Cooper rivers.

nots. The town had a large number of denominations and included New
England Congregationalists, Scottish Presbyterians, German Lutherans,
Baptists, and Quakers. A decade later, Sephardic Jews from Spain would
build a synagogue. The profusion of places of worship gave Charles Town
its nickname: the Holy City.

The growth of the town was more or less guided by Culpeper's plan,
although some of the large blocks were irregularly subdivided, producing anomalies in the street layout. The angle of Queen Street, for example, departed from the strictly orthogonal grid. Saint Philip's Church
protruded into the right-of-way of Church Street, causing an awkward
but picturesque vista. Johnson's Street (present-day Legaré) acquired a
two-block-long offset. A small central square marked the intersection of
the two main streets, Meeting and Broad.

By the eve of the Revolution, cosmopolitan Charles Town was the

American colonies' fourth-largest city, after Philadelphia, New York, and Boston—and probably the richest. This prosperity was reflected in the architecture. The earliest buildings had been wood, but after a number of fires, they were replaced by more durable masonry (the brick often brought from Britain in the form of ships' ballast). The most impressive residences were in the prevailing Palladian style. A surviving example, the imposing Miles Brewton House, with its two-story portico overlooking King Street, was built by a banker and prominent civic leader. Prosperous plantation owners had equally grand townhomes, where they and their offspring came, as one early historian put it, "for pleasure and for health, for business and for education." The civic monuments included Saint Philip's Church with its landmark steeple, a State House, and a new Exchange, whose materials (and probably design) were imported from England. A large marble statue stood in the central square—the first public monument in the American colonies—honoring William Pitt the Elder, the British politician who had supported the American colonies and led the repeal of the unpopular Stamp Act.

When the Marquis de Lafayette landed in Carolina in June 1777, on his way to join General Washington's army, he spent ten days in the city. "Charles Town is one of the best built, handsomest, and most agreeable cities that I have ever seen," he wrote to his wife, Adrienne. Coming from someone who knew Paris and London, this was high praise, although perhaps we should take the enthusiastic description of a nineteen-year-old setting out on a great adventure with a grain of salt. In the same letter Lafayette gushed: "The richest and the poorest man are completely on a level and although there are some immense fortunes in this country I may challenge any one to point out the slightest difference in their respective manner toward each other." Richest and poorest on a level? Obviously the marquis wasn't referring to the many African slaves. More than half of these were domestics, but they also worked as stevedores, drovers, and in the rice mills. Although city ordinances forbade teaching slaves trades—or reading and writing—these rules were weakly enforced, and there were black carpenters and masons, as well as black ironworkers who were responsible for the many decorative wrought-iron gates, fences, and balconies that graced the city.

Slavery had come to Carolina from the Caribbean. Large planta-

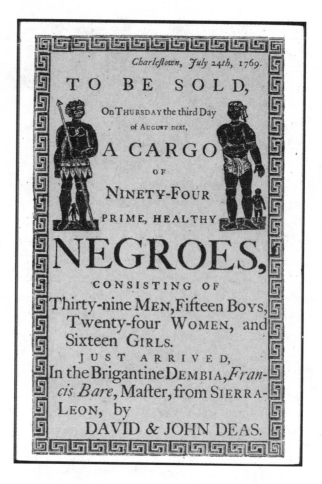

Slavery was at the heart of antebellum Charleston's
prosperity. An auction handbill of 1769.

tions worked by slave labor had been introduced to the West Indies by
the Spaniards and Portuguese, and were soon copied by the British. One
of their most successful island colonies was Barbados, which became
fabulously wealthy thanks to the cultivation of sugarcane. Many of the
original settlers of Charles Town were the offspring of well-to-do Bar-
badian planters seeking new business opportunities. They introduced
monoculture to Carolina (substituting indigo and rice for sugarcane) as
well as chattel slavery—and the harsh laws and self-serving racial atti-

tudes that accompanied it. These libertarian slaveholders replaced the Proprietors' ordered vision of a feudal society with an oligarchic, racially focused caste system dominated by merchants and plantation owners. The Barbadians also imported their own freewheeling boomtown culture, a "brittle, gay, and showy society, compounded of old world elegance and frontier boisterousness," according to the historian Richard S. Dunn.

The decades after the end of the Revolutionary War saw Charleston, as the city was now renamed, continuing to grow and prosper. The port expanded to accommodate the flow of rice, known as Carolina gold, as well as indigo and sea-island cotton, a superior long-fiber strain unique to the Lowcountry. Although federal law now forbade the importation of slaves, the demand for plantation labor increased, and so did the value of slaves, adding to the wealth of the largest slave owners. Most of the grand houses in the city date from this period. Many of these mansions were built in new districts beyond Boundary Street (today Calhoun Street) as the city expanded northward up the peninsula.

The indefatigable British political activist and writer Harriet Martineau visited Charleston in 1835 during a southern tour. She appreciated the hospitality of her hosts and the exotic charm of the city—"the groups of mulattoes, the women with turbaned heads, surmounted with water-pots and baskets of fruit"—but as a confirmed abolitionist, she was unsparing in her criticism of slavery. She described a visit to a slave market where she saw mothers and their children on the auction block. "We next entered a number of fine houses, where we were presented with flowers, and entertained with lively talk about the small affairs of gay society, which to little minds are great. To me every laugh had lost its gayety, every courtesy had lost its grace, all intercourse had lost its innocence." Such contrasts colored her impression of the city. "It seems to me a place of great activity, without much intellectual result; of great gayety, without much ease and pleasure."

By 1850, more than half of Charleston's inhabitants were black, the highest proportion of any American city. The outnumbered white population was deeply concerned about the threat of insurrection, its fears fueled by memories of the recent conspiracy of Denmark Vesey, a freedman carpenter. Vesey's planned rebellion, which was inspired by the

Haitian slave revolt and anticipated that of Nat Turner by a decade, was put down before it began. More than thirty black persons were either executed or deported, and the African Methodist Episcopal Church that Vesey had cofounded was razed to the ground.

Frederick Law Olmsted, who worked as a journalist before he embarked on his park-building career, spent a week in Charleston in 1853 as a correspondent for the fledgling *New-York Daily Times*. He left us this vivid picture of the effect of slavery on city life.

> In Richmond, and Charleston, and New Orleans, the citizens are as careless and gay as in Boston or London, and their servants a thousand times as childlike and cordial, to all appearance, in their relations with them as our servants are with us. But go to the bottom of this security and dependence, and you will come to police machinery such as you never find in towns under free government; citadels, sentries, passports, grape-shotted cannon, and daily public whippings for accidental infractions of police ceremonies. I happened myself to see more direct expression of tyranny in a single day and night at Charleston, than at Naples in a week; and I found that more than half of the inhabitants of this town were subject to arrest, imprisonment, and barbarous punishment, if found in the streets without a passport after the evening "gun-fire."*

The "gun-fire" referred to a nine o'clock curfew, after which time no black person—slave or freedman—was permitted to venture out without a note ("passport") from his or her owner or employer. Those caught without a note were flogged, and their owners could be fined.

The problem for slave owners, as Olmsted pointed out, was that slavery and towns were a poor match. Whereas slaves on a plantation were isolated, slaves in town were in daily contact with the world at large, which included black freedmen and foreigners, many of whom were northern abolitionists. "Slaves can never be brought together in cities but their intelligence will be increased to a degree dangerous to

---

* Olmsted had previously visited Naples when it was under the despotic rule of Ferdinand II.

those who enjoy the benefit of their labor," Olmsted observed. Hence the many restrictions on their freedom of movement. In Charleston, public places that might encourage assembly, such as parks and squares, were few and far between. The original central square, for example, was eventually built over and disappeared entirely. White Point Garden, a park at the tip of the peninsula, and the esplanades along the water were strictly off-limits. Forbidden access to hotels, taverns, and restaurants, black Charlestonians congregated surreptitiously in illegal grog shops and in freedmen's homes. The only places that slaves were legally permitted to gather were churches, which had pews reserved for black parishioners.

The Palladian mansions and single houses of Charleston make an attractive street scene today, but a bird's-eye view of the city in the mid-nineteenth century would have revealed a different reality. The spaces behind the houses were a warren of walled compounds that contained the slave quarters. These compounds resembled prison yards with brick walls sometimes as high as twenty feet. Back lanes were rare, as they would have allowed slaves to slip out unobserved. With half the population effectively locked away, the city at night must have been a reserved and quiet place. Indeed, the relaxed antebellum lifestyle of white Charlestonians, which "emphasized conviviality over diligence, dilettantism over specialization, and leisure over work," as one local historian puts it, existed largely behind closed doors—in homes, social clubs, ethnic associations, and library societies. Streets are normally the lifeblood of a city, but one has the impression that in antebellum Charleston they were places of strained encounters between masters and slaves, of surreptitious glances and averted gazes.

The city that Olmsted visited on the eve of the Civil War had long since passed its apogee. The advent of steam power signaled the end of the age of sail, and with it the end of Charleston's advantageous position on the Great Circle route. The British demand for rice and cotton, Carolina's chief exports, had fallen thanks to competition from India and elsewhere. The presence of slave labor discouraged the sort of European immigration that fueled the growth of northern cities. Lastly, the influential planter class, which disdained commerce and industry, preferred to preserve the city as a convivial second home and did little to encourage commerce. When the railroad reached Charleston, for example, the city fathers insisted that the terminus be located outside the city limits, which meant costly trans-shipping of goods to the port. To make matters worse, the state legislature passed a law that required free black sailors on all visiting vessels to be placed in jail until their departure, with the result that foreign ships increasingly bypassed the port. All these factors contributed to Charleston's decline. Visiting travelers described an atmosphere of genteel decay. To Thomas Gunn of the *New-York Evening Post,* Charleston resembled "a small, old-fashioned New York." The English actress Fanny Kemble, passing through on an American tour, found the place "a little gone down in the world, yet remembering still its former dignity." This was not just the impression of outsiders. Hugh Legaré, a prominent local lawyer and politician, described his native city as "mouldering away, in silence, amidst the unavailing fertility of nature." From the fourth-largest city in the country, Charleston had slipped to twenty-second place.

The Civil War sealed Charleston's fate. During a two-year siege, the district closest to the sea—the tip of the peninsula—came under naval bombardment. What escaped the cannonball was ravaged by a devastating fire that broke out as Union troops entered the city. Photographs taken immediately after the end of the war show the ruined shells of churches, collapsed houses, and rubble-strewn streets. The rubble was cleared and the city was rebuilt, but it never really recovered. Without the economic support of the slave-driven plantation economy, postwar Charleston became a shadow of its former mercantile self.

Being a backwater was not all bad. When Henry James visited Charleston in the winter of 1904, he was charmed by its "easy loveliness," its gardens, and its "silvery seaward outlook." He enjoyed hot chocolate and Lady Baltimore cake, a local specialty, in a tearoom on King Street. "Up and down and in and out, with my companion, I strolled from hour to hour; but more and more under the impression of the *consistency of softness* [emphasis added]." A curious phrase. James explained that he meant there was no trace of the truculent city whose inhabitants, by firing on Fort Sumter forty years earlier, had started the Civil War. That bellicose place, he reasoned, must have been much different. "Whereas the ancient order was masculine, fierce and moustachioed, the present is at the most a sort of sick lioness who has so visibly parted with her teeth and claws that we may patronizingly walk all round her," he wrote. He described a kind of emptiness. "How, in an at all complex, a 'great political,' society, can *everything* so have gone?" he asked himself. "Had the *only* focus of life then been Slavery?" His answer is interesting.

> To say "yes" seems the only way to account for the degree of the vacancy, and yet even as I form that word I meet as a reproach the face of the beautiful old house I just mentioned, whose ample spaces had so unmistakably echoed to the higher amenities that one seemed to feel the accumulated traces and tokens gradually come out of their corners like blest objects taken one by one from a reliquary worn with much handling. The note of such haunted chambers as these—haunted structurally, above all, quite as by the ghost of the grand style—was not, certainly, a thinness of reverberation; so that I had to take refuge here in the fact that everything appeared thoroughly to *antedate,* to refer itself to the larger, the less vitiated past that had closed a quarter of a century or so before the War, before the fatal time when the South, monomaniacal at the parting of the ways, "elected" for extension and conquest. The admirable old house of the stately hall and staircase, of the charming coved and vaulted drawing-room, of the precious mahogany doors, the tall unsophisticated portraits, the delicate dignity of welcome, owed nothing of its noble identity, nothing at all appreciable, to the monomania.

Little did James imagine that the future of Charleston lay precisely in rediscovering its "noble identity," its easy loveliness, and its beautiful old architecture. The fortunes of cities are often directed by outside forces. The Holy City had been built on slavery, and it was undone by Emancipation. That was true of many southern cities, but Charleston's former preeminence made it especially vulnerable. Yet there is a key variable in the life of a city: its inhabitants. Human creativity is unpredictable; exceptional individuals come along, and unexpected events follow. That is what happened in sleepy Charleston.

FOUR

Loving Charleston

A dance, a novel, and a renaissance

nowing my interest in Charleston, a friend sent me a You-
Tube link to a film called *City of Proud Memories*. The ten-
minute travelogue, made in 1934, was the kind of one-reeler
that once accompanied feature films in movie houses. The
opening shot shows a trolley car rolling down Meeting Street, but the
city is portrayed as having been largely bypassed by modern life, a place
of "old-time and almost an old-world charm and quaintness," as the
narrator intones. Instead of automobiles, we see horse-drawn carriages
and pushcarts, while black flower vendors and street musicians stroll
the palmetto-shaded sidewalks. "Papa Joe" hawks fresh shrimp, calling
out his wares in Gullah dialect. The atmosphere is more like a sleepy
Caribbean town than a modern American city. A rose-tinted picture, no
doubt, but probably not completely inaccurate.

According to the opening credits, *City of Proud Memories* was part
of the "Thrilling Journey" series, although I could find no record of any
other episodes. The film was produced by Lorenzo Del Riccio, an Italian
immigrant living in New York who had worked for Paramount Pictures
in Hollywood.* Del Riccio's company specialized in travelogues, but why

---

* Del Riccio is best remembered for inventing horse racing's photo-finish camera. While
at Paramount he also developed the wide-screen Magnascope projector, a forerunner of
CinemaScope.

did he choose Charleston? The little southern city had recently come to national attention. There was the dance craze, of course. The Charleston was *the* popular dance of the 1920s; the Ziegfeld Follies featured it, Fred Astaire sang about it, Josephine Baker introduced it to the Folies Bergère. The dance had debuted in 1923 as a number in a popular black Broadway musical, *Runnin' Wild*. The composer was the great jazz pianist James P. Johnson, who collaborated with the lyricist Cecil Mack. According to Johnson, the characteristic clave rhythm of the dance was inspired by Charleston dockworkers.

Two years after *Runnin' Wild* premiered, a bestselling novel featured Charleston as its setting. The title character of *Porgy* was inspired by an actual black street vendor known as Goat Cart Sam, and the novel's chief locale, a tenement called Catfish Row, was based on Cabbage Row, a set of pre-Revolutionary buildings on Church Street. The *New York Times* praised the novel as "a noteworthy achievement in the sympathetic and convincing interpretation of negro life by a member of an 'outside' race." The author was DuBose Heyward, a Charleston native who belonged to an impoverished old-line family. Heyward and his Ohio-born wife, Dorothy, a playwright, adapted the novel into a play that had a year-long run in New York and two national tours. *Porgy* was hardly the first favorable depiction of poor blacks in American literature, but the play was one of the first Broadway productions to be performed by an all-black cast—at the insistence of the authors.

Even before the play opened, George Gershwin had become interested in writing a musical based on the novel, and he invited Heyward to collaborate. The pair visited Charleston together, attending black churches, where they listened to spirituals—by Heyward's account, Gershwin was an enthusiastic participant in the singing. Heyward wrote the libretto and most of the lyrics, and the result was what Gershwin called a "folk opera." *Porgy and Bess*, which premiered in 1935, was performed by a classically trained all-black cast. Although not an immediate hit, the musical was revived in the 1940s and toured internationally in the 1950s. (*Porgy and Bess* did not play in Charleston until 1970 because its black cast refused to perform in a segregated theater.) White Charlestonians did not take pride in their newfound notoriety. A flapper's dance created by two black New Yorkers hardly accorded with

83–85 Church Street, the model for Catfish Row
in *Porgy and Bess.*

their genteel self-image, and while Heyward was a native son, neither did
his low-down novel and the subsequent play and opera.

Whatever Charlestonians thought, Catfish Row entered the American pantheon of imaginary literary places. In his novel, Heyward
described the tenement: "Within the high-ceilinged rooms, with their
battered colonial mantels and broken decorations of Adam designs in
plaster, governors had come and gone, and ambassadors of kings had
schemed and danced." The Charleston that Heyward knew—"an ancient,
beautiful city that time had forgotten before it destroyed"—was full of
such remnants. Throughout the late nineteenth century, its built heritage
(although it's unlikely anyone called it that) had been dealt hard knocks.

A 1906 sketch of the Old Exchange, one of many historic
Charleston buildings that survived the Civil War.

The Adamesque Joseph Manigault mansion, built in 1803, was ignomini-
ously subdivided into a rooming house. The gracious eighteenth-century
home of Heyward's own ancestor, a signer of the Declaration of Inde-
pendence, was converted into a commercial bakery.

Despite the ravages of the Civil War, the periodic destruction
caused by city-wide fires, and the disastrous earthquake of 1886, a surprisingly large number of public buildings survived: the Palladian Old
Exchange, which dated from before the Revolutionary War and had been
used as a post office during the Civil War; the County Records Building, popularly known as the Fireproof Building due to its pioneering
fire-resistant construction, designed by Robert Mills (a Charlestonian

and generally considered the first native-born American to be a professionally trained architect); the main building of the College of Charleston, with its imposing Greek temple front, the work of Philadelphian William Strickland; and Hibernian Hall, a Greek Revival building built for the Irish society by Strickland's protégé, Thomas Ustick Walter. The presence of three leading architects—Mills would design the Washington Monument, Strickland's Second Bank of the United States in Philadelphia ushered in the American Greek Revival, and Walter was responsible for the U.S. Capitol dome—attests to Charleston's architectural preeminence.

The Old Exchange and the College of Charleston are featured in *City of Proud Memories*. Another scene shows a small, windowless structure that is identified as the "historic powder magazine." The building wasn't from the seventeenth century and it wasn't built of tabby—lime and crushed oyster shells—as the narrator claimed, but it was the oldest surviving public building in the city. Dating from the early 1700s, the brick structure had served as a powder magazine during the Revolutionary War, and was subsequently used as a wine cellar, a printer's shop, and a stable. In 1902, it was purchased by the local chapter of the National Society of the Colonial Dames of America, which restored it and turned it into a small museum: an important moment in Charleston, for this was the first conscious effort to preserve an old building for purely historic reasons. Ten years later, the Colonial Dames acquired the disused Old Exchange.

The concern for saving old buildings was in part a reaction to immediate threats. Despite the placid image presented by Del Riccio's film, Charleston was not insulated from modern life. Car ownership was on the rise, for example, and the oil companies were competing to build gas stations that, on the densely built-up peninsula, inevitably meant making space by demolishing old buildings. The tipping point came in 1920, when the Ford Motor Company announced that it was going to tear down the venerable Manigault mansion and replace it with a car dealership. The hastily formed Society for the Preservation of Old Dwellings (today the Preservation Society of Charleston) forestalled the plan and purchased the house.

Another kind of threat was described by Albert Simons, one of the

founders of the Preservation Society. Simons, a Charleston native and
a University of Pennsylvania–trained architect, was interested in history, and long before it was fashionable he was recovering architectural
fragments from old buildings facing demolition and donating them to
the local museum. "It distresses me painfully to see our fine old buildings torn down, and their contents wrecked," he explained, "or what is
more humiliating sold to aliens and shipped away to enrich some other
community more appreciative of such things than ourselves." The "aliens" were chiefly northern antique dealers, who resold the old decorative ironwork, interior paneling, and mantelpieces to collectors and
architects. The home of DuBose Heyward's ancestor, also known as
the Heyward-Washington House because the president had slept there
during his week-long visit to the city in 1791, became a cause célèbre
when the current owner threatened to dismantle and sell the interiors.
This time the Charleston Museum joined the Preservation Society to
save the building. The Planter's Hotel on Dock Street was a different type
of conservation. The hotel had been a stylish watering hole before the
Civil War—Harriet Martineau had stayed there—but it was now vacant
and dilapidated. The building stood on the site of a Colonial-era theater, and after the owner donated the property to the city, Albert Simons
built a theater modeled on an eighteenth-century London playhouse in
the courtyard of the restored building. He reused period paneling and
mantels recovered from a Charleston mansion. Such "fabricated tradition" would be condemned by purists today, but it is an example of the
inventive spirit of these early preservationists.

Something unusual was happening. Charlestonians, perhaps for
the first time in their long history, were beginning to love their city—in
G. K. Chesterton's sense. This love was manifested not only in efforts to
preserve landmark properties; private individuals began to repair and
restore modest dwellings, not as museum pieces but as places to live. One
of the most active restorers was the redoubtable Susan Pringle Frost. A
member of an established Charleston family, an ardent suffragette, and
a leading founder of the Preservation Society, Frost was also a real estate
agent. In that role she bought decaying historic properties, renovated the
houses, and resold them. Her interest in the past often outweighed her
business judgment. "I have never commercialized my restoration work,

or my love of the old and beautiful things of Charleston," she told an interviewer. "I have lost heavily on Tradd Street." Frost was referring to her efforts to restore an entire portion of one of the city's oldest streets. Around the corner, on East Bay Street, was another of Frost's projects, a row of eighteenth-century houses. Subsequent owners painted the facades in different pastel colors—another "fabricated tradition"— giving rise to the name Rainbow Row.

Not only Charlestonians came to love Charleston. During the First World War, unable to vacation in Europe, wealthy northerners began wintering on the Georgia coast, and on the way they discovered the Lowcountry. Owning a Carolina plantation became fashionable, so much so that Simons referred disparagingly to "Wall Street planters." Despite the complaint, northern money played an important role in preserving the city. New Yorkers, especially, were prominent: Solomon R. Guggenheim bought and restored a mansion on East Battery; the celebrated architect John Mead Howells made his winter home in a renovated historic house on Tradd Street; and Loutrel Briggs, a landscape architect who would design many gardens in the Charleston area, bought and restored the Church Street tenement that was the model for Catfish Row.

Piecemeal conservation was all very well, but it was obvious that preventing further indiscriminate destruction of old buildings, and the introduction of intrusive uses such as gas stations and car dealerships into the historic district, required some sort of legislation. It was obvious that the historic buildings were important to the growing tourist industry, but the city could not simply ride roughshod over the rights of individual property owners. The solution lay in a new type of municipal regulation: zoning. In the early 1900s, the U.S. Supreme Court had upheld the right of cities to regulate land use through zoning, and most states adopted laws that enabled local governments to enact such ordinances. In 1931, as part of a city-wide zoning plan, and with the active support of preservationists such as Frost and Simons, the Charleston city council created a so-called historic zoning district at the tip of the peninsula, the city's oldest neighborhood. For the first time in an American city, zoning was used to preserve old buildings. The ordinance was based on a groundbreaking insight: that the historic sense of a place was not the result only of individual landmarks but of the experience of entire neighborhoods. What became known as the Charleston ordinance was subsequently copied by other cities, both small and large: Annapolis, Georgetown, and Saint Augustine, as well as New Orleans, Boston, and Philadelphia. It was at this time that the city created the BAR to oversee implementation of the historic ordinance.[*]

How did a small, poor, provincial southern city become a pioneer in historic preservation? Robert R. Weyeneth, a historian at the University of South Carolina, has identified several reasons. The first was the city's early history of great wealth followed by great poverty, the former producing some of the most refined colonial and antebellum urban buildings in the country, and the latter ensuring their survival. As we have seen, the old-line Charleston elites resisted change, and modernization largely bypassed the poor city. This had the effect of preserving the streets and buildings. In the early twentieth century, most fast-growing American cities showed little concern for their own history as they developed new residential areas and new commercial centers that left their old downtowns behind. Not Charleston. In 1930, the city was barely larger than it had been in the nineteenth century, the downtown was still the downtown, the wealthy neighborhoods remained at the tip of the peninsula, and the working-class neighborhoods were farther north. The city skyline of church steeples was unmarred by high-rise buildings. Economic lethargy only partly explains Charleston's preservation of the past, however. City of Proud Memories describes a place "where tradition reigns supreme and the possession of a proud old name is the proudest thing a man can have," a reminder of the enduring importance of ancestry among the Charleston elite. As Weyeneth observes, the "preservation of local heritage was frequently inseparable from preservation of family history."

This interest in preserving the past was further encouraged by a cultural flowering known as the Charleston Renaissance. "Renaissance" may be misleading—Charles Town was never a cultural mecca. It may have been the fourth-largest city in the colonies, but since more than half its inhabitants were prohibited by law from learning to read and

* The first architect on the board was the tireless Albert Simons, who served for forty-three years.

write, in terms of an active cultural life it was more like a small town. Moreover, the boomtown atmosphere, while it encouraged conspicuous consumption—including building and furnishing fine homes—did not necessarily stimulate intellectual pursuits, as Harriet Martineau had observed. The wealthy city produced no Emersons, Thoreaus, or Hawthornes. The College of Charleston was founded as early as 1785, but for years it attracted few students because wealthy families sent their children north to be educated—to New England and as far away as Britain. During his travels, Olmsted commented on the generally low level of southern culture: "From the banks of the Mississippi to the banks of the James, I did not (that I remember) see, except perhaps in one or two towns, a thermometer, nor a book of Shakespeare, nor a piano-forte or sheet of music; nor the light of a . . . reading lamp, nor an engraving or copy of any kind, of a work of art of the slightest merit."

The literary side of the twentieth-century cultural flowering was represented most prominently by DuBose Heyward, who also cofounded a local poetry society. The visual arts included a group of local painters such as Alice Ravenel Huger Smith and Elizabeth O'Neill Verner, who started magazines, sketching clubs, and art schools. Northern painters such as Childe Hassam and Edward Hopper "discovered" Charleston and added to the mix. It was natural that architects should be drawn into this circle. Smith and her architect father together wrote *The Dwelling Houses of Charleston, South Carolina* (1917), a thick compendium illustrated with her evocative drawings. The book was published by Lippincott in Philadelphia, and was instrumental in bringing the city's historic architecture to national attention. *Dwelling Houses* included photographs and drawings by Albert Simons, who taught art appreciation at the College of Charleston and, with his architectural partner, Samuel Lapham, Jr., edited a comprehensive survey of the historic district's early buildings. Simons's cousin, Samuel Gaillard Stoney, produced a similar study of Lowcountry plantations.

Old buildings were not only cherished architectural treasures— and family heirlooms—they were also reminders of a vanished way of life. To V. S. Naipaul, who visited Charleston in the 1980s, southerners' attitude toward the past was not simply nostalgia but a kind of cult. "It

The artists of the Charleston Renaissance took the
historic city as their subject. Alice Ravenel Huger Smith
drew the kitchen courtyard of the Miles Brewton
House in 1914.

wasn't only the old houses and the old families, the old names, the antiquarian side of provincial or state history," he wrote. "It was also the past
as a wound: the past of which the dead or alienated plantations spoke,
many of them still with physical mementoes of the old days, the houses,
the dependencies, the oak avenues. The past of which the more-black-
than-white city now spoke, the past of slavery and the Civil War."

To black Charlestonians, the past meant something quite different, of course. The two perspectives remained separate. Although writers such as Heyward were sympathetic to black culture, the Charleston
Renaissance was strictly a white affair. Even the Society for the Preservation of Spirituals, which was dedicated to the collection, transcrip-
tion, and performance of Gullah gospel music, and of which Heyward
was a member, was all-white.* A talented black painter such as Edwin A.
Harleston, a Charleston native who was a graduate of the art school of
the Boston Museum of Fine Arts and thus better trained than most of
his white Charleston contemporaries who were self-taught, worked in
isolation. In 1926, he was invited to exhibit in the Charleston Museum
by its director, but the invitation was quickly rescinded by the museum
trustees. Although the museum played an important role in preserving
the past, throughout most of the 1920s that institution, like the public
library, was off-limits to black Charlestonians.

Although the Charleston Renaissance predated the better-known
literary Southern Renaissance, except for Heyward, none of its figures
achieved national prominence. Nevertheless, in a small city such as
Charleston, with its overlapping social circles and interrelated established families, the effect of this artistic activity was significant, especially as the focus of the movement was the city itself. As Weyeneth
puts it: "Artists and writers alike discovered a sentimental charm in the
crumbling structures of the old city, and they created images that promoted a powerful, nostalgic aesthetic."

It's easy to pooh-pooh nostalgia, but the attitudes toward the past
that were formed in the Charleston Renaissance had an important effect
on the city. While other cities embraced urban renewal in the 1950s
and 1960s in the name of progress, Charleston, secure in its backward-
looking self-importance, stubbornly resisted change and maintained its
old ways. The sometime laborious procedures put in place by the historic
ordinances and the BAR prevented the wholesale destruction of downtown neighborhoods that was a common feature of so many American

---

* Members of the Society toured nationally and performed at Franklin Roosevelt's White
House.

cities, and despite the occasional high-rise apartment building, the peninsula largely preserved its historic scale. Moreover, the nostalgic aesthetic provided the foundation for the economic revival of the city as a major destination for holidayers and cultural tourists. In the process, it also paved the way for Historic Renovations of Charleston, Tully Alley, and the building adventures of George Holt and his friends.

Part II

FIVE

Palladio and Polystyrene

The continued allure of Andrea Palladio,
from Thomas Jefferson to today

I got to know George more or less by chance. In March 2003, I was in Charleston to give a talk at the invitation of Vince Graham. Vince, a soft-spoken Georgian then in his mid-thirties, was a developer. We had met a decade earlier in Beaufort, a Lowcountry coastal town where he was building a small subdivision—his first real estate project. I was impressed by the design, which was inspired by old Beaufort's narrow treed streets and antebellum architecture. We had kept in touch. In the intervening years, Vince had gone from success to success. His current—and most ambitious—project was a planned community named I'On in Mount Pleasant, a suburban city across the Cooper River from Charleston.

I'On was an example of New Urbanism. This type of planning is based on walkability and visual diversity, and emphasizes neighborhood features such as scale, density, and the pedestrian experience. New Urbanism rejects the "towers-in-the-park" ethos promoted by International Style architects and planners such as Le Corbusier, and this strong anti-modernist streak favors established architectural traditions. Houses in New Urbanist developments tend to have pitched roofs, porches, bay windows, shutters, and picket fences. To assure the design quality of the houses in his project, Vince screened more than a hundred small, local home builders and invited ten of them to join what he called the I'On Guild, whose members would have the exclusive right to buy lots and build in the development. He created a formal induction ceremony and ordered up monogrammed caps and T-shirts. To develop what he called "a culture of the right way to do things," he organized dinners, ran workshops, and held an annual ceremony with awards in categories such as Best Carpentry and Best Masonry. He also invited visiting lecturers, which is where I came in.

My wife, Shirley, and I drove down to Charleston during the university's spring break. Vince lent us his house, a small book-filled cottage in I'On. We had some free time before the talk and decided to go into Charleston. We had visited the historic district a few years before, and I asked Vince if there was something recent that we should see. He mentioned Tully Alley and gave us directions. I was impressed. I'm an admirer of Addison Mizner's work, and the marigold house with its fanciful Moorish motifs was straight out of the Mizner playbook—and entirely unexpected in staid Charleston.

Just before my lecture, which was held at the I'On community clubhouse, I was telling Vince about our favorable impression of Tully Alley. He pulled over a small, wiry man and introduced him as responsible for the project—it was George Holt. He and Vince were obviously friends. We chatted briefly, but my mind was on my lecture. My topic was the villas of Andrea Palladio, the great Renaissance architect and the subject of my latest book. Palladio was originally trained as a stonemason, not as an artist or an architect, and I though that would appeal to my audience. There were about forty people, mostly builders and contractors and a few residents. They were attentive during the talk and forthcoming during the lively question period. After the lecture, Shirley, who had been talking to George while I was signing books, brought him over. "Guess what?" she said. "He's building a real Palladian house." Somewhat diffidently, George suggested that if I was interested and had the time he'd be happy to show me the house, which was in a Charleston suburb. I didn't know what to expect, but after seeing Tully Alley I was curious.

We went the next day. George's project was in Otranto, a neighborhood in the small suburban city of Hanahan, north of Charleston, where George had grown up and where his parents still lived. Otranto derived its name from an eighteenth-century colonial plantation belonging to Dr. Alexander Garden, a noted botanist after whom the gardenia is named. The house he built still stood, a low structure with deep, shady porches. The estate itself survived intact until the 1960s, when it was subdivided, and it was now covered with cul-de-sacs, driveways, two-car garages, and pleasant but unremarkable brick ranchers and split-levels.

We had no trouble finding George's house. It was the only construction site in the neighborhood; a dumpster and a portable toilet stood in the muddy front yard, and workers' pickup trucks filled the driveway. The house facade was distinguished from its neighbors by its rudely plastered stucco walls and a large portico of the sort that most people associate with small-town banks. This one had a temple-like pediment supported by four square piers. The one-story house was not large, but thanks to its proportions it appeared massive, its ponderous simplicity suggesting great age, an impression reinforced by the lack of contemporary details and the roughness of its finishes. I took all this in quickly. It was starting to rain and we hurried into the shelter of the portico.

George, wearing a plaid shirt and a battered baseball cap—his contractor's uniform—was waiting for us. Before we went in, I examined the piers of the portico. Close-up, their bulk was impressive. They were not smooth, but made of stacked-up blocks of concrete, each about thirty inches square and a foot thick. George explained that the blocks were hollow and were filled with concrete and steel reinforcing bars. He told us that he precast the blocks using several molds of slightly different size, to avoid the impression of mechanical uniformity; the rough surface was produced by smearing the interior of the molds with a mixture of vegetable shortening and sand. The slight variation in color was the result of varying the amount of umber dye that was mixed with the cement. The concrete would be painted with three coats of linseed oil, which would soak in unevenly and liven up the color. George said that he modeled the piers on photographs of Palladio's Villa Sarego outside Verona, whose columns are made out of roughly carved individual stone drums, stacked up like piles of huge donuts. George thought that round columns would look pretentious in these suburban surroundings, so he made them square instead: "Square piers seemed cozier to me than round columns."

Some of Palladio's early villas do have square piers, although "cozy" is an odd word to choose to describe these rugged supports. As George spoke, I realized that he was no simple contractor. He clearly had studied Palladio—the Villa Sarego was not one of the master's famous works—and the details of the portico suggested a sophisticated understanding of classical design. Subtle visual refinements, such as the slight variations in the color of the concrete and in the construction of the piers, were not a part of most modern architects' vocabulary, however. George was an anachronism—an old-fashioned master builder.

The monumental front doors were about ten feet tall. We went inside. We had to duck to avoid the scaffolding; a crew of plasterers was at work on the interior. The walls and ceilings of the entry hall, which led directly into a living room, were unfinished plasterboard, but the general outlines of the space were evident. There were niches for built-in bookshelves and an opening for a fireplace. The living room had an impressive sixteen-foot ceiling, and the hall was enlivened by intersecting arches supported on concrete columns. George told me that the fiberglass molds for the columns had been made for him from specially fabricated wooden originals. The surprisingly large, undecorated imposts resembled crudely carved boulders. "The imposts are based on ones I saw in a Justinian cistern in Istanbul," he said. "Their roughness is meant to tone down the interior and keep it from looking too polished."

Palladio's villas in the Veneto usually have basements and attic stories, neither of which was present here, but the house was distinctly Palladian in a number of other ways: the symmetrical front facade with its central entrance portico; the monumental piers; the large double doors and tall ceilings. Palladio built his villas with heavy masonry walls, and I noticed that here the external walls were almost a foot thick. George explained the construction. The walls were built of blocks manufactured of recycled polystyrene, a material commonly used for packaging. The lightweight blocks, bonded with Portland cement, were four feet long and sixteen inches tall, much larger than conventional cement blocks. As the blocks were assembled, steel reinforcing bars were placed horizontally and vertically in the cavities, which were later filled with concrete.

Once in place, the blocks were plastered, inside and out. These types of blocks are sometimes called insulated concrete forms because the blocks act as permanent formwork for the reinforced concrete and also provide insulation for the finished wall. George said that this was the first time he had used this material, an Austrian product manufactured in Texas. He liked it because it was resistant to rot, insects, and fire. And also to hurricanes—he referred to the house as a bunker.

The combination of Palladio and polystyrene reflected George's pragmatic approach to building. Unlike some modern classicists, he was not overly concerned with historical correctness—the Byzantine imposts in the living room, for example, have no precedent in Palladio's work, nor did the room layout adhere to the strict symmetry that characterizes Palladio's villa plans. "I always found Palladio a little stiff," George said. "In any case, my client didn't like the formality of a symmetrical plan." However, the temple front of the central loggia was definitely Palladian. The tympanum, or triangular face of the pediment, which in a Renaissance villa would have displayed the owner's coat of arms, and which most modern architects would have adorned with a roundel or a lunette, was downright plain: simply butt-jointed wooden boards. George had gone to a lot of trouble to re-create the generous scale of a Palladian villa: massive piers; tall front doors; and very tall casement windows (actually French doors used as windows). But he was not fussy about details. I found his fondness for blemishes and crudeness compelling. Most contemporary Palladian houses combine Palladian motifs with flawless workmanship, but one of the things that makes Palladio's Renaissance villas so attractive is precisely their lack of precision, their unexpected mixture of ancient Roman monumentality and Veneto rusticity. Ionic columns support clay-tiled roofs, carved stone moldings sit next to rough plaster—palatial architecture in a farmyard. There would be no farmyard next to the Otranto house, just a front lawn and a driveway, but the contrast was similar: something special side by side with something everyday. As I later told Vince, George's suburban project was the most Palladian house I had seen other than the originals.

Palladian architecture has deep roots in Charleston. The city's colonial prosperity coincided with the ascendancy of the Palladian style in Britain, and the homes built by wealthy Charlestonian merchants and planters followed the prevailing fashion. Because there were no professional architects in colonial Charleston, the houses were designed either by their owners or by carpenter-builders. These amateur architects based their plans on so-called pattern books, the eighteenth-century equivalent of DIY guides. Architectural enthusiasts might have a copy of Palladio's *The Four Books on Architecture*, originally published in 1570 as *I quattro libri dell'architettura* and available in an English translation since 1720.

The Charleston town houses modeled on Palladio's designs for country villas were called double houses, which had nothing to do with the single house, but described the plan: two banks of rooms, one on each side of a central stair hall, a traditional British arrangement. The Miles Brewton House, built in the late 1760s, is a good example. The front of this brick building is dominated by a two-story portico in the form of a Roman temple. The portico was probably influenced by Drayton Hall (1738–42), a Lowcountry plantation house located a short distance up the Ashley River from the city and considered one of the oldest Palladian houses in North America. Drayton Hall's delicate two-story portico is loosely modeled on Palladio's Villa Cornaro, described in *Quattro libri*. The proportions of the rooms, the symmetrical placement of the windows on the main facades, and the imposing monumentality are all derived from Palladio. The plantation house stands on a tall basement, and the main floor is reached by an impressive exterior stair. The effect was originally even more imposing, thanks to two flanking outbuildings linked to the house by curved arcades, or hyphens, a Palladian device much favored by colonial builders—George Washington used hyphens at Mount Vernon.

The designer of Drayton Hall was likely its owner, John Drayton. He had a collection of pattern books, so his version of Palladio was filtered through eighteenth-century British eyes. The walls of his house were red brick with white trim—not Italian at all—many details were carved wood instead of carved stone, the original roof was tin or sheet iron rather than clay tiles, and the column spacing of the portico was

Palladio provided the model for Drayton Hall, 1738–42,
a plantation house outside Charleston.

considerably wider than prescribed by the master. The inspiration was
also not solely Palladian. Drayton adapted the floor plan from a popular
pattern book, James Gibbs's *Book of Architecture*, and based the design of
the imposing fireplace in the main public room on another widely used
handbook, William Kent's *Designs of Inigo Jones*. Jones had introduced
Palladio to the British in the sixteenth century, so Drayton Hall is three
times removed—from Drayton to Kent to Jones to Palladio. And there
are other anomalies. The side elevations are clumsily unsymmetrical and
the elevation facing the river is downright awkward. Whether this awk-
wardness is the result of an amateur's lack of mastery, or of colonial
pragmatism, is hard to tell. The most radical departure is the staircase.
The stairs in Palladio's villas were always hidden in secondary spaces,
but the monumental double staircase of Drayton Hall is prominently
located in an entrance hall. As far as we know, this is the first such colonial stair, a feature that would become a hallmark of many later Ameri-

can homes. John Drayton adapted and altered Palladian ideas to suit the conditions and way of life of his time, just as George would do with the Otranto house more than two hundred years later.

Twenty-six years after Drayton Hall was completed, Thomas Jefferson started to build his house at Monticello. He likewise took the Villa Cornaro as his model. Jefferson's carefully drafted drawing shows a two-story facade that is less Georgian and more Palladian than Drayton Hall. The design includes flanking wings, a Doric frieze, and properly spaced and proportioned columns, closely following Palladio's prescriptions. Jefferson started to build in 1768. The work was slowed by the war, and by his later responsibilities as minister to France and secretary of state. Then, unexpectedly, he had a change of heart. His time in Paris, and his travels in France and Italy (though not as far as the Veneto), had sharpened his eye and broadened his architectural horizons; simply creating a faithful copy of the Villa Cornaro would no longer do. Deciding that his house should be on one level, Jefferson demolished the newly built second story and enlarged the footprint, in the process making several of the rooms octagonal and adding semi-octagonal bay windows. Such geometry has no precedent in Palladio, and Jefferson's source was probably *Select Architecture,* a pattern book written in 1750 by the English architect Robert Morris.

Jefferson's other major alteration was the addition of a dome. His copy of *Quattro libri* contained two domed villas, and like Palladio's villas, Monticello was situated on a hilltop, the dome acting as a kind of architectural trope of the topography.* Palladio's domes were masonry. Jefferson had no skilled masons among his plantation slaves, but while in Paris he had come across a technique for constructing domes out of wood. Since his dome was a last-minute addition, it required compromise: the dome did not cover a central hall, as in Palladio's designs, only an awkwardly accessible and little-used attic. Jefferson may have been a little ashamed of this improvised solution. Years later, he wrote to a friend, the architect Benjamin Latrobe: "My essay in architecture has been so much subordinated to the law of convenience, & affected also

---

* In *Quattro libri,* Palladio describes one of the hilltop sites as *"un monticello"*—a small hill— which was likely Jefferson's inspiration for the name of his home.

After Monticello, Thomas Jefferson designed this simple version of
a Palladian house: Edgemont in Albemarle County, Virginia, c. 1796.

by circumstance of change in the original design, that it is liable to some
unfavorable & just criticism."

Whatever Jefferson's reservations, Monticello is a distinctive building, and as a result Jefferson was frequently asked for architectural advice
by his friends and neighbors. One of these was James Powell Cocke, who
owned a plantation in Albemarle County, fifteen miles from Monticello.
There is strong evidence that Edgemont, the house that Cocke built in
1796, was based on sketches provided by Jefferson. The design is a dis-
tillation of Palladian motifs. Jefferson's surviving sketch shows a simple
three-bay facade with a hipped roof and a central pedimented portico
with four Tuscan columns. The result resembles the facade of George's
Otranto house, except that Jefferson's version has a pronounced base.
I showed a copy of the sketch to George. "I've never seen that drawing
before," he told me. "Oddly, I gave much thought to adding a similar

base skirting the house at ground level but decided that since the column bases weren't very high that it would look overdone. I now wish I had done it." Two self-taught architect-builders inspired by the work of a distant Renaissance master had the same idea—not so odd at all.

Why did house builders such as Drayton and Jefferson—and George—turn to Palladio? It was surely not simply that Palladio's book provides detailed architectural solutions—all pattern books do that. Palladio was not merely an inventive designer, he was consciously seeking to discover the secrets of his ancient Roman predecessors, whose ruined buildings he studied and carefully documented on his frequent visits to Rome. The fragmented remains that he saw were temples, not houses, so he was obliged to imagine what Roman villas *might* have looked like. In doing so, he carefully explained the rationale for his conjecture. *Quattro libri* has been so influential not because it is easy to copy, but because it is easy to understand. The text is clear and to the point; the accompanying drawings include all the necessary information. That may be the reason that over the centuries so many architects, talented professionals as well as amateurs, have been attracted to Palladio. The prescriptions never feel like pedantic rules but more like a colleague generously sharing insights that inspire rather than constrain.

I asked George what had led him to Palladio. He said that he thought that the prominent corner lot called for something special, but that a Byzantine house would have been too "gimmicky." Instead, he opted for a simplified Palladian villa. "I had an idea that it would look as if the house had been there before anything was built, as if the other houses around it had been constructed later," he said. Which is exactly the way it has turned out. Like Dr. Garden's plantation house, which we drove past on the way in, George's house looked as if it had been there forever. It was the bungalows and split-levels around it that looked like interlopers.

Six months later, I returned with George to see the finished house. The owners had moved in. The lawn was freshly sodded, and potted shrubs stood ready for planting. The stucco walls were painted a warm ochre

George Holt designed a Palladian bungalow for his sister
in the suburbs of Charleston, 2003.

that contrasted with the dark green of the windows and shutters and the
umber portico. The mottled colors of the pier blocks varied slightly, as
George said they would.

We were greeted at the front door by George's clients: his sister
Julia and her husband, Alan. She was a hospice nurse, he a high school
science teacher; they had two teenaged boys. The proud new homeowners showed me around the house. Although they had moved in only six
weeks earlier, the rooms looked comfortably occupied. The large living
room—home builders would call it a great room—had striped sofas in
front of the fireplace; Julia's upright piano was at one end of the room,
a television-watching area at the other. The shelves were full of books.
I mentioned to George that except for the Byzantine columns, whose
rough stone capitals were now painted the same creamy color as the
walls, the details were rather simple. It was a question of the budget, he
explained. "I love fabulous moldings, but a room can look good without
all that ornament. It's mainly a question of the proportions."

An arched doorway led to the bedrooms; on the opposite side, another opened to the dining room and a small kitchen with a walk-in pantry. These rooms overlooked a large patio, about sixteen by twenty feet, at the heart of the house. This was George's alternative to the suburban backyard. The patio was not a Palladian feature, more like something you would find in a Spanish hacienda. Arched openings were supported by concrete half-columns with what look like turtles on the capitals and twisted vines instead of flutes. George said that the boys liked turtles— the patio also had a shallow turtle pond—and as for the twisted vines, "they have no historical model; I was just having fun." The paving of the patio remained unfinished. Building the house had obviously stretched Julia and Alan's finances, and they told me that they planned to complete the work themselves.

I asked Julia, a cheerful, dark-haired woman in her thirties, how they came to build the house. "We'd lived in our previous house for fifteen years, and it no longer worked for us," she said. "I didn't like living on two floors—I was having problems with my knees." Julia wanted a really big pantry and a laundry room with a proper folding table and linen cupboards. She and Alan didn't mind if their bedroom was small, but they wanted a dressing room. The living room, where they spent a lot of time, had to be spacious; Alan wanted a small study. They also needed a guest suite for his elderly parents. As a nurse, Julia was concerned with handicap access: wide doors, large bathrooms. Julia and Alan had decided against buying an old house, since old houses in Charleston often suffer from mildew and other environmental problems that could trigger their allergies—they both suffered from asthma. Julia and Alan didn't feel they could afford an architect, so they looked at catalogs of mail-order house plans. It was difficult to find something suitable.

From time to time during their search they would show plans to George and ask his opinion. He was rather critical. One day, he showed up with sketches of his own. "I really didn't want to take it on," he said. "Building in the suburbs didn't appeal to me—I'm a downtown architect. But she was my kid sister, and I wanted to help." Julia was delighted. "We knew that it would be something special. Every house George builds is different. But I trusted his judgment."

George developed the plan around the inner patio. "We had never thought of having a courtyard," Julia said. "As you can see, most of the light in the house comes from there. We love it." It took a long time to work out the details. "They wanted a lot," said George, "but they didn't have enough money, so the plan kept growing and shrinking. We were able to get it down to just over three thousand square feet. It took me a year to finish the design."

George had not planned to be the contractor. Then he came across the polystyrene block-building system. He explained to Julia and Alan that he had never used the material before and wanted to try it; they liked the idea of a concrete house and agreed to the experiment. George offered to build the walls himself—at cost—and to help find a contractor to complete the rest of the house. "We interviewed a number of builders," said Julia, "but it became obvious that they didn't really understand the design." At one point, the builders stopped coming. Worried, Julia called Cheryl and asked her what was going on. Who was going to build their house? George? "Oh yes, absolutely," Cheryl said. "There's no way he would let anyone else build the house for you."

After our visit, George mentioned that he was building something for Vince Graham, my developer friend who had introduced us several months earlier. George said it was an unusual project. Would I like to see it? I was getting used to his offhand demeanor, and if he said something was unusual, that sparked my interest. "Let's go," I said.

Turrets and Domes

Vince dreams of a castle, George meets Andrew,
Andrew builds a church

Georgethe and I drove to Sullivan's Island, which overlooks the
entrance to Charleston Harbor. This is the site of Fort Moultrie, which played an important role in both the Revolutionary War and the Civil War. The island served another
historic function. It is sometimes called the black Ellis Island, for it was
here that nearly half of all enslaved Africans transported to the American colonies were disembarked and quarantined after the horrific Middle Passage. Today the island is a holiday beach town.

Our destination was a small stone church on Middle Street, the
island's main thoroughfare. Ralph Adams Cram, who wrote a handbook
on religious architecture, would have called it a country chapel, and he
would have approved of its simple English Gothic features: buttressed
rubble granite walls, a trefoil window, a belfry steeple. Vince Graham
came out to greet us. He was in the process of converting the building
into a residence for himself. That surprised me. He had struck me as a
practical, down-to-earth sort of person, hardly the type to undertake
what appeared to be a rather quixotic venture.

Why did he want to live in a converted chapel? I asked. The answer
was a convoluted story. The Chapel of the Holy Cross had been built in
1891 to serve the Episcopal summer residents of Sullivan's Island. The

architect was W. W. DeVeaux, based in New York but originally from Charleston. Less than fifteen years later, the U.S. Army, which was in the process of enlarging Fort Moultrie, took possession of the building to use as a post chapel (the displaced Episcopal congregation built a new church down the street). When Fort Moultrie was deactivated after the Second World War, ancillary buildings were sold off and the chapel changed hands again, becoming a Lutheran church. Twenty-five years later, after the Lutherans had moved on to a larger home, the deconsecrated chapel was sold to a private individual, who converted the structure into a beach house.

Vince acquired the chapel in a roundabout way. One of the principles of New Urbanism is to locate civic buildings within residential communities—a common practice in the past—and Vince's vision for I'On had always included a neighborhood church. He had set aside a plot of land for that purpose. A local Baptist congregation was interested—it planned to share the building with a Jewish congregation—but finally decided that it needed a larger lot. Vince attended the Church of the Holy Cross on Sullivan's Island, and he discussed the possibility of a satellite church in I'On with his pastor. At this time, the old converted chapel on Middle Street came on the market. Vince thought it might be possible to move the building to I'On, and because the chapel had once belonged to the selfsame Episcopal congregation, his pastor was open to the suggestion. In 2002, Vince put down a deposit on the property.

Vince had assumed that the chapel would have to be dismantled to be moved, but when he consulted a house mover he learned that it might be possible to move the building whole. The house mover introduced him to a Scottish mason who had been involved with moving the Cape Hatteras Light, which had been threatened by tidal erosion and had to be relocated half a mile inland. If you could move a 210-foot-tall brick lighthouse, surely you could move a small chapel? The operation would require raising the chapel from its foundations, laying railroad tracks from Middle Street to the water's edge, loading the building onto a barge, and floating it across Charleston Harbor and up Hobcaw Creek, which adjoined the I'On property. The new community was in its early stages, so there was plenty of room to lay a second set of tracks leading to the final building site. The chapel weighed five hundred tons, and the total moving cost was estimated at half a million dollars. "I went ahead and arranged a bank loan," Vince told me. "It was a lot of money, but I could justify it because of the publicity. The Discovery Channel was interested in filming the event, which would have been a huge boost for I'On."

It was at that point that the Sullivan's Island town council, learning of the plan, decided to block the move and passed an ordinance creating a new historic district that included the chapel. As a developer, Vince was used to such tactics and he was prepared to fight the last-minute legislation, but the Holy Cross pastor was reluctant to involve the church in a lawsuit. Thus, the move was shelved. Rather than forfeit his deposit, Vince decided to go ahead with the purchase, figuring he could resell the building and at least break even. "The chapel was on the market for three days," he said. "Then I called the broker and told him I had changed my mind. I wanted to keep it."

Vince was single, but he looked forward to marrying, and he had become intrigued with the idea of owning what he called a "family place on the beach." He imagined turning the chapel into a sort of medieval castle; he would call it Mugdock Castle, after the fourteenth-century stronghold of the Clan Graham in Scotland. As a first step, he commissioned Alex Skellon, the Scottish mason who had been involved in the Cape Hatteras lighthouse move, to extend the stumpy belfry, whose wooden steeple had long since disappeared, and turn it into a corbeled and battlemented turret.

By 2003, when George and I visited, work on the chapel interior was under way. The partitions erected by the previous owner had been removed, and so too had a crude sleeping loft at one end. The bare nave was small but striking; the tall ceiling supported by an open timber structure of trusses and hammer beams contributed to the impression of a medieval hall. A dim light came in through the windows—the original stained glass had been removed years before when the Holy Cross congregation had moved out of the building. "I greatly admired the fireplace in George's home and I felt something similar was needed for Mugdock," Vince told me. He commissioned George to design and build a massive baronial fireplace made of patterned concrete with a raised hearth and a tall hood. That was the project that George wanted to show me.

The front of the fireplace mantel included a series of blank pan-

Vince Graham converted Holy Cross Chapel on
Sullivan's Island into Mugdock Castle.

els that were intended to receive mosaic inserts. George said that he
was having trouble finding someone to make them. The talk of mosaics
reminded me of one of my Penn students. Shortly before I left on this
Charleston trip, he had dropped by my office to show me a beautifully
crafted mosaic icon that he had made himself. The panel, about a foot
square, depicted Christ Pantocrator holding the New Testament in one
hand and making a blessing with the other, a classic Byzantine motif. I

The hall of Mugdock Castle. George's baronial fireplace is on the right.

told George about my student and his interest in Byzantine mosaics, and said that I would send him contact information as soon as I got home.

My student's name was Andrew Gould. We met when he enrolled in my seminar on architectural criticism. Generally, architecture students are more comfortable expressing themselves visually rather than verbally, so a successful seminar depends on having at least one or two vocal students to keep the discussion going. Andrew was one of those. Of slight build, with a tall brow and delicate features, he was articulate, although he had an odd way of speaking, a kind of lockjaw New England drawl that reminded me of William F. Buckley, Jr.* His rather formal dress—

---

* I later learned that Andrew's way of speaking had nothing to do with his New England roots, his upbringing, or his schooling, but was the result of childhood therapy to cure a speech impediment.

jacket and tie when most students wore sweatshirts and baseball caps—
reminded me of Buckley, too. The seminar topic that year was the role
of style in contemporary architecture. Unlike many of the participants,
who were resistant to the suggestion that modern architecture had anything to do with style, Andrew was open to the idea. The final essay
assignment required analyzing a modern building in terms of its style.
He chose Lloyd's of London, designed by Richard Rogers. "High tech
is my favorite modern style," he told me later. "It overtly plays up the
machine aesthetic. I find that interesting, since I'm attracted to things
like music boxes, clocks, and ships." The paper earned him an A+, a rar-
ity in my classes.

Andrew had grown up in a Victorian house in Brookline, Massachusetts, an old suburb of Boston. His father was an environmental
engineer and his mother a marine biologist. Andrew was an unusual
boy. "I was not raised churchgoing, but began attending church on my
own when I was thirteen," he told me. "I chose a famous Anglo-Catholic
church in Boston, the Church of the Advent near Beacon Hill, which has
a very grand liturgy and a spectacular professional choir. I don't think
you could find a church in the world that has a more perfectly medieval-
ist liturgical ethos to its services." The Church of the Advent is a beautiful
Early English Gothic structure designed by the notable Boston architect
John Sturgis in 1888. By curious coincidence, the young Ralph Adams
Cram also attended this church, and later designed its Lady Chapel and
the choir screen. Living in Brookline, Andrew was surrounded by inter-
esting religious buildings, including work by such distinguished archi-
tects as Cram and Goodhue, Richard Upjohn, and Robert S. Peabody.
One of his favorites was the Temple Ohabei Shalom, a large Byzantine
Revival synagogue designed in 1925 by the Boston firm Blackall, Clapp
& Whittemore and modeled on Hagia Sophia.

Andrew received his undergraduate degree from Tufts University,
where he majored in art history. He spent a study year at University
College London because he wanted to learn about the Victorian Gothic
Revival and the British Arts and Crafts movement. While he was at University College he joined the choir society, and had the opportunity to
visit Rome on a tour. "It was the Byzantine mosaics in Rome that struck
me more than anything there, and put me on the path towards con-

version to Byzantine architecture. In any case, I had wanted to be an architect ever since I was a little kid." After graduation, he applied to several East Coast architecture programs and was accepted by the University of Pennsylvania. The summer before he started, he accompanied his parents on a vacation trip to Istanbul. Like Cram, Andrew was overwhelmed by Hagia Sophia. "As soon as I walked in I had this strange flash of insight that the interior could be seen as a sort of naturalistic image of the New Jerusalem described in the Book of Revelation—an icon of heaven."

Andrew was interested in history and historic styles, and he had had the impression that among the Ivy League schools, Penn was open to traditional design. He soon discovered that this was not the case. "The studio teachers did not tolerate traditional design, only avant-garde modern," he said. "Each professor taught what was analogous to a different style, although they didn't think of it as such. I went along with that—I wasn't trying to pick fights." But he didn't abandon his interest in traditional architecture. During the summers, he worked for the Church of the Advent designing and building carved Gothic-style furniture, including a lectern and a display case. It was at this time that he made the mosaic icon that he had showed me. To replicate the luster of the mosaics he had seen in Rome and Istanbul, Andrew used opalescent stained glass, Italian marble, and glazed ceramic, as well as Italian smalti. He was becoming a skilled craftsman, obsessive about detail.

Back in Charleston, despite his setback with the old chapel, Vince continued his plan to build a church in I'On. He was approached by Father John Parker, the pastor of a small Eastern Orthodox congregation that was currently renting a store in I'On's town center. The religious bookshop was used as a makeshift place of worship on Sundays, and Father John wanted a proper church. Vince offered a building plot in one of I'On's residential neighborhoods and introduced him to Richard Economakis, an architecture professor at the University of Notre Dame, who prepared some preliminary sketches. Vince showed the sketches to George, who thought the building looked large and a bit complicated for such a small congregation. Vince arranged for the pastor and several members of the congregation to visit George's house on Charles Street. They were impressed by the Byzantine architecture. In the meantime,

Economakis's wife had fallen gravely ill, and he was obliged to withdraw from the project. The congregation turned to George. He told them that he thought a traditional Byzantine-style church could be built that would fit their budget, which was less than $1 million.

"I like Byzantine architecture, but I knew nothing about the Orthodox religion when I accepted this project," George told me. Eastern Orthodoxy was the result of an eleventh-century schism between Constantinople and Rome. The schism had an architectural impact, for while church architecture in western Europe changed over the centuries—Romanesque succeeded by Gothic, classical, and Baroque—Orthodox church architecture remained largely unchanged. There were regional variations in Greece, Russia, and eastern Europe, but all maintained the tradition of domes—onion domes in Russia, flatter domes elsewhere. In the United States, Orthodox traditions have often been interpreted rather more loosely: the Greek Orthodox Annunciation Church outside Milwaukee, designed by Frank Lloyd Wright, includes a distinctly un-Byzantine saucer-like dome; Marlon Blackwell's Antiochian Saint Nicholas Eastern Orthodox Church in Springdale, Arkansas, is a minimalist steel box with only vestigial Byzantine features; and Santiago Calatrava's Greek Orthodox church at Manhattan's Ground Zero, begun in 2015, has a very un-Byzantine translucent dome.

The Holy Ascension congregation in Mount Pleasant belonged to a conservative strain of Orthodoxy, and it wanted something traditional. George modeled his design on churches of the middle Byzantine period, which had simple cruciform plans and large domes over the crossing. He placed a sanctuary at the east end, flanked by a sacristy and a prothesis. The church was entered through a narthex at the west end.

In 2004, shortly before George started working on the church, Cheryl announced that she was retiring—she was not in the best of health and the demands of managing the day-to-day operation of the company were proving too demanding. Her retirement would turn out to be tragically short. "She often complained of not feeling well," says George. "We sort of got used to it." But this time it was serious. She was often tired and was diagnosed with sleep apnea. Her overall health worsened and, two years later, after a short stay in the hospital, she died of congestive heart failure. She was only fifty-three. "She loved Charleston's rich history," her obituary read, "and made a lifelong career of refurbishing Charleston's historic homes." That rang true—without her organizational skills, it's unlikely that George and Jerry would have been able to realize their ideas. The obituary described George as her "life companion." That rang true, too.

George had seen Cheryl's retirement as an opportunity to wind up Historic Renovations of Charleston and focus his energy purely on design. The church would be his first such project. He was used to making rough sketches and working things out on the building site; now he had to produce detailed drawings that a contractor could follow, and for that he needed someone with architectural training. A short time later, he contacted Andrew Gould in Philadelphia. "George telephoned me twice," Andrew recalls. "The first time we discussed our shared interest in Byzantine architecture. The second time he told me about a project that he was working on, an Orthodox church, and asked if I would be interested in coming to Charleston to make construction drawings under his supervision." At first, Andrew was hesitant. He was graduating that spring and had planned to return to Brookline—in any case, he had never been south of Philadelphia. "As a New Englander, I think Andrew was skeptical of moving to the South," said George. There were several more phone calls. Unknown to George, Andrew had a personal interest in the Holy Ascension project. "I had just become engaged," said Andrew. "Julie was a Methodist and I was Episcopalian; we decided that we would convert and be married in the Orthodox Church. It was almost a practical necessity, because neither of us liked the other's denomination, but we were both attracted to Orthodoxy." The opportunity to take part in building an Orthodox church was too good to pass up. Andrew and Julie decided to move to Charleston after his graduation, stay for the summer, and see how things went.

"George got the church to rent us the ground-floor apartment in the Pink House on Saint Philip Street and provide us with furniture," said Andrew. "Julie and I were taking instruction from Father John, and he was concerned that we weren't yet married. When the two beds were delivered they were placed at opposite ends of the apartment; the church was very explicit about which belonged to whom. They kept tabs on us."

It was a busy time for Andrew: preparing to marry, taking instruction in Orthodoxy, working at his first architecture job.

It was Andrew's task to translate George's diagrammatic sketches into a set of detailed construction documents that could be used to elicit bids from contractors. "I did my best," Andrew recalls, "but I soon realized that I didn't know how to make real construction drawings." Not having had the opportunity to work in an architect's office, he had no practical experience—he needed help. The church hired a licensed architect who was about to retire to be the architect of record. He reviewed Andrew's work and taught him how to prepare proper construction documents. "It's what I should have learned at Penn, but in all my time there I was never shown a set of construction drawings," said Andrew. He also benefited from the advice of the project's structural engineer, a member of the congregation.

Andrew's job was not simply technical. The church decided it needed a parish hall, and he added a low wing with an arcaded gallery. He also designed an entrance porch at the west end of the nave. George's plans did not include details, and Andrew worked on those, too. His approach to design was unusual. "I tend to feel that almost every project requires a historical fantasy to define the design concept," he once told an interviewer. For the church he imagined the following scenario: What if Russian Orthodox immigrants had come to Charleston in the nineteenth century and built a church? "That historical fantasy is not far-fetched," Andrew told me. "There are a variety of old churches in Charleston built by different immigrant groups in various styles and for different liturgical rites, so it is relatively easy to imagine that Russians could have done the same had they been here at the time." He leaned to Russia because that was the country of origin of the Orthodox Church in the United States to which the Holy Ascension congregation belonged. (The first American Orthodox churches had been built by Russian immigrants in Alaska.) Walking around Charleston, Andrew identified typical local architectural patterns: masonry construction with a stucco finish, a particular cornice detail, hand-crimped copper roofs, the use of southern heart pine on the interior, strong colors on the exterior, intimate walled gardens with brick paving. He combined these local practices with the characteristic onion domes and three-bar crosses of Russian Orthodoxy.

Andrew's approach was unusual for a modern architect, but it was not unprecedented. In 1910, when Ralph Adams Cram was commissioned to design a new campus for Rice University in Houston, he faced a difficult problem. "A level and stupid site, no historical or stylistic precedents (not even that of old Mexico of which Texas had been a frontier part so many generations ago); no ideas imposed by President or Trustees," he recalled in his autobiography. Although Cram was campus architect at Princeton and believed that Gothic was a suitable style for collegiate buildings, he determined that English Gothic spires and flying buttresses would be out of place on the hot Texas plain. "We wanted something that was beautiful, if we could make it so, Southern in its spirit, and with some quality of continuity with the historic and cultural past." His solution was a new Gothic style, not an outright invention but a historical fantasy. Cram asked himself, What if Gothic had emerged in the southern Mediterranean region rather than in northern Europe? "I reassembled all the elements I could from southern France and Italy, Dalmatia, the Peloponnesus, Byzantium, Anatolia, Syria, Sicily, Spain, and set myself the task of creating a measurably new style that, while built on a classical basis, should have the Gothic romanticism, pictorial quality, and structural integrity." This unique blend was achieved in rose-hued brick, multicolored marbles, and glazed, iridescent tile.

There were several parallels between Andrew and Cram, not only their ties to Boston and their attendance at the Church of the Advent. Cram was a devout Christian and, like Andrew, he had undergone a sort of epiphany in Rome. During a youthful Italian trip—he was twenty-three—Cram attended midnight mass in a Baroque church, a transformative experience that led him to convert to Anglo-Catholicism. The same trip confirmed his intention to become an architect. Unlike Andrew, Cram was largely self-taught, but both men pursued a historical interest—Cram in Gothic, Andrew in Byzantine—both were talented draftsmen, and both liked to think their way through an architectural problem.

By the time that Andrew completed the construction drawings for the church, the summer of 2004 was coming to a close. He and Julie decided to stay in Charleston; they both liked the city, and he wanted to see the church built. They were received into the Orthodox Church and were married the following January. The ceremony took place in Pennsylvania, where Julie's parents lived; Father John came up from Charleston to concelebrate.

The construction drawings for the Holy Ascension Church were sent to two large builders for bids. The first bid came in at $1.7 million, the second at $1.4 million; the church's budget was $800,000. Andrew looked for someone less expensive. "We approached a general contractor who did low-end work such as strip malls. I told him that that there would be no specialized subcontractors, that we would use some of George's old crew, and that I would be on the site to supervise. That got the price down to one million." In order to further reduce the cost, Andrew simplified the details and substituted cheaper materials—asphalt roofing shingles instead of copper, plasterboard instead of hand-laid plaster—reasoning that he could upgrade the materials after construction began. Now they were down to $800,000. To get a construction loan, the congregation had to raise $250,000. "We had lots of small donations," said Andrew. "About half came from parishioners and half from outside. The traditional design helped because many Orthodox churches built today are not very high quality, and people appreciated the difference." The project was put on hold until the fund-raising was completed.

When construction did commence, the work progressed as Andrew had planned and he was able to reintroduce higher-quality materials. The domes got their copper cladding, and the interior was hand-finished lime plaster. To reduce costs, members of the congregation undertook to do some of the work themselves: the framework for the onion domes, the wooden doors, the copper three-bar crosses, and much of the detailed carpentry. A group of volunteers laid the southern heart pine floor. Under Andrew's direction, they built the iconostasis, the wooden icon screen that separates the nave from the sanctuary—the icons themselves were painted by a Russian-American artist in California. A garden designer friend of George's contributed a garden plan, and the parishioners did the landscaping work. The church was consecrated in May 2008.

"George and I share a preference for Byzantine, but this church is a

What if Russian Orthodox immigrants had come to Charleston in the
19th century and built a church? That was the question George Holt
and Andrew Gould asked themselves when they designed the
Holy Ascension Church in I'On, Mount Pleasant, South Carolina.

hybrid," Andrew told me, "more Byzantine on the inside but more Russian on the outside." The exterior had the vertical proportions of a Russian Orthodox church, and the smaller domes, which Andrew added to
George's design, were what Russians call "helmet domes" because they
resemble the headgear of medieval Tatars. The tall hemispherical dome
over the crossing was Byzantine, as were the columns supporting the
arcades that separated the nave from the side aisles. Andrew cast the
concrete columns using George's fiberglass mold (the one he had used
for his sister's house). He carved the molds for the Ionic capitals and
imposts himself, modeling them on those of the Basilica of Saint John,
a sixth-century Greek ruin in Ephesus. The columns were wet-sanded
until their surfaces were perfectly smooth, their greenish patina the
result of several coats of linseed oil.

Holy Ascension Church is more Russian on the outside and more
Byzantine on the inside. Andrew carved the column capitals and made
the *choros* chandelier below the crossing.

When I visited the finished church, the crossing was full of scaffolding and three visiting iconographers from California were painting
the interior of the dome and its supporting drum with images of Christ
Pantocrator and the prophets. My chief impression of the interior was of
inward-looking solidity. Byzantine churches, unlike Gothic, tradition-
ally have few windows—the walls are blank and the natural light comes
from apertures high up in the drum of the dome. There is no stained
glass. At Holy Ascension, the sense of solidity was emphasized by the
massive sixteen-inch-thick walls, two wythes of cement block. Andrew
had the masons chip the corners to create a rounded effect when the wall
was plastered. The heaviness of the masonry contrasted with a large, delicate, circular chandelier that hung on long chains beneath the dome.
Andrew's model was a medieval lighting frame that he had seen in the
Metropolitan Museum of Art. "The chandelier is called a choros after

the circular space that it adorns," he explained. "In ancient Greek, choros was the word for a circular clearing in the forest, a meadow . . . churchmen boldly adopted this word to denote the circular liturgical space under the dome, a sunlit clearing in the forest of columns." The Holy Ascension choros consisted of a twelve-sided band of metal fretwork supporting lights and adorned with decorative motifs and text. To overcome the prohibitive cost of bronze casting, Andrew drew the fretwork in AutoCAD, had steel plate cut by a robotic plasma cutter, and developed an oxidized patina that resembled old wrought iron. He assembled and installed the pieces himself. The text was a famous verse from the Book of Revelation: "There shall be no night there; and they need no candle, neither light of the sun; for the Lord God giveth them light: and they shall reign for ever and ever."

The copper helmet domes on the exterior are an exotic presence among the porches, dormers, and bay windows of I'On's residential neighborhood. Yet thanks to Andrew's historical fantasy, Holy Ascension does not appear out of place. The yellow ochre of the stuccoed walls can be found in many older Charleston buildings, and the central dome recalls the cupolas of the First Presbyterian Church on Meeting Street. The low wing containing the parish hall is a comfortable domestic presence, as is the adjacent garden, which forms a sort of horticultural overture to a more intimate walled garden at the entrance to the church. Bell-ringing is a Russian Orthodox tradition, and a low timber frame with four bells stands on one side of the garden. One of the most attractive features of the building is its human scale, the result of a happy relationship between the larger elements such as the rounded volume of the apse and the swelling dome. Another is its crafted details: the hand-crimped copper roofs, the carved capitals, the glass roundels of the arched windows. "One of the most common mistakes made in modern buildings is that they are over-scaled and under-detailed," Andrew observes. "That is to say, the architectural features are very large and they do not have enough detail for that large size." At Holy Ascension, scale and detail are in happy balance.

SEVEN

Andrew's World

How do you add to a beautiful old building?

Vince completed the conversion of the old chapel on Sullivan's Island into Mugdock Castle in 2008. The nave now contained a living area, with an open kitchen at one end and a sleeping loft at the other. That was alright for a bachelor, but Vince envisioned family get-togethers, which would require more space, including guest bedrooms. He had discussed a rear addition with George, who had made some rough sketches, but when it came time to start, George was occupied with another project and recommended that Andrew take over. That was fine with Vince, who had been impressed with the Holy Ascension Church. The Mugdock addition would be Andrew's first independent commission.

How do you add to a beautiful old chapel or, indeed, to any old building? One tactic is to embrace continuity by matching the architecture of the original. That is what Christopher Wren did when he was called upon to complete the gatehouse—Tom Tower—of the Great Quadrangle of Christ Church, Oxford, in 1681. The college had been built by Cardinal Wolsey a hundred and fifty years earlier. Wolsey's castellated Late Gothic was out of fashion—thanks in no small part to Wren, the country's leading classicist—but Wren nevertheless chose the antique style for the addition. As he succinctly explained, the tower "ought to be Gothick to agree with the Founder's worke."

Wren's sensible view would not pass muster with most historic preservationists today. They are guided by the Venice Charter, or the Venice Charter for the Conservation and Restoration of Monuments and Sites, to give it its full name. The charter, which was drawn up in 1964 by an international group of architects, scholars, and building conservators, describes standards for restoring and conserving historic buildings. These rules mandate that any replacement of missing or unfinished parts to a building "must be distinguishable from the original so that restoration does not falsify the artistic or historic evidence." Matching new construction to old is denounced as "false history." According to this reasoning, Wren should have built a classical tower, to emphasize that his addition was from a different period than the rest of the college. The assumption that a building represents coherent historic and artistic intentions is an art historian's view. In fact, buildings, unlike paintings and sculptures, are not static creations; construction takes a long time and changes are often made during that extended process, interiors are regularly modified by successive generations, and on the exterior the weather takes its toll. In addition, building functions change, and as old uses disappear, new ones have to be accommodated. Thus, most old buildings are accumulations of many layers, each new at one time, and each eventually becoming old. If every layer were "distinguishable," as the Venice Charter demands, the result would be visual pandemonium.

Nevertheless, the U.S. Secretary of the Interior's Standards for the Treatment of Historic Properties, which were adopted in 1977, were based on the Venice Charter: "Design for the new work may be contemporary or may reference design motifs from the historic building. In either case, it should always be clearly differentiated from the historic building." Modernist architects, who take it as given that whatever is built today must be "of our time," have enthusiastically embraced this mandate. This has produced some distinctly odd results. None is odder than Robert Venturi and John Rauch's 1970s addition to the Allen Memorial Art Museum at Oberlin College in Ohio. The original art museum was designed in 1917 by Cass Gilbert, a talented eclectic who was adept at many styles and whose notable works include the Woolworth Building (Gothic), the Supreme Court of the United States (classical), and Battle Hall at the University of Texas at Austin (Spanish-Mediterranean). The

Oberlin museum, which faces the college green, is an Italian Renaissance palazzo with patterned sandstone and a delicate, vaulted loggia that recalls Brunelleschi. Gilbert had recently visited California, and he added a fountain court that is more like a hacienda patio than a Tuscan *cortile*. On the other hand, the doorway leading to the library is an actual antique, transported whole from Venice. Gilbert, who designed several buildings at Oberlin, died in 1934, and four years later, the director of the museum, Clarence Ward, an art historian and self-taught architect, designed a large addition housing an auditorium, classrooms, and offices. Ward matched the addition to Gilbert's building. He placed the new wing on the far side of the fountain court, in the rear, which made it clearly subservient to the original. The addition blends seamlessly with Gilbert's architecture so that the two are indistinguishable today. Most visitors would be forgiven for assuming that the entire building was designed by the same architect—which it was, at least in spirit.

Subservience was the last thing on the minds of Venturi and Rauch, whose addition includes a gallery, work spaces, and a new library. The new architecture is aggressively assertive: the roof of their addition is flat rather than hipped, its overhanging eaves are paper-thin rather than modeled, and the windows are conceived as continuous ribbons of plate glass rather than apertures. The sandstone and granite match Gilbert's building exactly (they came from the same quarry), but they are patterned in a garish and distinctly un-matching checkerboard. New and old meet in an abrupt collision of forms. "Our squarish gallery with strip windows and big overhang recalls on the outside a high school gym of the 1940s," explained Venturi. "But why, I wonder, does an addition to an art museum have to take as its reference system a high school gymnasium?" asked Robert A. M. Stern in a critical magazine article. "Why can't the new building look like the building it's added onto? At the very least, why can't it look like some other museum one has seen or could find in a book somewhere and not a gymnasium?" Perhaps the answer is that at some subliminal level Venturi and Rauch, who in 1976 were still neophytes with only a few small houses under their belts, were intent on cheekily thumbing their noses at one of the great masters of an earlier generation. Take that, Florentine palazzo!

Vince didn't want a contrasting modern addition; he wanted the new building to resemble a castle keep. But he also wanted an interior that was full of light and had views of the nearby ocean. This put Andrew in a quandary. Medieval keeps generally had small openings such as embrasures and arrow slits, which produced characteristically dark and moody interiors. But if he simply substituted large windows, the result would risk becoming a caricature, like a White Castle hamburger stand. His solution was to create another piece of historical make-believe. "I imagined the addition as a late Victorian building, crenelated but with large windows and whimsical castle styling." Andrew's inspiration was a famous Charleston landmark, the Old Citadel on Marion Square. The building had been designed by Frederick Wesner in 1829 as an arsenal, and enlarged—and medievalized—by Edward B. White twenty years later, after it had become a military academy. The result was a potpourri of battlements, machicolations, corbeled turrets, and narrow-arched windows. This sounds Disneyesque, but the prim Victorian architecture is actually quite sober. Sobriety appealed to Andrew, who found Vince's castle conceit to be a little frivolous, especially his latest additions: two gas-powered flambeaux fixed to the facade of the chapel, and a small swivel cannon installed in the turret, which Vince insisted on firing off on national holidays, much to the alarm of his neighbors.

Andrew had learned a lot from working with George. "George does things in a way that makes sense to him, which is often unconventional and different from the industry standard, and when it comes time to execute there can be problems. I learnt that if I wanted to build things differently, I would have to stay ahead of everybody at each step. I check all the documents, and explain what I want to the subcontractors." Staying ahead meant poring over building regulations and zoning codes. When Vince bought the chapel it included an ungainly 1960s A-frame addition at the rear containing three bedrooms: "a relic of the disco era," he called it. Vince demolished the A-frame, which had severe mold problems. To simplify permitting, Andrew kept the same footprint for the new building as the A-frame. "We maxed out the zoning envelope," he says of the four-story addition. The town, perhaps still smarting from Vince's proposed move of the chapel, turned down his application for a building permit on the grounds that the new addition was too close to an existing sewer line. "They claimed that the sewer had a twenty-foot wide easement, even though there was no documentation to back that up," said Andrew. After lengthy negotiations, the issue was resolved: Vince let the town have an easement on his property to access a sewer manhole, and Andrew reduced the depth of the addition by a few feet. In the process, he was obliged to replace the straight stair with a more compact spiral stair that, as he observed, actually improved the design. When Sullivan's Island created a historic district to thwart Vince's plan to move the chapel, it also formed an architectural review board modeled on the Charleston BAR. The Sullivan's Island board had no objection to the castle-like appearance of the addition.

The addition was finished in 2010. The following year, I was in Charleston for an academic conference, and Vince showed me around the completed building. We exited the old chapel through a small back door. "Now we're entering Andrew's world," Vince said. We found ourselves inside a round tower that housed the spiral stair. Medieval newel stairs consist of keyhole-shaped stone treads with the broad ends built into the wall and the narrow ends forming a continuous column; Andrew followed this technique, but substituted precast concrete for stone. Before going upstairs we descended three steps and entered a low space under the building, partly enclosed by arched openings. The undercroft, which felt like an open-air cellar, had a heavy timber ceiling supported on fat, round concrete columns with chunky Romanesque capitals. The floor was brick. A long, heavy wooden table and benches made it a perfect spot for candlelit dinners.

We went back in and ascended the spiral stair. The ceiling of the tower, painted blue with stenciled stars, resembled a night sky. The second floor contained two small bedrooms with their own bathrooms, and two tiny rooms with built-in children's bunk beds, effectively ship's cabins. The nautical theme was reinforced by the planked wooden partition walls. The exterior walls, on the other hand, were thick masonry, just like the Holy Ascension Church. Andrew was critical of ersatz construction. "I don't really care about the look of the building," he once told an interviewer. "I don't want the look of masonry, I want the masonry."

The third floor contained what Vince called the Summer Hall—as opposed to the Winter Hall of the chapel—an airy, two-story-high living room with a beamed ceiling, from which was suspended an octagonal wooden chandelier. Daylight streamed into the room—I counted thirteen large windows, designed like French doors, some high up in the wall. Beyond, I caught a glimpse of the blue expanse of the ocean. "You should see it in the spring when all the doors are open to catch the sea breeze," said Vince. Adjoining the hall was a small bedroom suite with a built-in bed that resembled Jefferson's alcove bed in Monticello. A paneled Tudor-looking open stair on one side of the hall led up to an identical bedroom suite on the fourth floor. Opposite the stair was a massive Indiana limestone fireplace, somewhat simpler in design than George's baronial version, as befitted this bright room. The mantel included reliefs of winged dragons, modeled by Andrew on Celtic manuscripts. The work was by Mary May, a local carver, originally from Minnesota. Charleston, with its wealth of restoration projects, had attracted skilled building artisans from around the world; the masons, carpenters, blacksmiths, and plasterers who worked on Mugdock came from Britain, France, Germany, and the Czech Republic. The iron light fixtures throughout the building were Andrew's work, as was the stenciled starry ceiling of the stair tower. The muted interior color scheme was chosen by a British interior decorator friend of Vince, Renée Killian-Dawson. "The Summer Hall was conjured up out of the bouillabaisse of the sum of the parts that it represented," she explained to me in an e-mail. "The sheer folly and hopeful exuberance of the nature of the building, the time period it was representing in architectural style, the actual environment it rested in, its ecclesiastical neighbor—the Winter Hall—Vince's Scottish heritage and all that implies, and the idea of a certain kind of purity in the materials. I wanted to use colors that could only have been duplicated either at great expense or with plants at the time the Italian Gothic style was at its zenith." All the eco paint was a dead-flat finish, applied by brush.

The French doors opened onto an outdoor gallery wrapped around three sides of the hall. An outside stair led to a second gallery, whence one ascended to a roof terrace, or "rampart," as Vince called it. Although surrounded by battlements, the terrace had modern conveniences such as water and gas connections so that it could be outfitted with a wet bar and a barbecue and turned into a dining aerie. The view was splendid. Beyond Vince's turret and the rooftops of Sullivan's Island, we could see the cable-stayed Ravenel Bridge, which connects Mount Pleasant to

Andrew Gould's medieval-Victorian-contemporary
addition to Mugdock Castle.

Charleston. Immediately to the south we looked down on the bermed
fortifications of Fort Moultrie, and beyond it the Atlantic. I watched
a container ship silently glide across the water, bound for the North
Charleston Terminal.

The southern facade of the addition was impressive. The lower portion of the white stuccoed walls was battered, which, together with the
corbeled battlements, reinforced the impression of a castle keep. The gal-
leries, whose unpainted wood was already turning gray, were supported
on heavy timber brackets joined by steel strapwork—that looked medieval, too. So did the arched windows whose shutters, pea green with
a broad plum stripe, reminded me of heraldic gonfalons. Andrew had
painted a vertical sundial on the south-facing wall, with radiating lines
marking the hours and two curves showing the position of the winter
and summer solstice. "It must have been quite a mathematical feat drawing these things in the old days," he said. "You couldn't just copy another
sundial, because the lines are unique for a given latitude, longitude, and
wall orientation. Fortunately, my computer program allows me to model

the sun path and cast virtual shadows so I could generate those hyper-
bolic curves accurately." A digitally designed, hand-painted sundial:
Andrew's world, indeed.

A visitor to Mugdock Castle fifty years hence might be forgiven if
she thought the building dated back to a much earlier period than the
first decade of the twenty-first century. She might have the same impression as the author of this description, written more than a hundred years
ago.

> [The house] does not stare with newness; it is not new in
> any way that is disquieting to the eye; it is neither raw nor
> callow. On the contrary, it almost gives the impression of a
> comfortable maturity of something like a couple of hundred
> years. And yet there is nothing sham-old about it; it is not
> trumped-up with any specious or fashionable devices of spu-
> rious antiquity; there is no pretending to be anything that it
> is not—no affectation whatever.

That writer was the noted gardener Gertrude Jekyll, and the country house she was describing was Munstead Wood, her own home in
Surrey. Built in 1897, it had been designed by her friend and collaborator,
Edwin Lutyens. Munstead was one of the young architect's first major
commissions—he was twenty-seven, Andrew's age when he designed
the Mugdock addition. "The house is not in any way a copy of any old
building," wrote Jekyll, "though it embodies the general characteristics
of the older structures of its own district." Lutyens incorporated half-
timbering, hand-hewn beams, buttery sandstone walls, steep roofs, and
prominent chimneys. Although he used recycled roofing slates, old age
was implied rather than simulated. Thanks to its traditional forms and
old-fashioned details, Munstead Wood is a reminder of the past—not a
replica, a reminder.

Buildings last a long time, and an old building such as Munstead
Wood, which is more than a hundred years old and still occupied, belongs
to both the past and the present—*its* past and *our* present. But buildings
can evoke a third time dimension. The half-timbering and pegged beams
of Munstead remind us of the medieval heritage of Surrey's rural build-

ings. The evocation of earlier times—whether it is Lutyens evoking the Tudor age, Palladio recalling ancient Rome, or Andrew summoning up Victorian Charleston—enriches the experience of architecture. Compared to this, a building that willfully forswears history may be handsome and useful, and it may tell us something about when it was built, but it tells us precious little more. It is flatter and thinner—a dish without spice. A building like Mugdock is a richer preparation, telling many stories and conjuring up many images: the Old Citadel, William Morris, even *Ivanhoe*.

Andrew and George were rapidly becoming collaborators. They worked together on a number of projects. One of these was for Bob Holt and involved turning a shuttered Baptist church into rental apartments. The old building, a utilitarian brick structure built in 1947, was a far cry from a Gothic Revival chapel—the *Post & Courier* architecture critic described the church as a "handsome warehouse." Andrew and George subdivided the space into twelve loft apartments. The project, which was in a fringe area at the north end of the Charleston peninsula, was aimed at "working professionals," and the prices were low enough that qualified first-time buyers were eligible for a grant from the city. The tiny one-bedroom units included metal spiral stairs, wood-burning fireplaces, and quirky industrial details.

Another project for Bob Holt was a new building on Tully Alley. George and Jerry had sold the lot facing Cannon Street to Holt, who turned the front house into a hostel. An inspection of the rear house revealed a problem: the structure was slowly sinking and required a new foundation. The old frame house was raised up in the air and a two-foot-thick reinforced-concrete foundation large enough to support a new adjoining building was poured underneath. The new building housed a rental apartment and office space. George designed a square two-story Palladian villa with an apartment on the first floor, surmounted by rooms around a central atrium. The floors and roof were framed in wood and the exterior walls were cement block with reinforcing bars and concrete in the cavities. George wanted to try a new technique, laying the blocks without mortar to speed up construction. The experiment was not a success. The blocks were not precise enough, and the masons complained that it was difficult to keep the walls plumb. As before, Andrew drew up the construction documents and worked on the details. He designed a stenciled pattern for the ceiling of the atrium. He and his wife, Julie, laid a mosaic floor using debris from a granite countertop manufacturer. The atrium was leased as work space, and for a number of years George and Andrew had their office in the building.

George and Andrew were both attracted to traditional construction details in their projects: thick masonry walls, sturdy timber framing, brick floors. But unlike George, Andrew was not interested in simulating the appearance of old age. Although he used recycled bricks in the undercroft of the Mugdock addition, he generally made no attempt at weathering—new materials looked new. He was consumed with workmanship. "George and I are opposites," said Andrew. "When I design a building from scratch I tend to do a box and then focus on the details. George focuses on the concept and the details are secondary." This was less a result of their different backgrounds than of temperament. Andrew was a born craftsman, fastidious and, at heart, a conservative. George was an artist, intuitive and emotional, always willing to upset the applecart, an iconoclast. They had, in many small matters, different tastes. "I find microwaves and toasters to be quite useful," George observed, "but the only reason there are modern appliances in Andrew's kitchen is because Julie insisted." There was also the question of music. "We both like to listen to music while we work," George told me. "My favorite is Euro-Trance dance music. Early on Andrew and I had to deal with this because he hates Euro-Trance and I find his Byzantine and pre-Renaissance religious chants so depressing that, if asked, I'd recommend them as an accompaniment to suicide."

Odd couples often make good collaborators. Ralph Adams Cram described his longtime partner, Bertram Goodhue, as "my alter ego."

What ability I had stopped short at one definite point. I could see any architectural problem in its mass, proportion, composition, and articulation, and visualize it in three dimensions even before I set pencil to paper. I had also the faculty of planning, and I generally blocked out all our designs at quarter-scale. There my ability ceased. I had neither the power nor the patience to work out any sort of decorative detail. At this point Bertram entered the equation, to go on without a break to the completion of the work. And the detail was marvelous, no less. Historic data . . . might serve as a basis, but what in the end issued from his fertile imagination and deft fingers had suffered a sea-change into something rich and strange.

For Cram, the appeal of the past was more than architectural—it was intellectual and even moral, which gave his early independent designs a cool, archaeological quality. "I was so anxious to demonstrate the continuity of tradition (theologically as well as artistically) in Christian culture," he wrote. Goodhue, on the other hand, was an aesthete with little interest in either history or religion. He was happiest giving his inventive spirit free reign. Both men were self-taught, and they learned from each other. Of his partner, Cram wrote: "He came to see problems more in the large, as consistent and unified conceptions, where detail was *only* a detail." Conversely, Cram himself "realized the inherent value in his [Goodhue's] originality and modernism." This complementary partnership lasted twenty-two years. Eventually, diverging artistic interests pulled the two men apart—Goodhue was drawn to Art Deco modernism, which didn't appeal to Cram, and went on to design such masterpieces as the Nebraska State Capitol and the Los Angeles Central Library. Cram, who did not share Goodhue's restless creativity, continued his exploration of Gothic, although the eclectic Rice campus and the Art Moderne Doheny Library at the University of Southern California show that he could broaden his architectural palette when required.

George and Andrew's partnership was just beginning. Whether it would survive the strains of creative collaboration, only time would tell. What they shared, and what brought them together, other than a fascination with Byzantine architecture and an affection for tradition, was a desire for beauty. This sounds old-fashioned, even corny, but it's the only way I can put it. George once told me that he always felt depressed when he returned from one of his trips to Istanbul: "That city was so beautiful and Charleston seemed so bleak by comparison." Andrew was charac-

teristically blunter: "Nowadays we don't live in a beautiful culture," he
once told an interviewer. "We live in a world where most things around
us are accidental, ill-considered, often deliberately sinful, and so modern people grow up without any obvious guide in their lives as to what is
beautiful and what is ugly." The desire to create beauty drew both men
to earlier periods—Byzantine, Romanesque, Gothic. The attraction was
intuitive and emotional for George, more intellectual for Andrew.

At the heart of George and Andrew's collaboration was the shared
belief that many of the answers to today's questions could be found in the
past. This belief represents a rejection of the central tenet of modernist
architecture, that a modern age requires uniquely different, even revolutionary, buildings. Cram addressed this issue in his autobiography,
which was published in 1936, by which time the Modern movement was
already well established. Cram recognized that new functions demand
new means of expression.

> For a stock exchange or a department store, a moving pic-
> ture palace, a garage, or a hangar, a skyscraper, a cocktail bar
> or for the conventicle of any of the newer forms of religious
> emotion and experience, it would be as irrational, perverse
> and misleading to revive the motives and the forms of the
> past ages as it would be to design a Greek railroad train, a
> Byzantine motor car, a Gothic battleship or a Renaissance
> airplane.

Conversely, he argued, human institutions that maintain a strong
link with the past and had changed little in the last seventy-five years—
the home, the school, the place of worship—did not require new forms
of expression. "Just as I think it would be absurd to build a school of
mechanical engineering or a chemical laboratory after the stylistic fashion of an Oxford college, or a gymnasium like a Medieval abbey," he
wrote, "so I hold it is equally absurd and perfectly pointless and ungram-
matical to couch a school of liberal arts, a library, or a college chapel in
the terms of a garage, a department store, or a skyscraper office building." This was a pointed criticism of an art school that looked like a factory (Walter Gropius's Bauhaus), or a college residence that resembled an

office block (Le Corbusier's Pavillon Suisse). Cram was mistaken when he assumed that modernism was a passing fad—"episodical and evanescent," he called it—but his judgment that traditional institutions ought to express themselves through traditional architecture has been vindicated. Most Americans accept modernist office buildings and airport terminals, but their homes have tended to remain traditional in appearance. Similarly, Collegiate Gothic has persisted, and new versions have recently reappeared on several university campuses, not least Oxford and Cambridge, and Princeton and Yale.

The present-day revival of traditional styles, which began about forty years ago, has led to an ideological rift between modernists and traditionalists: the former condemn the latter as nostalgic and backward-looking, while traditionalists criticize modernists for their idiosyncratic, hyper-expressive designs. George and Andrew's preference for traditional building materials and techniques was pragmatic rather than ideological. As we have seen, George used masonry construction because it was resistant to the climate; Andrew preferred tried-and-true details because they were more durable. The pair's attraction to Byzantine distinguished them from most so-called modern classicists, who tend to find inspiration in the Renaissance. George and Andrew's hands-on involvement in the building process likewise set them apart, although I would not describe them as Luddites. George was willing to experiment with new materials, such as the polystyrene blocks he had used in his sister's house. Andrew did have a preference for traditional crafts, yet he had no reservations about using a computer when he designed a sundial, or a laser cutter to produce decorative ironwork, and while he made watercolor renderings of buildings to show clients, his construction drawings were produced digitally. His Victorian addition to Mugdock Castle was not merely an exercise in historical style; it was livable and comfortable. As Cram succinctly put it, "*From* the past, not *in* the past."

In his autobiography, Cram frequently emphasized the importance of steadfast and supportive clients. In Vince Graham, Andrew was fortunate to have a client who shared his concern for durability in building and his enthusiasm for old-fashioned craftsmanship. I asked Vince what it was like to work with someone who could be as finicky as Andrew.

"Actually, I found it easy," he said. "Whenever I brought up a suggestion to revise a detail Andrew had drawn, he would patiently explain his
rationale, which usually led to my agreeing with his way of thinking. On
the rare occasion when I insisted on doing things a different way, I later
regretted it." Vince was interested in architecture, which was a big part
of his work, but he was not an architect. His career had developed quite
differently.

EIGHT

The Education of a Developer

"They Had It Right the First Time"

"I come from a long line of inquisitive contrarians," Vince Graham once told an interviewer. "There is an undercurrent of trying to do things differently in my family." His great-grandfather was Micajah Clark Dyer, celebrated in Georgia for being granted a patent for a flying machine as early as 1874, more than twenty-five years before Kitty Hawk. The patent describes a dirigible-like contraption powered by flapping wings and paddles operated by the pilot. There is no evidence that it ever flew, but Dyer, a farmer, is said to have launched gliders from a mountainside ramp near his home in Blairsville. According to family lore, his widow sold one of these flying machines to an Atlanta businessman who resold it to the Wright brothers. Vince's great-uncle, Festus E. Kitchens, was a physician who lived in Coral Gables, Florida, and was a volunteer trainer of the fledgling University of Miami football team in the 1930s. The grateful university named a football scholarship after him and invited him to choose the first recipient. "Doc" Kitchens obviously had a sense of humor, for he selected his younger sister, Nina. Vince's grandfather was a builder, and his father was a developer who built residential condos in Atlanta. "He would find unusual or difficult sites inside the Perimeter that had been ignored and figure out a way to develop them," Vince told me.

Vince grew up in suburban Atlanta. After finishing high school, he applied to several colleges and was accepted by the University of Virginia. "I had never been north of the Carolinas, so this was a fresh start for me." With his family history in building, he had considered architecture, but he was discouraged by the complicated application process, which required a portfolio of drawings, and he enrolled in economics instead. Jefferson's campus, with its Pantheon-like library and central lawn, made a big impression on the young man.

Vince's first job after graduation was with an Atlanta bank. He didn't enjoy the work, nor was he satisfied with the suburban lifestyle offered by that city. He remembered Jim Chaffin, a University of Virginia alumnus whom he had met while fund-raising for his fraternity. (Vince was president of Pi Kappa Alpha, the same position Chaffin had held two decades earlier.) Chaffin's real estate company specialized in developing resort and recreational communities. "I asked him for a job," said Vince. "He didn't have any openings at the time, but suggested that I stay in touch. I left the bank and worked as an independent commercial real estate broker, helping my father on the side with an Atlanta development project. Meanwhile, I kept badgering Chaffin. Eventually, he relented, and in July 1989 I went to work on a property that he and his partner, Jim Light, had acquired in South Carolina."

Chaffin and Light's coastal property was about a hundred miles south of Charleston. Spring Island was three thousand pristine acres that had previously been a quail-hunting plantation. Their plan was to build five hundred houses on very large lots, leaving much of the island in its natural state and providing hunting and fishing preserves, horse-riding trails, and a golf course. According to Vince, Chaffin described the buyers, saying, "One-third are interested in hunting, one-third in golf, and one-third just want to be there." Vince's job as project manager was to oversee the implementation of the master plan.

Spring Island is located halfway between the resort community of Hilton Head Island and the town of Beaufort. "When I moved there, I looked at both places as possible living options," Vince recalled. "Hilton Head was like Atlanta with palmetto trees—I'd had my fill of that." He settled on Beaufort, a charming historic coastal town. Founded only forty years after Charleston, it had been a colonial shipbuilding center and had grown wealthy in the antebellum period thanks to the surrounding sea-island cotton plantations. The little main street was surrounded by compact neighborhoods with narrow, heavily treed streets and stately houses with deep verandas. You could walk everywhere. Vince loved it, not only the place but also the leisurely pace of Lowcountry life. The contrast between where he lived and the community that was taking shape on Spring Island was not lost on him. "I noticed that as Spring Island was built up, there was a veiled resentment toward newcomers, as there was now less privacy and exclusivity than before. The mindset in Beaufort was completely different. When I moved there, people were welcoming." Equally important, the budding developer noticed that the highest property values in Beaufort were in the oldest, densest neighborhoods.

Six weeks after he started working, Vince wrote a long memorandum to Chaffin and Light. He titled it "Thoughts on Spring Island Master Plan." It is the brash statement of a twenty-five-year-old with no actual experience in property development, but brimming with ideas. Low density was not the only way to create value in real estate, he wrote. "Homes on Bay Street across from the water in Beaufort rarely come on the market. When they do they fetch prices of $1 million or more. Larger homes on the back streets go for $500,000 and up. Homes near the Battery in Charleston go for much higher. And none of these have a golf course, pool, or hunting and equestrian facilities." Vince proposed that a portion of Spring Island be developed as a sort of village—he called it New Jamestown—with houses close together on small lots.

> The houses would have the same characteristics of those in Beaufort (wide front porches, high ceilings, formal gardens and architectural detail), but would be enhanced with modern floor plans, air conditioning, and fire protection. The street scene would have all of the streetlights, sidewalks, decorative street nameplates, etc, which make the pedestrian orientations of Charleston, Beaufort, and Savannah so inviting. There could also be a park in New Jamestown with a walkway on the waterfront and perhaps a day dock where invitees from Hilton Head and Beaufort could tie up to come watch a band in the park gazebo and fireworks on the Fourth of July.

Two months later, Vince followed this up with a second memo, titled "Another Two Cents' Worth," in which he elaborated his contention that, under the right circumstances, homeowners might actually be attracted to density.

> Today we think of each home as its own castle, standing by itself to insure privacy rather than incorporating privacy in the individual home design. We think we must have a big lot because we wouldn't want our neighbors too near us and we enjoy spending two hours of our free time each week cutting the grass. Then we go to a Charleston or a Beaufort and think "isn't this charming . . . wouldn't it be neat to live here." And these towns, with their homes oriented so closely, continue to be sought after because they are classic and *are what people want!*

"I never got a response to my memos," Vince recalled. "My bosses seemed to appreciate the thoughts, but it felt a bit like being patted on the head." He shared his ideas with Charles Fraser, a retired developer who lived in Sea Pines Plantation on nearby Hilton Head Island. Fraser, who basically invented the resort golf course community, was a legendary figure in the real estate world. He had started Sea Pines in the 1950s and pioneered such innovations as covenants, deed restrictions, and environmental controls. In the process he trained a generation of young developers, known as Charlie's Angels—Chaffin and Light were among them. When Vince started working at Spring Island, Chaffin introduced him to Fraser. "We became friends," said Vince. "He was incredibly generous, shoveled books at me, told me what field trips to take, and invited me to be part of Sunday afternoon excursions aboard his sailboat, *Compass Rose.*" Fraser had started his career as a developer when he was Vince's age and equally inexperienced, and he must have seen something of himself in the young fellow Georgian of Scottish descent.

Fraser encouraged Vince to pursue his unconventional ideas about traditional communities. "You need to check out a place called Seaside," he said and mentioned its planner, Andrés Duany (Vince recalls that he pronounced it with a southern twang, "An-dray Dwainey"). Seaside was a beach community on the Florida Panhandle, planned in the early 1980s by Duany and his wife, Elizabeth Plater-Zyberk. Their project, which was inspired by small southern towns, was influential out of all proportion to its size, and it sparked a resurgence of interest in traditional town planning that led to the New Urbanism movement.

Vince never got to Seaside, but he did get his hands on a videotape of a lecture by Duany. The hour-long talk was a full-throated jeremiad denouncing the evils, as Duany saw them, of contemporary American suburban planning, the focus on low density, the privileging of cars, the poor environmental qualities, and the inability to engender a feeling of community. The solution to these shortcomings, according to Duany, was a revival of the principles that had guided the growth of American towns in the past: density, walkability, human scale—the very things that Vince admired in Beaufort and Charleston. "I must've watched that tape at least a half dozen times," Vince told me. For the first time, he heard someone articulate what until then had been personal musings.

One difference between a developer and a planner is that, unlike a planner, who depends on clients to implement his ideas, a developer can take the initiative—as long as he is prepared to shoulder the risk. After two years with Chaffin and Light, Vince felt ready to strike out on his own. His idea was simple. The most expensive residential real estate in Beaufort was in a historic neighborhood on the Beaufort River called Old Point. Why not create a comparable neighborhood, but with smaller and less expensive houses? Vince found a waterfront parcel for sale on Lady's Island, directly across the river from Old Point. The property was about fifty acres, about the same size as the historic neighborhood. He called his project Newpoint. The advertisement that Vince wrote for Newpoint summed up his philosophy: "They Had It Right the First Time."

What Vince did next was both artless and ingenious. He measured his favorite street in Old Point—the pavement width, the size of the tree planting strip, the dimensions of the sidewalk, the setbacks of the houses—and simply duplicated it. He also copied the dense arrangement of houses. Instead of one-acre lots, which was the usual practice for new residential developments on Lady's Island, Newpoint's lots were as small

The historic district of Old Point in
Beaufort, South Carolina.

as zoning allowed—one-quarter of an acre—and only sixty feet wide,
which meant that houses were close together. Alleys provided access to
garages in the rear, something that Duany recommended. Vince wasn't
building any houses: he planned to sell lots to builders and homeowners.
He had read about Seaside, and he wrote a simpler version of its architectural code, mandating traditional features such as pitched roofs, front
porches, and picket fences.

One of Charles Fraser's dictums was "Find the best piece of land
on your site and give it to everyone." At Sea Pines, Fraser did not build
on the dunes, for example, and he left wide swaths of open land leading
to the beach to accommodate public walkways. Vince thought that the
best piece of Newpoint was the riverfront. So, instead of following the
conventional practice of subdividing the waterfront into exclusive lots,
he turned more than half of the frontage into a public park. Now everyone living in Newpoint had access to the water and the view. And, just as
he had described in his Spring Island memo, he built a public boat dock
and a gazebo.

Another of Fraser's sayings was "It's really smart to be second,
first," that is, to be the first to copy a good idea. Real estate developers

A narrow treed street in Newpoint, Vince's pioneering
development on Lady's Island.

generally shy away from innovation—the business is risky enough as it
is. But Vince, ignoring Fraser, was doing exactly that: trying something
new and—at least in his experience—untested. He financed Newpoint
through a creative bootstrap operation. Together with his partner, Bob
Turner, a boyhood friend whom Vince had earlier recruited to Spring
Island, he negotiated an installment purchase plan with the owner of the
land. Then he found investors: his parents, fraternity brothers, friends,
even his banker. He called these early buyers Charter Members. "Altogether, the initial lot purchase contracts were close to the amount of the
first installment—half a million dollars. With those contracts in hand,
the bank issued a letter of credit, which effectively served as a bond to
guarantee infrastructure funding, and allow a plot to be recorded. So
we simultaneously closed on the land and lots the same day; with funds
from the latter used to pay for the former." Sales were slow at first; at one
point, Vince had to write a personal check on his credit card to make
up an installment payment. But once there were enough houses to create a portion of a street, people could see what they were getting, and
sales picked up. The buyers were mostly locals—this was not a resort
community—professionals, small business owners, as well as several

Marine pilots and their families from the Beaufort Naval Air Station.* After the first year, the price of a typical lot, which had been $20,000, doubled, then doubled again. Soon quarter-acre lots in Newpoint were outselling one-acre lots in neighboring developments. In addition, the lots facing the park and the water view were selling at a premium, even though they were not directly on the water. Vince's guess had been right: people valued—and were prepared to pay for—neighborliness.

When Shirley and I first visited Beaufort in 1994, we were drawn to the town by memories of seeing Lawrence Kasdan's *The Big Chill,* which was filmed on location in Old Point. One day I came across an ad for Newpoint in the local business guide—the striking headline "They Had It Right the First Time" caught my attention—and we drove over to take a look. That was how I met Vince, who was barely older than some of my students. He showed us around. The development was only two years old, and already one hundred of the one hundred and thirty lots had been sold. The street modeled on Old Point was almost complete, and it really did resemble the original. The property was heavily wooded, and Vince had done his best to save as many trees as possible—even slightly kinking one of the streets to accommodate a giant live oak. The presence of large trees gave Newpoint a settled look. So did the variety of the houses, which were brick, clapboard, and stucco. A few were designed by architects, but most were the work of local home builders. The houses were modest in appearance, except for those on the lots facing the waterside park, which were rather grand, like the mansions on Charleston's Battery. These larger houses were accessed from Waterside Drive. Most new developments on Lady's Island tend to have quaint street names such as Chickadee Lane and Salt Marsh Cove; Newpoint street names were distinctly un-cute, except for Prescient Avenue. An economist would recognize Hayek Street and Mises Road, although he might wonder about the origin of Fraser Street.

---

* Beaufort and the Naval Air Station are the setting of Pat Conroy's novel *The Great Santini* (1976).

New Urbanism in Old Charleston

The ups and downs of real estate development

At the time that Vince was building Newpoint, the first large New Urbanist community was going up in Gaithersburg, Maryland, just outside Washington, D.C. Kentlands, a large, ambitious project planned by Duany and Plater-Zyberk, received national media attention. "When it comes to neighborhoods and towns, they can make 'em like they used to," wrote *Time*, which singled out Kentlands in its "Best of 1991" issue. That may have been premature, for the following year, the project fell victim to the real estate developer's greatest enemy: an unexpected economic downturn. A major recession stalled the real estate market and Kentlands, still incomplete, went into receivership.* That made tiny Newpoint—unbeknownst to Vince—effectively the first financially successful application of the ideas pioneered at Seaside.

Vince first realized that he had achieved something special when Charles Fraser brought Disney executives to visit Newpoint. The entertainment company was building a residential community—the future town of Celebration—near its property in Orlando, Florida, and the head of Disney's real estate division, Peter Rummell, another of Charlie's Angels, had asked his old mentor for advice. Fraser introduced Rum-

---

* Kentlands was eventually completed. It was so successful that it gave rise to a second traditional development next door, Lakelands.

mell to Newpoint. In May 1995, Fraser and two coach-loads of planners, builders, and architects arrived to tour Vince's development. "The Disney people had come all that way to see a little project done by us country boys," Vince recalled.

On the strength of his success at Newpoint, Vince developed two small groups of houses, one in Beaufort and one in neighboring Port Royal. But what he really wanted was a chance to try something on a larger scale. He was living in Newpoint, and spending time in Charleston, when he learned of an interesting opportunity. The town council of the suburban city of Mount Pleasant, which lay just across the Cooper River from Charleston, had recently adopted a master plan that explicitly incorporated New Urbanist principles to guide future development and called for a compact mix of residential, commercial, and civic uses. A sympathetic municipal government was just what he was looking for.

The Mount Pleasant master plan identified a large parcel of vacant land—243 acres—as a potential site for a new residential development. The so-called Jordan Tract belonged to a family-owned construction company based in Columbia, South Carolina. The company specialized in building roads and highways, and it had acquired the land decades earlier in order to quarry sand. Now it wanted to sell the property—to the right buyer. Vince invited the company's president, David Jordan, to visit Newpoint. Jordan was favorably impressed, and they reached an agreement. Vince, who had formed a partnership with his father for this project, couldn't afford to buy the entire site at once. "I told Jordan that he would have to be our banker," recalls Vince. "We signed a rolling option that enabled us to buy the land in portions, a minimum amount each year, over a period of six to eight years. This was organized in such a fashion that if the project failed at any point, Jordan would be able to sell the rest of his property."

Vince needed a town planner, and he approached two of the leading New Urbanist firms, Duany Plater-Zyberk and Dover, Kohl & Partners, both based in Miami. He expected two bids, but he was surprised when the planners suggested that they would do the project together and share the fee. "In the old days we used to do that often," Andrés Duany told me. "New Urbanism being a movement, we played as a team." Vince wanted the planners to get a feeling for the urban architecture of the region, and in May 1995, the two teams, led by Duany and Victor Dover, met him in Savannah. They toured the city, spent the night at Newpoint, and drove to Mount Pleasant, where they visited the historic neighborhood of Old Village, which Vince saw as a model for his project.

Duany and Plater-Zyberk had developed a technique called a charrette, an intense public exercise in community urban design whose purpose was to familiarize concerned citizens with New Urbanism and, not least, to defuse local opposition to development. The charrette assembled all the parties with an interest in the project: public officials, municipal planners, fire marshals, traffic engineers, conservationists, environmentalists, community groups, and neighboring property owners. The participants were asked to voice their concerns and, on the spot, the architects and planners drew up design options. These options included not only street plans but also illustrative views that gave the layperson an idea of what was to come. Drawings were presented to the participants, and in turn provoked more discussion. This interactive design process unrolled over several days, and if all went well, the end product reflected the diverse concerns of the various interest groups. Equally important, with a broad base of support the project was more likely to garner official approval during the subsequent permitting process.

The week-long Mount Pleasant charrette took place in a historic house on King Street in downtown Charleston. Vince was concerned that the Miami planners should understand the casualness of Lowcountry life, so he took them on walking tours of Charleston's historic district. He showed them his favorite street, Legaré Street, pointing out its subtle twists and turns. Vince is a businessman, but he has a quirky side; he organized what he called a "land-blessing ceremony" that required the slightly bewildered Miami planners to wade into the tidal flat of Hobcaw Creek. During that visit to the Jordan Tract, a member of the team came across an old burial ground. One of the grave markers commemorated Jacob Bond I'On, an early landowner and a local dignitary who had served in the Revolutionary War. "Great," said Vince, "we'll call the development I'On."

At the end of seven days, the master plan was ready. The street layout was dictated by three large excavations left over from the sand quarrying. The deep pits were turned into lakes; one retained its rectangular shape, one was slightly modified to soften its outline, and the third was altered to appear more naturalistic and became part of a five-acre bird sanctuary. The plan was divided into six neighborhoods, each with its own character: denser and more town-like near the entrance; more formal around the lakes; looser and more countrified in the marsh-front area near Hobcaw Creek. Three-quarters of the creek's edge was reserved for public use and included a walkway, a boat dock, and a club-house. The lakes were likewise surrounded by public walks. Unlike Newpoint, which contained only single-family houses, I'On would have three-story apartment buildings, schools, churches, several neighbor-hood corner stores, and a small village center.

Before the proposal could be voted on by the Mount Pleasant town council, it had to be approved by the planning and zoning commis-sion. Although the town had adopted a master plan, it had not revised its zoning map, and the Jordan Tract was zoned R-1, meaning single-family houses on quarter-acre lots. Hence, before the proposed I'On plan could go ahead, the site would have to be rezoned. In August 1995, Duany presented the plan to the zoning commission during a standing-room-only meeting. Following several public hearings, the commission recommended rezoning by a 7–1 vote. The subsequent meeting of the town council was crowded with supporters and opponents of the proj-ect. Sensing from the initial discussion that there might be resistance by some on the council to the apartment buildings as well as the overall density of the project, Vince asked for a deferment. He instructed the planners to reduce the number of apartments, increase the size of the lots facing the creek, and cut the amount of commercial space by a third. These changes dropped the total number of homes from 1,240 to 850. The revised plan was presented to the town council at another packed pub-lic meeting. More than seventy people asked to speak. According to the Charleston *Post & Courier,* the majority of speakers were in favor of the project. Nevertheless, the town council rejected the rezoning application by a 5–4 vote. The final vote was cast by the mayor, who bravely sided with the minority.

What happened? "Among the mistakes I made was to hold the charrette in downtown Charleston," Vince told me. "We should have had it in Mount Pleasant. Some hot issues did surface during the charrette, but we did not anticipate running into the buzzsaw of NIMBY opposition." The Not-In-My-Backyard reaction of I'On's immediate neighbors was centered on a fear of increased car traffic, the presence of apartments, which were seen as incompatible because they attracted tenants rather than homeowners, and the higher density, which was perceived as a threat to surrounding property values. It didn't help that during his characteristically impassioned presentation, Duany had referred to the surrounding Mount Pleasant neighborhoods as "cookie-cutter" and "urban sprawl." That got people's backs up.

The I'On neighbors had firm prejudices: density was bad; renters were undesirable; houses on smaller lots reduced property values; new construction would be shoddy and of poor quality. The last objection was supported by the recent subdivisions built in Mount Pleasant, which tended to be generic and mass-produced—people simply didn't believe Vince's claim that I'On would be different. Opponents loudly disputed traffic studies that showed that a new connector road, which would be paid for by the developer, would alleviate local congestion. One of the chief opponents, a retired engineer who had worked for the City of Charleston, called a proposed traffic roundabout a "circle of death." All Vince's attempts to mollify the opposition proved fruitless.

This would have been an opportune time for Vince and his father to forfeit their deposit with Jordan and withdraw from the project. Instead, they decided to carry on. "At that point, we had a lot of time and money invested in the project," said Vince. "Imagine playing poker and you think you have a winning hand. Through several rounds of betting, you've got a lot of money in the pot. Are you going to walk away? No!" The gambling analogy is appropriate. A developer is risking his money on a bet—a bet that he can ultimately convince people of his vision, a bet that some unknown factor will not suddenly arise and sink his project, and a bet that the economy will remain strong in one or two years' time, when his lots come on the market.

The Grahams were stubborn, but they realized that they had to make concessions. "We tried to decipher what kind of plan would be supported by those council members who had voted against the application," Vince explained. The local lawyer who was advising them recommended removing all the commercial space. They were not willing to go that far, but they did reduce it by half, which made it the same size as the shopping street in Mount Pleasant's Old Village. And they agreed that the apartment buildings would have to go. That reduced the density to three units per acre, about the same as Old Village, and much lower than what they had originally intended.* I'On would consist only of detached single-family houses. One of the architects who worked on the charrette later criticized this uniformity. "There's too much repetition and not enough building types," he told me. The uniformity did not meet New Urbanist ideals, but it was necessary to get the project approved, and it also mimicked Old Village, which is what Mount Pleasant residents were used to. Vince knew that neighborhood well, since he had bought and restored a house in Old Village and had moved there the previous year.

In January 1997, now a year and a half after the charrette, the revised master plan was presented to the planning commission, which again voted in favor of the rezoning. In March, after several noisy public meetings, the town council approved the revised plan by a 6–3 vote. Emboldened, Vince ordered work to begin. That summer saw the construction of roads and infrastructure, and a year later ground was broken on the first house. Meanwhile, the opponents of the project were not idle. They presented a petition to the town council signed by 3,500 registered voters, requesting that either the rezoning be overturned or that a public referendum be held on the matter. The council voted to uphold the rezoning, but agreed to the referendum. Vince challenged the legality of such an action, and a circuit court judge ruled that a municipality could not hold a referendum on a zoning issue. The opponents (though not the municipality) appealed this decision and the matter ended up in the South Carolina Supreme Court, which unanimously upheld the lower court ruling.

I'On could proceed, but there were political repercussions. In the next municipal election, the opponents of I'On targeted the city councilors who had voted for the project, and five of the six, including the mayor, were defeated at the polls (the sixth chose not to run). Not only was a new town council in place, the chief critic of I'On was appointed to the

---

* The density of the original plan of I'On was similar to Charleston's historic district, about five units per acre. Tully Alley, with its tiny houses and narrow lanes, is about ten units per acre.

planning commission and eventually became its chairman. This meant that although Vince's plan was approved, he faced a distinctly hostile town council and planning commission. His proposal that 10 percent of the approved homes be town houses modeled on Rainbow Row in Charleston was turned down. When he applied for a building permit for a Montessori school on one of the sites approved for a "civic use," the town argued that a school was not a civic function. Vince contested this decision, and that case went to the South Carolina Court of Appeals, which ruled in Vince's favor.

Meanwhile, construction continued. At first, average lot prices were in the neighborhood of $30,000. "We probably left money on the table in the first year or two," Vince recalled. "Our aim was to get quality homes built quickly, to establish momentum, create value, and enable prospective buyers to walk down a street of completed homes to get a feel for what was to come." Within a year the average lot price had gone up to $40,000, and in two years it was in the $50,000 to $60,000 range. The year that Shirley and I stayed in I'On—2003—the development was five years old, lakefront houses were selling in the high six figures, and one sale had even exceeded $1 million. The agreement with Jordan required the development to be built neighborhood by neighborhood, which proved to be an advantage. Because the lots were not sold all at once, Vince and his father were able to benefit from the rising prices. Home builders as well as individuals clamored to buy lots. Vince resisted the offers of large builders who wanted to buy blocks of land. Instead he formed the I'On Guild and limited sales to approved small builders, who were required to follow an architectural code that set guidelines for houses and landscaping. Vince hired a local architectural historian, Macky Hill, to review the designs. Hill prepared an illustrated handbook, *Principles of Lowcountry Vernacular Design,* to help home builders get it right. The handbook described the right and the wrong way to build porches, balconies, front entrances, and dormers. "Some of the most imposing formal walls and fences are perforated with 'windows,' or openings," instructed the section on fences and walls. "In a way, these are the friendliest since the owner has gone to great lengths to create a beautiful garden, and has spent even more effort to make sure anyone passing by can peek in to share the view."

The paradigm for New Urbanism at that time was the small town, but I'On emerged as an unusual hybrid. The lakes, bird sanctuary, and view of tidal wetlands brought to mind Fraser's green and secluded Sea Pines Plantation; on the other hand, the narrow treed streets were more like Newpoint. The combination had wide appeal. In 1999, Vince and his father were named Charleston's Developers of the Year. In 2002, only five years after I'On began, the National Association of Home Builders gave the project its Platinum Award for the best smart growth community in the country. Vince's final vindication occurred when two of the individuals who had vociferously opposed his development—the leader of the citizens' group who later chaired the planning commission, and the lone dissenter on the planning commission—both bought homes in I'On.

In a *New Yorker* profile, John McPhee recounted that when Charles Fraser was starting his career as a developer on Hilton Head Island, he confided to his mother, "I may never make any money, but I want to create something beautiful." In fact, Sea Pines was a financial success, but the statement is revealing. The popular image of the developer is that of an amoral salesman. This is certainly true in many cases—if there were such a thing as a developers' guild, its motto would be "Give the people what they want." But a developer is not only a buyer and seller of real estate; he is also a builder, and hence—like an architect—he is liable to be motivated by creative impulses. McPhee compared Fraser to a painter: "Sea Pines Plantation appears to be something painted by a single hand, in greens, grays, and browns. . . . Most of the houses have cedar-shake roofs and bleached-cypress siding, the intention being that they should blend into their environment like spotted fawns."

Vince sometimes refers to himself as a civic artist. When I'On was under construction, he and his younger brother, Geoff, who worked with him on the project, did what Vince called "fine tuning." New Urbanist developments sometimes include Georgian-style crescents, squares, and boulevards, but I'On's street layout was more casual. "We added street deflections, mixed up lot sizes, and tweaked side lot lines so that they didn't run perpendicular to front lot lines," said Vince. "We had both lived in Beaufort and Charleston and we were partial to informality." Many of these decisions were made in the field. For example, a large tree intended to be saved might not be located in the exact place shown on the tree survey and would require adjusting the street, or an alignment might be slightly altered to emphasize a view. In the early days of the project, such changes frustrated the contractor as well as the township. "The friction was never about substandard quality or us wanting to make adjustments that were technically difficult," Geoff told me. "It was because so much of the conventional development process depends on predictability, and we were liable to make last-minute changes." In time, things ran more smoothly, as Vince's cost estimates became more accurate and as people got used to his way of working.

Vince and Geoff were following in the footsteps of Camillo Sitte, a nineteenth-century Viennese architect who is best remembered for his influential handbook, *City Planning According to Artistic Principles*. The stated aim of this planning handbook, which was published in 1889, was to reform city planning. Sitte objected to the standardized city blocks and monotonous rows of regularly aligned houses that characterized "hygienic" town planning in the late nineteenth century. "Modern city building completely reverses the proper relationship between built up area and open space," he wrote. "In former times the open spaces—streets and plazas—were designed to have an enclosed character for a definite effect. Today we normally begin by parcelling out building sites, and whatever is left over is turned into streets and plazas."

As the title suggests, Sitte considered city planning to be an art. People had always admired the streets and squares of medieval and Renaissance towns and cities, and Sitte was convinced that their beauty was not accidental. He analyzed the old towns of Italy and Germany. He was particularly interested in irregularity, which, he sensed, contributed to the beauty of medieval towns. He noticed that in German medieval towns, for example, the cathedral was never located in the center of a square but always to one side. Even as simple a thing as a fountain or a statue in an open space benefitted from being placed off-center. Similarly, traditional squares were rarely actually square but often irregular in outline. His book was replete with drawings that illustrated his findings. Sitte's critique of city planning was well received, and it particularly resonated in the United States, where the gridiron plan had long been paramount. An American edition appeared in 1945, and in his introduction, the New York architect Ralph Walker wrote that the fifty-year-old book was more relevant than ever. And so it remains today.

Vince came across Sitte's book while he was working on I'On. It was recommended to him by his sister, Tamara, a landscape architect. Sitte taught that plan drawings are a poor tool for conveying the three-dimensional reality of urban spaces, which is why Vince and Geoff did much of their fine-tuning on the spot. "Take a walk. You'll see," read the I'On website. What I saw when I walked around the community were subtle shifts of perspective, visual adjustments in the way that a view of a building opened up suddenly as I turned a corner, the pleasing irregularity of a winding street. In many cases, the irregularities were so understated that they were felt rather than seen.

Not all of Vince's plans for I'On came to fruition. During the charrette, one of the architects suggested that the two lakes should be connected by canals. Vince liked the idea, and he commissioned George to design a cluster of fourteen houses along one of the canals. While the plan layout of Tully Alley and Charles Street had been constrained by existing conditions, here George was free to indulge his imagination. His little fragment of a Venetian *sestiere* included a variety of canal-side houses—small and large—linked by alleyways and courtyards and a pedestrian bridge over the canal. A small piazza by the water had outdoor steps that could be used as outdoor seating. "We imagined showing outdoor movies, sort of like *Cinema Paradiso*," Vince recalls. George's plan required widening the existing canal and replacing the wooden bulkhead with concrete shoring, which proved costly. So was the house construction, which George and Andrew, who prepared the construction documents, insisted be masonry. Vince was unable to convince his partners that the extra expense was justified, and George's plan was shelved. The canal-side lots were developed more conventionally.

Despite the construction of the Holy Ascension Church, which was located in one of the residential neighborhoods, Vince had not given up on the idea of a small church in the village center. The pastor of the Holy Cross congregation on Sullivan's Island was still interested. Vince commissioned an Atlanta architectural firm to design a Gothic

Canal-side houses in I'On, Vince Graham's planned community
in Mount Pleasant, South Carolina.

Revival chapel, but the final construction cost proved too steep. Macky
Hill came up with a solution. He had been studying eighteenth-century
Lowcountry "chapels of ease," small places of worship built on outlying
plantations that were far from established parishes, and he suggested
that a similar simple structure might work for I'On. When even this
proved too expensive for Holy Cross, Vince and Geoff built the chapel
themselves and leased it to the congregation, with an option to purchase
in the future. The secular building functions as a meetinghouse. "To
pay expenses, we rent it out for weddings and community events," said
Vince. "Andrew is designing a decorative garden wall and gate, and we
plan to add a bell tower."

Several longtime I'On residents approached Vince about the possibility of reserving gravesites in the old burial ground where Jacob Bond
I'On was buried. The ground was a designated historic landmark, hence
off-limits, but Vince owned the adjacent parcel, and he and Andrew

explored the feasibility of building a memorial park that would include burial places, an open-air chapel, and even a pet cemetery. Meanwhile, Andrew designed a small outdoor columbarium attached to the meetinghouse. The brick niches were in a private walled garden reached by a secluded wooden gate surmounted by a Doric pediment, also in brick. Vince had another project in mind for the parking lot next to the meetinghouse. On a holiday visit to Bruges, he had seen what Belgians call *Godshuizen*, "God's houses," which were fourteenth-century almshouses for the elderly poor, built in the form of miniature houses. Why not adapt the idea for contemporary seniors in I'On? Vince commissioned George to design five attached three-story buildings, each with three micro-apartments complete with elevators and private porches.

A good developer is like an impresario, orchestrating public events, bringing new acts to town. When Charles Fraser started building Sea Pines, he and his wife, Mary, invited new residents to a party every Saturday night. They did this for the first ten years of the project. "I was only twenty-seven and not very knowledgeable," Fraser told me, "but I knew it was important to introduce people to each other." To the same end, Vince organized festivals and a farmers' market in the I'On village square, and concerts in the outdoor amphitheater beside one of the lakes. Nearby he built a boathouse with dinghy and kayak storage. Providing land for churches was part of the same strategy. Getting people together, whether they were playing tennis, taking the kids to soccer games, or worshipping, was all a part of encouraging community. "A lot of developers talk about creating community," Vince told an interviewer. "I really don't think that's what we do. Community can't be created by one person, it has to emerge from people living or working some place. But you can create the conditions that enable it. That's what I try to do— create conditions where people can connect with one another."

I'On was becoming a community. It was an attractive place, but it was basically a homogenous collection of detached houses—in effect, a better suburb. Vince was not discouraged. Like most developers, he was focused on his next project. He had found a site where he thought it might be possible to create the dense and varied urbanism of historic Charleston. It would be a challenge, but with Newpoint and I'On under his belt, he was sure he could succeed.

Townscapes

*Vince starts a new project; George lays out
a medieval neighborhood; Andrew designs
a mountain village*

The property that Vince had his eye on was in North Charleston, only three miles up the Cooper River. Originally called the North Area, the land had been strictly agricultural until 1895, when the Charleston city council, in a rush of civic high-mindedness, bought a long-neglected rice plantation—six hundred acres—to turn into a rural park for day-tripping townspeople. Such alternatives to urban parks were not uncommon in the late nineteenth century; in the 1880s, Frederick Law Olmsted had laid out a Lido-like park outside Detroit on Belle Isle. Olmsted had since retired and left his practice in the hands of John Charles and Frederick, Jr., his stepson and son, and it was their firm, Olmsted Brothers, that Charleston commissioned to design its park. The Olmsteds' report to the Charleston city council extolled the virtues of the site: "The views over the river, and its bordering salt meadows and distant woods, are very beautiful. . . . There exist many grand old live oaks, which are alone worth the trouble of a trip from the city to see." In addition to preserving the live oaks and the surrounding pine woods, and laying out the usual walks, bridle paths, and carriage drives, the Olmsteds converted the abandoned rice fields into a network of saltwater lagoons for pleasure boating. Their plan included a nursery, an athletic field, and a promenade along the river, as well as a program to control malarial mosquitoes. Chicora Park, as it was called, would be linked to the city by an existing trolley line, and a future parkway was part of the plan.*

Construction started immediately and progress was rapid. In their 1900 report, the park commissioners described tree planting, path and roadway building, and lagoon construction. A gardener's cottage and the keeper's lodge were completed and work was about to start on converting the plantation house into an inn. Yet the following year, learning that the Navy Department was considering establishing a shipyard in the region, a new city council, eager to attract industry, changed course and sold the property to the federal government. That was the end of Chicora Park.† The Navy filled in the lagoons, replaced the plantation house with an administrative building, and built officers' quarters among the live oaks. Along the riverbank it erected piers, ship berths, and the largest dry dock on the eastern seaboard.

As the city fathers hoped, the presence of a shipyard and the attendant industrial activities stimulated economic growth. In 1912, hoping to capitalize on this bounty, a group of Charleston businessmen founded the North Charleston Development Corporation. The corporation acquired five thousand acres of forestland immediately to the north of the shipyard and hired P. J. Berckmans & Company, an Augusta, Georgia–based landscape architecture firm, to subdivide one thousand acres into residential and industrial lots. The project was promoted as the New South Garden City. The idea of garden cities, which were satellite communities that combined the amenities of urban living in a country-like setting, had originated in Britain at the turn of the century as a reaction to the crowded Victorian industrial metropolis. The concept rapidly spread across Europe and as far afield as Canada, Brazil, Japan, and Australia. The first American garden city was Forest Hills Gardens in Queens, New York, planned in 1909 by Frederick Law Olmsted, Jr. He described

---

* "Chicora" was the name of a mythical El Dorado–like kingdom in South Carolina, sought by sixteenth-century Spanish and French explorers.
† Charleston used the proceeds from the sale to build a sixty-acre city park, Hampton Park, planned by John C. Olmsted.

The garden suburb of North Charleston, laid out in 1914.
The Mixson site (shaded) is at lower left.

the design as "the kind of accidental plan which has generally resulted
from unpremeditated city growth, combining straight streets with subtle
deflections, bends and variations in width," which sounds a lot like what
Vince and Geoff would do at I'On.

The master plan of North Charleston was the work of one of Olmsted Jr.'s Harvard students, William Bell Marquis, a recent graduate now
employed by Berckmans. Marquis loosely modeled the residential neighborhoods on Forest Hills, laying out a grid of meandering streets with
sites reserved for parks, playgrounds, and schools. The most striking fea-

ture of the plan was a large circular park with eight radiating avenues that resembled the spokes of a wheel. The main commercial street led from the park past a railway station to the trolley stop. Factory sites lined the banks of the Cooper River, and farmland on the periphery acted as a green buffer. The design, though not as refined as Forest Hills, was a commendable effort for a beginner.

Construction started in 1914; the circular park and the radiating avenues were laid out and the trolley line was extended. The new town was to house thirty thousand people—the prescribed population for a garden city—an ambitious goal at a time when the entire population of Charleston was only fifty-five thousand. Like many visionary real estate ventures, North Charleston had a rocky start. The First World War expansion of the Navy yard proved temporary and the anticipated industrial growth of the surrounding area failed to materialize. As a result, the lots remained unsold, and in 1925, with little to show for its efforts, the North Charleston Development Corporation was forced into receivership. The projected city limped along under a succession of owners. The construction of a new bridge between Charleston and Mount Pleasant directed suburban growth to the east rather than the north, and by 1930 the population of North Charleston was barely two thousand.

Following the outbreak of the Second World War, thanks to the establishment of a full-fledged Navy base and the revival of the shipyard, industries—and people—began moving into the area. The Cold War expansion of the shipyard, which serviced ballistic missile submarines, attracted more workers, while a new interstate highway provided a convenient link to the city. The national trend toward suburban living benefited North Charleston, and in due course, it grew into an incorporated city, annexing not only the Navy yard but also Charleston International Airport and the adjoining Air Force base. By 2010, the population of North Charleston was approaching that of Charleston itself.

North Charleston far outgrew the Marquis plan, which survived as a "historic neighborhood" called Park Circle. Prewar garden cities such as Forest Hills Gardens are distinguished by their charming domestic architecture, but the houses of Park Circle, which dated from a later era, were unremarkable suburban ranchers and bungalows. The bones of Marquis's plan were still there, however. The circular park remained and now contained a community center and two baseball diamonds; shops and businesses lined the busy little main street. The trolley stop was gone, but there was an Amtrak station. The broad radiating avenues gave a pleasant sense of organization to the place.

"I was looking for somewhere to build a more affordable version of I'On," Vince told me. It was natural that he should turn to North Charleston. The city was less affluent than Mount Pleasant—the median household income was about half, and real estate prices were correspondingly lower. The demographic makeup was different, too. Like the members of Sunsetter Lodge on Saint Philip Street, many of the African American families who left the Charleston peninsula had moved to North Charleston. As a result, while Mount Pleasant remained a predominantly white community, North Charleston had a racially mixed population that included a significant number of Hispanics.

What also attracted Vince to North Charleston was the dynamic local government. In the mid-1990s, the Navy announced that it was closing its base, and the city took active steps to ensure its own future. The naval base, which the federal government had handed over to the city, became the basis of an ambitious twenty-year development plan to be undertaken by the city and a private developer. The so-called Noisette Project was the largest urban revitalization project in the United States, covering thousands of acres and including a riverfront park, as well as residential neighborhoods and a brand-new downtown. North Charleston was hot.

The property that interested Vince was in the historic district of Park Circle, forty-four acres bisected by Mixson Avenue. The parcel was currently the site of John C. Calhoun Homes, a residential complex that had been built in 1941 by the Defense Homes Corporation, the wartime federal agency responsible for providing emergency housing for defense workers. Calhoun Homes, one of several similar projects in North Charleston built to house shipyard workers and their families, consisted of two hundred one-story, prefabricated wooden buildings, each containing one or two dwellings. The no-frills architecture and hurriedly conceived layout resembled a military base.

Following the end of the Second World War, the Defense Homes Corporation was wound down and its housing projects were sold off to their occupants. Over time, as the original families moved out, Calhoun Homes was turned into inexpensive rental housing. "The property was owned by a group of a hundred or so small investors, mostly elderly retirees," Vince told me. Many of the owners had once lived in Calhoun Homes themselves and remembered it as a vibrant community, but the project had since fallen on hard times. "When we came along it was pretty rough, basically a slum-lord situation," said Vince. "About half of the homes were dilapidated and boarded up, and there were drug and prostitution rings in others. The property was for sale and had been under contract, but the deal had fallen through. The investors really wanted to get out."

I talked about the property acquisition process with LeGrand Elebash, who managed Vince's company, the I'On Group. Elebash had met Vince years before—he was one of the Marine fighter pilots who had bought a house in Newpoint. After retiring from the military, he got a Harvard MBA, moved to Charleston, and joined Vince's company. Elebash told me that there had been another buyer interested in the Mixson Avenue property. "We were successful, but it wasn't chiefly a money issue. The other buyer wanted to do repairs and basically keep Calhoun Homes as it was. We planned to create a new neighborhood, and that appealed to the owners." Once the property changed hands, the occupied houses had to be vacated before demolition could begin. "We gave the tenants, most of whom were African Americans, six months' notice. To help them relocate we partnered with a local nonprofit to hold a housing fair to which we invited North Charleston landlords. We also assisted with moving expenses. Before the demolition we organized a 'Farewell to Calhoun Homes' party. The demolition took several months because some of the houses had asbestos cement siding and vinyl asbestos kitchen floors and required remediation."

In 2005, a year after acquiring the property, Vince organized a charrette, as he had done with I'On. Instead of bringing in out-of-town planners, he hired Tim Keane to lead the workshop. Keane, a Charlotte, North Carolina, native, had recently left his post as director of planning for the City of Charleston to start his own consulting firm. He had previously taught at the University of Miami, where Elizabeth Plater-Zyberk was dean, so he was familiar with New Urbanism. He was assisted by Jacob Lindsey, a landscape architect. Keane brought in Rick Hall, a traffic engineer who had worked on many New Urbanist projects, including I'On. Vince suggested to Keane that he engage George as a consultant. According to Elebash, "Vince hoped that George would provide the architectural spark for the project." At first George was reluctant to take part—he didn't believe in design by committee—but he had known Tim Keane for a long time and respected him, and he finally agreed. He engaged Andrew as an assistant.

The week-long charrette took place in a storefront on North Charleston's main street and involved local officials as well as the public. George found the first day discouraging. "The charrette seemed to be mostly a cheerleading session," he recalled. "I didn't know what to do with myself." Partway through the first afternoon he left and went home. George wasn't quitting—he felt a sense of commitment to Keane and Vince. Vince had described the prospective buyers as small professional households and first-time homeowners, which meant that the houses had to be affordable. George went through his project files and pulled out all the plans of small houses that he had built over the years. He chose half a dozen and redrew the ground-floor plans at one-sixteenth scale, photocopied them onto different-colored paper, and cut them out. The next day he brought the paper cutouts to the charrette. He asked for a detailed one-sixteenth scale plan of a corner of the site. He and Andrew sat down with the drawing and tried to imagine how a village might have developed over time. According to G. K. Chesterton, towns began when people gathered around a sacred stone or a sacred well. There were no sacred stones on the Calhoun Homes site, but there were a dozen giant live oaks. People gravitate to trees, George reasoned, and using the cutouts and the site-plan drawing, he and Andrew began arranging houses around one of the large trees. Then they did this around a second tree. They sketched a street connecting the two clusters and placed houses along the street. And so on. It was like a game. The rule was that the houses could be freestanding or attached, but they couldn't have front gardens or backyards, and each house had to have space for parking. Another rule was that you couldn't go back and rearrange the cutouts once you had placed them.

George's unusual technique was an attempt to achieve the organic quality of Tully Alley in a project that was designed on paper. The resulting layout simulated the four conditions recommended by Christopher Alexander: it was designed in a piecemeal manner; it was unpredictable in the sense that it did not follow a master plan; it was coherent— punctuated by open spaces surrounding trees. And it was full of feeling: the irregular layout resembled a medieval town, the buildings at odd angles, the streets snaking through—and sometimes even under— the buildings, widening here and narrowing there. Parking was handled haphazardly, as it is in old towns. Some of the houses had garages, some cars were in small parking lots in the back, some were in mews-like alleys, others were simply parked in front of houses on the street. "George thinks of urban design as designing buildings," Andrew told me. "The streets are what is left over."

As the plan filled up, the game became more complicated. Some of the houses were given private gardens, while some of the balconies protruded over the sidewalk. One perimeter block had an inner courtyard that served as a car park. Small, three-story apartment blocks popped up at the edges. A square opened up to accommodate a fire truck turnaround. A village green developed around the largest live oak; a pedestrian street led into the green next to a large building consisting of commercial spaces and live-work units on the first floor and courtyard houses above. The large building and the village green provided a focus to the neighborhood.

By the end of the charrette George and Andrew, who had been working on their own, had produced a large collage consisting of glued-down rectangles of colored paper—one hundred and fifty houses in all. They showed the plan to Vince. He had recently returned from a visit to Italy and was enthusiastic about the village-like arrangement; he decided that the plan should be the first phase of Mixson, which is what he was calling the project. George and Andrew spent several weeks refining their plan. George detailed the house plans, while Andrew drew the

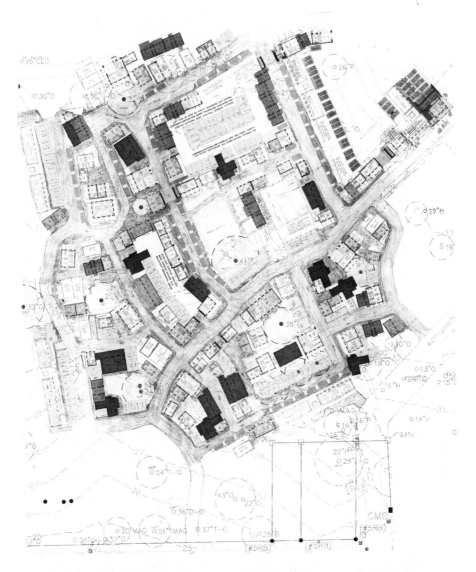

George Holt's organic plan for a neighborhood in Mixson resembles a
medieval town. The houses are grouped around existing live oaks.

Andrew Gould's rough sketch of proposed houses shows the variety
and dense urbanism that characterize Mixson.

elevations and a digital site plan that showed the precise locations of the
streets, lots, buildings, and trees.

George and Andrew's plan occupied seven acres in the southwest
corner of the site. The rest of the project was designed during the charrette: Mixson Avenue was redirected to slow traffic; shops were grouped
around a square; residential lots were arranged on gently winding streets.
Andrew described the overall result as "a typical New Urbanist plan
intersecting with a medieval village." Vince had a local engineering firm
translate Andrew's site drawing into a plan that he could present to the
city. The plan met with a positive reception. The North Charleston city
council had taken the lead in the redevelopment of another old Defense
Homes Corporation project, and it was anxious to see new construction
on the Calhoun Homes site. After the success of I'On, Vince's credibil-
ity was high. "The city was extremely liberal with the rezoning," Vince
said. "We were able to increase the total number of homes from the original three hundred and fifty to nine hundred and fifty, which is a gross
density of more than twenty units per acre, much higher that we could
achieve at I'On. The new zoning included attached houses and some
apartments, as well as shops. We were even allowed to create roadways
beneath buildings to reach rear courtyards, which is unprecedented."

Mixson was a $200 million project, and although Vince's company was the managing partner, the bulk of the financing came from a group of private investors. With the site cleared and remediated and planning permissions in hand, the value of the property had increased considerably. As a result, the investors decided that it was time to sell and let someone else undertake the lengthy—and risky—process of actually building and marketing houses. In 2006, Vince, who was intent on building Mixson, hunted around and found a buyer. Jamestown Properties was a large German-backed real estate investment fund with its U.S. headquarters in Atlanta, and more than $10 billion of assets under management, mostly in New York. These were existing buildings, but recently Jamestown had started developing new projects such as the Chelsea Market on Manhattan's Lower West Side and Ponce City Market in Atlanta, and it was looking to expand into the Charleston area.* I asked Elebash if an international real estate fund was a good fit with a small developer such as the I'On Group. "Institutional capital can be very rigorous," he said. "There are lots of financial controls and reporting requirements because of responsibility to investors—in this case German pension funds. This can be burdensome for the developer, and it can sometimes be difficult to align goals." Vince agreed. "Mixson was a huge project for us, but it was a drop in the bucket for Jamestown. The novel concept, its location in North Charleston, and the market timing made the project challenging. Jamestown's revolving door of asset managers, and its skepticism about our ability to build at the density planned, made it even more difficult to be on the same page with regard to the vision."

An example of the problem of aligning goals was the church. Vince had met the pastor of nearby Saint Peter's African Methodist Episcopal Church. "Saint Peter's is kind of tucked away, and they had approached us about buying land on Mixson Avenue to give them more visibility," Vince recounted. "My idea was to reroute the avenue to go around the church and locate the new building in a manner that terminated the vista, the same way that Saint Philip's does on Church Street in Charleston." The city approved the idea, and Vince referred the pastor to Andrew,

* In 2018, Jamestown sold Chelsea Market to Google for $2.4 billion.

who did some preliminary sketches. "Unfortunately, Jamestown balked at the cost of realigning the avenue, and nothing ever happened. That was too bad, because in addition to making the street more interesting, the project would've made the church part of the neighborhood. The congregation had many members who were interested in living in Mixson."

At I'On, lots had been sold to builders, but George's complicated plan required a different approach: selling finished houses. Vince started a construction company, hired an experienced home builder as manager, and commissioned an architectural firm to prepare the construction drawings. George attended meetings with the construction and marketing team. Differences soon surfaced. George had designed the houses using cement blocks for durability, but the construction people wanted to substitute lightweight aerated cement blocks, which were less expensive but which George thought were too fragile and would get easily damaged. The marketing people wanted to change George's unconventional house plans. The final straw was when the marketing manager insisted on wall-to-wall carpeting in the bedrooms, which George always avoided in his projects because of mold problems caused by the humid climate. George comes across as easygoing, but when it comes to his work he can be stubborn. "I could see that this wasn't going to work out," he says. Andrew told me that George felt betrayed. George said that "betrayed" was too strong a word, but he was definitely disappointed. "I felt bad about letting Vince down, but at the end of the year [2005] I withdrew from the project and asked that my name be taken off the drawings."

Vince was not completely surprised by George's decision. "I knew that trying to marry George with production builders would not be easy. George and Andrew focus on the integrity of materials and design and that became difficult here," he said. He added, "It was probably partly my fault for not being more involved." With the real estate market in full swing, Vince was spread pretty thin. At the same time that he was starting a new construction company to build Mixson, he was working on a project in downtown Charleston and exploring two other development opportunities in North Charleston for Jamestown Properties. He was also involved in several out-of-state projects. One of these was in North Carolina's Appalachian Mountains, in the vicinity of Highlands, a resort town about a two-hour drive from Atlanta. In the 1930s, the famous golfer Bobby Jones had developed Highlands into a golfing mecca. There were now seven golf course communities in the area, the summer occupants attracted by the cool weather and the mountain scenery. Vince's project was ten miles from Highlands in Cashiers, which he described as "basically a highway crossroads trying to be a town." Vince's partner was Steve Zoukis, who had just retired as a partner in Jamestown Properties and owned a large parcel of forested mountainside in Cashiers. The plan was to develop the ten acres of open land near the highway as a residential community and leave the rest of the parcel in its natural state.

In spring 2007, Vince organized a charrette for Cashiers. He wanted George and Andrew to take part, but George wasn't interested. It had nothing to do with his experience at Mixson; it was the rural location that put him off. "I'm hardly what one would consider an outdoorsy type," he said, "and I don't know anything about mountain villages." Andrew, on the other hand, was game—and he was familiar with the area. After building Holy Ascension Church he had received commissions from other Orthodox congregations, including one in the mountain hamlet of Candler, North Carolina, not far from Cashiers.

The plan produced by the Cashiers charrette was a casual arrangement of buildings, close together and adapted to the hilly terrain. The "main street" included buildings with commercial spaces on the ground floor as well as a small square. The houses scattered on the hillside were a combination of small cottages, single-family houses, and town houses, most with verandas or front porches. Andrew was responsible for the design of the buildings. This time his "historical fantasy" was that the new development was an old neighborhood that predated the adjacent highway. He had visited the historic Moravian community of Old Salem, in Winston-Salem, and he thought that its simple domestic architecture would make a good model for Cashiers. Many of the structures in Old Salem were timber-framed, a traditional construction method their

Andrew's vision of a compact mountain village in Cashiers, North Carolina.

builders had brought from Bohemia and Moravia. Andrew was familiar with the technique since he had used it to build a barn-like parish hall in Candler, and he proposed timber framing for Cashiers. "We like to build things the way they used to be—solid, purposeful, and understated," Andrew wrote in a report on the project.

> The temptation with traditional architecture is to overcomplicate it. Many new structures in the mountains make use of every possible "mountain style" or "rustic" ornament, more for fashion than for practical purpose. As a result some new construction seems more like a theme-park imitation of traditional building, and is better suited for tourists than for simple living. In contrast, our buildings are based on careful study of the actual massing and details of old buildings, with a respect for their practical purpose. We also understand that the closer together buildings are, the simpler they need to be, so that they complement and do not compete. We propose a neighborhood of subtle and reposeful beauty, which, in its simplicity, will highlight the richness and grandeur of the

natural landscape. It's an old-fashioned design philosophy that involves a little more practicality and humility than is fashionable these days.

Andrew's sketches showed a severe architecture with few classical details, more like a nineteenth-century mill town than a twenty-first-century resort village. The project commenced. Zoukis hired an Atlanta architect to design a clubhouse on the ridge of the property, and several of the older buildings along the highway were renovated as shops; Vince and Zoukis were working with other property owners at the crossroads on a comprehensive master plan for the larger area. Andrew was pleased to see his ideas taking shape.

George and Andrew were done with Mixson, but not with North Charleston. In early 2007, a little more than a year after George withdrew from the Mixson project, his brother, Bob, asked him to help with a development on a four-acre property he had bought on Sumner Avenue in a neighborhood north of the historic Park Circle district. This neighborhood was less urbanized, with suburban ranch houses, strip malls, and mobile home parks. The property was vacant and heavily wooded with live oaks, palmettos, magnolias, pines, and cedars. Bob's plan was to build small, inexpensive houses. To that end, he wanted George and Andrew to work with a modular home manufacturer in North Carolina. Modular homes are prefabricated in a factory and shipped to the building site on trailers. A typical home might require between two and four modules, framed in wood and completely finished inside and out. The modules are placed on foundations, side-by-side or stacked. Once completed they are indistinguishable from conventionally built houses. The advantages of factory production are higher quality, better control over costs, and a reduction in work done on the building site—once foundations and infrastructure are ready, the modules are trucked in and the project can be completed in short order.

George and Andrew met the manufacturer. The design of modular homes is constrained by the dimensions that can be transported on the highway, as well as by the demands of the factory. George designed six different models, small houses with two bedrooms, ranging from 850 to 1,300 square feet. All of the houses were freestanding, and the majority were two stories. To introduce variety, Andrew added different roof shapes (gable and hipped), different porch configurations, and different exterior cladding (wood siding and stucco).

George and Andrew arranged the colored cutout house plans on the site drawing, just as they had previously done with Mixson. They adjusted the lots to suit the houses. "In dense projects where the intention is to have as many single-family homes as possible, it's best to work out the house plans in advance," says George. "Most urban planners go in the opposite direction, and lay out the lots first. The result is that houses have to be designed to suit different lots, which is expensive. Alternatively, having rows of tiny, similar-size lots on straight streets doesn't produce an interesting layout."

There were no straight streets in George and Andrew's plan. "We located the houses to save as many of the trees as possible," says George. "The casual arrangement gave a feeling of warmth, and the impression that the neighborhood had developed over time instead of being built all at once." Each house required two parking spaces. There would be no garages; parked cars were shoe-horned in wherever possible, beside and in front of houses, sometimes in tandem, sometimes in group lots. Although the site was rectangular, these requirements produced building lots that were highly irregular. In the center of the site, opposite a public green, George designed a three-story building with apartments above and commercial spaces below.

George and Andrew presented the project to the mayor. "He was pleased with our work and was personally involved in arranging the approvals," says Andrew. The permitting process required some changes to the plan. A city councilman objected to the commercial building, so that had to be removed, although the central green remained. The road configuration was simplified. The city required a drainage easement down one side of the site, which slightly reduced the available building area. To compensate, George added a seventh model that was raised up to allow a carport under part of the house. The final count was fifty-five houses, or fourteen houses per acre, a lower density than Mixson but

George and Andrew designed tightly packed modular homes
on Sumner Avenue in North Charleston.

very dense for a detached-house development. The Sumner Avenue project was approved in mid-2007.

Just as Cashiers and Sumner Avenue were about to start construction,
the national economic slowdown that is sometimes called the Great
Recession reared its head. The effects were felt almost immediately.
Banks stopped lending, homebuyers stopped buying, builders stopped
building, and, as a result, the housing market quickly collapsed. Little projects such as Cashiers and Sumner Avenue collapsed with it. So
did the Noisette Project. What about Mixson? Twenty-seven houses had
been built, and the underground infrastructure for phase one was in
place. "When the economy started to turn bad in 2008, and housing
sales stalled, Jamestown threatened to walk away," says Vince. "The project was essentially frozen, which made it difficult to market homes. Prospective buyers with homes under contract forfeited their deposits. By

then we had invested ten million dollars in the project. The three million dollar construction cost was a recourse loan, which meant that I was personally responsible, so I had no choice. The investor group I managed lost its ten percent interest to Jamestown, which purchased the project and the home construction debt for about forty cents on the dollar."

It was Vince's first major setback. "We really threw our hearts into that project," he says ruefully. "We invested so much money, time, and emotion into building the first phase. We had a fully supportive local government—the mayor and his wife even purchased a home there—and we were incorporating lessons from every development we had ever done. What a missed opportunity!" Yet he took the reversal in stride—he had no choice. Success in real estate is often a matter of timing, and the timing of outside events is beyond the developer's control.

Vince's vision was dead, but not the project. Jamestown was large enough to weather the recession, and it planned to build conventional rental apartments along the avenue; the rest of the project would have to wait. I visited Mixson a few years later. The original twenty-seven houses followed George and Andrew's designs, although the details were not what they would have done—Andrew called them "plasticky"; still, the general effect was charming. A covered pedestrian passage led to a little square surrounding a large laurel oak. Loggias and verandas overlooked the space. One of the buildings was brick, and the rest were plastered and painted in light colors: ochre, yellow, pink. The sidewalks of the narrow, winding street were lined with buildings three and four stories high, some accessed by outdoor stairs. A porte cochère led to an irregularly shaped rear courtyard lined with garage doors. This was very different from I'On: not a green garden suburb but a dense piece of traditional urbanism. My impression was of an old Parisian *quartier*. A Jeep Cherokee and a Volvo station wagon were parked on the street, but an old Citroën Traction Avant would not have been out of place. Nor would I have been surprised to see a caped *gendarme* strolling down the street. I'm being fanciful, but the truth was that walking around Mixson felt like being in a painting . . . by René Magritte. One minute you were on a back street of the Left Bank, but turn a corner and you were brought up short by the surreal spectacle of a barren field dotted with large trees—the rest of the cleared Calhoun Homes site. It was eerie and a little sad.

It appeared that George's idea of organic planning was destined to remain unfinished. That was a shame. Mixson would have demonstrated that the dense, piecemeal urbanism that made Tully Alley so attractive could be successfully adapted to a large planned development. What George didn't know was that he would be given a second chance. At the very time that he was withdrawing from Mixson, his friend Jerry was putting in motion events that would eventually culminate in another medieval street. Not in the northern suburbs or the Appalachians, but in downtown Charleston.

Part III

ELEVEN

The Monopoly Game

*Rebuilding the old and building the new
in downtown Charleston*

I t all began in 2005, when Bob Holt approached Jerry with an offer to buy the Pink House on Saint Philip Street. This was the house that George had rebuilt after it collapsed, the place where the Tully Alley adventure had begun. Jerry, who had bought out George and Cheryl's shares and was using the house as a rental property, accepted Bob's offer. The Internal Revenue Service allows commercial sellers to defer capital gains on real estate if, within a specified time period, they reinvest the gains in a "like-kind exchange"—that is, if they buy a similar property. The amount of the gains is deposited with a "qualified intermediary," usually a specialized bonded company that, at the time of purchase of the new property, remits the deposit to the seller. Jerry had done this before. Briefly put, he had six weeks to buy another house.

These days Jerry had more time to spend attending to his real estate investments—he was no longer flying. Twelve years earlier, he had been in Atlanta, completing his semiannual training at Delta's flight simulator facility, when driving late at night he was broadsided by a truck and injured his back. "I managed for two years with spinal injections, physical therapy, exercise, and FAA-permitted meds," he told me. Eventually, he needed cervical spine surgery. "You can't take serious pain medications and fly, and since the injured area was getting worse, I knew the clock was ticking, and in the winter of 2004, I had to leave the cockpit for good." We're sitting in the attic study of his home on Charles Street. Photographs of airplanes hang on the walls, and a fighter pilot's helmet sits on top of the bookshelf. "I was 47," he recalls. "With more time on my hands I upped my involvement in the real-life Monopoly game that George and I had started."

Two weeks before the like-kind exchange deadline, Jerry found a suitable property in Cannonborough, a neighborhood immediately west of Elliotborough. By curious coincidence, the location was only four blocks from the house on Perry Street, where the two-decades-old Monopoly game had started. The Cannonborough house was a small, narrow, one-story structure with three rooms and a piazza on the south side: in effect, a poor man's single house. Such structures, common in Charleston, date from the decades following the Civil War and are popularly known as freedmen's cottages, although recent evidence has shown that they were built by whites as well as emancipated slaves. The house at 266 Ashley Avenue dated from the late 1890s and was built by one Prince Anderson, a baker. In 1917, Anderson sold the house to another African American, Daniel Blythewood, a carpenter, who lived there with his large family. It was likely Blythewood who added the two bedrooms in the attic. The house changed hands several times, until in the late 1970s it became a rooming house. By the time that Jerry bought it, the building was in bad shape. The exterior wooden siding was largely rotten, the sagging piazza was missing a column, and a makeshift 1950s addition was awkwardly tacked on to the rear.

George and Andrew were no longer working on Mixson, and they helped Jerry with the project. They started by demolishing the rear addition, then turned to the interior, whose walls and ceilings were covered in beat-up plaster wallboard. Removing the wallboard unexpectedly revealed the original heart pine tongue-and-groove boards underneath. The heartwood of longleaf pine, rare today, is prized for its strength, hardness, and red coloration. Since the boards were in good condition, they could be saved. Thus began an unusual renovation. Most wood-frame buildings are renovated from the outside in—that is, the exterior cladding is replaced first and the interior is finished last. Here, because the interior wood finish would be preserved, the process was reversed.

The old tongue-and-groove interior finish was left in place and the rotten exterior siding was removed. After new wiring and plumbing were installed, closed-cell foam insulation was sprayed into the cavity, the framing was wrapped in a moisture barrier, and new wooden siding was nailed onto the exterior.

George had a friend who was a historic preservationist, and he and Jerry commissioned her to perform a forensic analysis of the interior paint finishes. An examination of paint scrapings under a stereomicroscope revealed as many as seventeen layers of paint. A typical wall in the house had a lime wash primer and multiple coats of oil paint: worn patches of vibrant orange, brown, and blue. The stair hall had an additional layer of wallpaper dating from the 1940s. George and Jerry decided to preserve the many paint layers. They removed the wallpaper and washed the walls and ceilings. Then, instead of adding a new coat of paint, they sealed the mottled surface with clear shellac. Rotted or damaged boards were replaced by old wood from elsewhere in the house. Thus they were able to consolidate the front parlor and the stair hall. Upstairs, they repaired the knee walls of the attic bedrooms with reused boards; the ceilings were new. Most of the kitchen walls were new, although the cupboard doors were a quilted mosaic of old boards. The result, which hardly met Charter of Venice standards, was an interesting potpourri. There was nothing traditional about the kitchen appliances, which included a built-in refrigerator, a downdraft cooktop, a wall oven, a concealed microwave, and a drawer dishwasher. Nor was there any attempt to blend the new with the old. New fixtures, new track lighting, new doors, and new wall cladding contrasted with the beat-up heart pine.

Old buildings generally display the evidence of their many occupants—additions, subtractions, modifications—but preservationists tend to favor consistency. Jerry, George, and Andrew were more pragmatic. Instead of reproducing a single historical moment in time, they created a palimpsest that preserved yesterday—and the day before yesterday—and combined them with today. We've become so used to consistency in renovation that it comes as a shock to see shiny stainless steel kitchen fixtures next to hundred-year-old chipped paint. George remembers that when the workers were applying the shellac to the walls, an elderly neighbor stopped by to visit. "She was a sweet old lady and she commiserated with us about how expensive everything was these days. Her advice was to not worry because in the future we'd find the money to paint the inside properly."

The dark-red heart pine floor was washed but not sanded before being coated with clear urethane, so its age showed through. The new, six-over-six, multipaned, double-hung wood windows replicated the originals; on the other hand, the fireplaces were stripped of plaster and their wooden mantels removed to reveal the brick beneath—a modern aesthetic. Andrew, who designed the trim, made the interior doors with planks and diagonal bracing, traditional in character but quite different from the paneled doors they replaced. The stair balustrade, which showed the wear and tear of a century of use but was otherwise sound, was merely washed. "We don't like to throw old things away," says Jerry.

Despite the reuse of old materials, the cost of renovating the freedman's cottage was considerable, and by the time that the work was finished in 2008, Jerry had invested much more than the current market value of the rebuilt house. His intention was to recover this money by renting the renovated house and building more rental buildings at the rear. The narrow lot was very deep—180 feet—and it had a large water oak on the property line. A Charleston ordinance allowed higher density for workforce housing, and George proposed that a substantial block of narrow town houses could eventually be built immediately behind the freedman's cottage. In the meantime, Jerry applied for building permits for two houses at the back of the lot. The first was a rental house, designed by George and Andrew. While working on Mixson, George had become fascinated by very small houses, and he saw this as an opportunity to design a house with a footprint of less than three hundred square feet. George was a devotee of masonry construction, but he wanted to try a wood-frame building with what he called double-hull siding—that is, siding installed with a space behind it to promote air circulation and prolong the life of the wood. "Since the house would be held by Jerry for at least a decade, it was a good property for conducting experiments," George explained. Jerry was amenable. "I knew we would be building more houses and I wanted a wooden house in the batch; since all of the neighboring houses are wooden, it seemed like a good idea," he said. He

When Jerry Moran renovated a freedman's cottage on Ashley Avenue,
it turned out to be the beginning of an ambitious project.

appreciated the irony of the situation. "As usual, I set out to be an investor and wound up running a not-for-profit school of the building arts."

The house was located near the large water oak. "We needed the
house to be narrow with no porch extension, so as not to crowd the tree,"
Andrew explained. "We were able to get a setback variance that allowed
us to push the building back to within three feet of the property line. As
with almost all our infill houses, it was the site plan and the footprint
that drove the design." The house was a simple box, only thirteen-and-a-
half feet deep by twenty-one feet wide, and three stories high. The wood
framing was two-by-sixes, diagonally sheathed with planks, filled with
sprayed-on closed-cell foam insulation, and finished in yellow pine clapboard siding mounted on battens.

The floor plan was straightforward: just one room stacked above
another, the main living space on the ground floor, and a bedroom and
a bathroom on each of the two upper floors. This arrangement reminded
me of a historic Philadelphia type, known locally as a bandbox or trinity.
These inexpensive Colonial-era workingmen's homes, many of which

George and Andrew designed the compact little
Blue House with a footprint of less than three hundred
square feet.

survive in the back lanes of downtown Philadelphia, consist of three
stacked rooms (Father, Son, and Holy Ghost) connected by a narrow
winding stair. Philadelphia trinities were usually built in rows, but
George's freestanding house had windows on all sides, which enlivened
the tiny interior. So did the fireplace in the living room and the intricate
interior-wall paneling that used heart pine salvaged from the freedman's
cottage. The kitchen was separated from the living room by an arched
opening. George designed a similar compact kitchen as in the freedman's cottage, without overhead cabinets, and with refrigerator and
freezer drawers and a farmhouse sink. The boxy exterior with its hipped

roof was straightforward, but to reduce the impression of verticality, Andrew designed the top floor to resemble an attic story. A shallow skirt roof extended across the facade at the second floor level to further reduce the height and to provide shelter for the front door. The attic was painted white, the lower floors were blue, and the windows were white with dark-blue shutters. Inevitably it became known as the Blue House.

At this time, George and Andrew decided to formalize their collaboration. "We now thought of ourselves as partners," says Andrew. They hung out their shingle which, in 2008, meant creating a website. They called it New World Byzantine and included early houses such as George's house on Tully Alley and Otranto, Andrew's work on Holy Ascension Church and Mugdock Castle, as well as unbuilt projects such as Mixson, Cashiers, and Sumner Avenue. "We are contemporary designers who believe that answers to modern questions can usually be found in the past," read the introductory text, which was a sort of manifesto.

> We choose to build out of solid, traditional materials; they last for hundreds of years, and you can feel the difference between a thick wall and a thin one. Our buildings don't just look like old buildings—they are built in the same ways. We prefer solid masonry construction and massive wooden beams because they feel good, and we refuse to use plywood structurally inside our houses, because it doesn't seem to stand the test of time, and we don't like the smell.

The second house at the back of Jerry's lot was designed by Andrew for his own family—which now included baby Madalene. Andrew and Julie were still living in the rented apartment in the Pink House on Saint Philip Street and they wanted a place of their own. Jerry sold Andrew a thirty-foot-wide lot behind the Blue House. "Andrew had no credit rating at that point, and since I had a line of credit with the bank, I covered the construction loan," says Jerry. "Once his house was built, Andrew was able to get a regular bank mortgage and pay me back." Jerry generously sold the land at cost.

The footprint of Andrew and Julie's house was slightly larger than

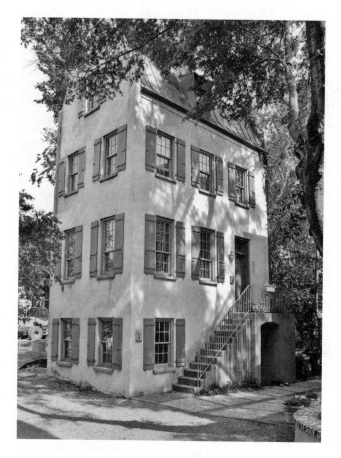

Julie and Andrew Gould's house. Andrew's "historical
fantasy" was an Anglo-Dutch house from 1690.

the Blue House—twenty-four feet wide by fifteen feet deep—but the overall layout was similarly straightforward: a living room and eat-in kitchen
on the main floor, above that a bathroom and a bedroom for Andrew
and Julie, and a small bedroom for Madalene on the attic floor—only
slightly more than a thousand square feet. Andrew needed a workshop,
but the zoning permitted only three stories. "I cut a deal with the zoning administrator," he says. "He accepted a taller house with a first-floor
workshop as long as I placed that floor well below the flood level, so it
couldn't legally be used as a bedroom." An exterior stair with a wrought-
iron railing ran up the side of the house to the front door.

The four-story-high walls were built of cement blocks, the floors and roof framed in wood. The cavities of the blocks were filled with concrete and reinforcing steel—Andrew was not taking any chances with hurricanes. He was characteristically fussy about the construction. Except for the roof sheathing, he didn't use plywood, and there was no engineered wood; all the ironwork hardware was solid—no plastic. The floor above the main living space was supported on exposed four-by-six joists mortised into an eight-by-twelve heart pine beam that ran down the center of the house; it took half a dozen workers to manhandle the massive piece of timber into place. The solid wood windows were double-glazed to reduce sound transmission from the nearby Cross-town Expressway. Andrew built the doors, cupboards, and bookshelves himself; most of the interior walls were paneled in wood and painted. The Early Colonial color scheme was chosen by Renée Killian-Dawson, with whom Andrew had worked on Mugdock Castle. Like the freedman's cottage and the Blue House, the house was heated and cooled by a geothermal heat pump. Additional heat was provided by a Rumford fireplace in the living room. This eighteenth-century invention—Jefferson had a Rumford at Monticello—has a tall and shallow firebox to reflect more heat, and a streamlined throat to reduce the draft and increase efficiency. The hearth and the firebox were lined with reused bricks.

Andrew and Julie's house, with its traditional construction and old-fashioned solidity, recalls an earlier time, as do its window seats, carved spiral balusters, and comfortable old furniture. Instead of using fancy stainless steel hardware, Andrew made simple wooden cupboard latches and used surface-mounted strap hinges. "I'm attracted by Charleston's early, pre-Georgian Colonial architecture," he tells me. "The historical fantasy here is that this is a house from 1690 or thereabouts. It's definitely inspired by the Pink House on Chalmers Street." That Pink House is well-known in Charleston because it's widely considered the oldest surviving stone building in the city.* Built of limestone from Bermuda, with a pantile gambrel roof and narrow, vertical proportions, it looks more Dutch than English. So does Andrew and Julie's tall house. The

---

* In the early 1900s, the architectural historian Beatrice St. Julien Ravenel had her studio in the Pink House.

gray, unpainted stuccoed walls with their rough, uneven finish are punctuated by tall windows with heavy wooden shutters that, with the vertical proportions, give the tall building the appearance of a watchtower. The terne metal of the gambrel roof and the windows and shutters are painted shamrock green and lend this sober little house a cheerful mien. Like a serious person winking.

The experience of developing Tully Alley and Charles Street had taught Jerry the advantage of grouping several lots together, which made it easier to add additional buildings and satisfy the city's parking requirements. Once he had refinanced the freedman's cottage and the Blue House, and Andrew had repaid his construction loan, Jerry had the cash and credit to consider further expansion. He spoke to his neighbor to the north about pooling their land. The owner of the rental house, a doctor, wasn't interested, but he agreed to sell Jerry the vacant back half of his lot, as well as an easement wide enough for an access lane. That enlarged Jerry's property by 50 percent.

The house on the south side of the freedman's cottage was a decrepit two-story structure, most of which was "forfeited to the elements," as Jerry put it. The owners, an elderly African American couple who couldn't afford proper maintenance, lived in two rooms on the upper floor—the first floor was vacant. Because of Jerry's renovation next door, their property had increased in value and they had become the target of interested developers. "The vultures were circling and offering all sorts of crazy deals," he says. The couple approached Jerry with an offer to sell. They were asking an impossibly high price, so he turned them down. Over the next three years there were further negotiations and the price came down, until finally Jerry made a cash offer that was accepted. "They were thrilled to move into a new suburban house," said Jerry. "I believe they had one of their children move into the same new house as well."

The old house was in such bad condition that Jerry and George, fearing it might collapse, immediately gutted the interior and put in cross-bracing to stabilize the walls. They also demolished a flimsy addition at the rear. The deep lot extended 150 feet back to the Blue House, and was large enough that the zoning permitted two additional houses. Then Jerry received an unexpected offer. Mark and Diane Gould, Andrew's parents, were interested in buying the entire back part of the lot. They had recently retired, sold their house in Brookline, and moved to Charleston to be close to their grandchild. The new location would be perfect. Jerry agreed; naturally, Andrew would design his parents' new home.

"My parents had always lived in wooden houses," Andrew explained, and so he opted for wood construction. He had become interested in timber framing. Timber framing, sometimes called post-and-beam, is a traditional construction technique dating back to the Middle Ages that uses heavy timbers pegged together. Andrew had already built two timber-framed structures in Candler, North Carolina, a parish hall and a rectory, and he had used timber framing in the unrealized Cashiers project. The experience had taught him that while timber frames were effective in large spaces, they were less suited to houses, whose partitions and closets obscured the timber frame and left awkward parts of it exposed. He thought that a hybrid solution made more sense: use the frames for the larger living spaces, but build the rest of the house conventionally. For his parents, he designed a two-story cottage with a veranda on each level. The structure of the verandas, as well as the main supports in the living room, were heavy posts and beams joined with oak pegs in the traditional manner; the exterior walls were lightweight wood framing. With a compact footprint only twenty-four by twenty-six feet, the first floor housed the main living spaces, while the second floor contained the master bedroom, a study alcove, and a tiny guest room.

Andrew submitted the design to the BAR together with three other houses that he and George had designed for the Ashley compound. "The more you present at once, the less scrutiny they give to each one," Andrew explained. Two of the houses were on the back portion of the lot that Jerry had bought from his doctor neighbor. The fourth was on a lot that Jerry had optioned, next to the Crosstown Expressway. Because this house was the tallest and most prominent, Andrew and George assumed that it would come in for criticism. Instead, the board approved it, calling it a "creative design." Unexpectedly, the project that became the focus

The timber-framed porch of Mark and Diane Gould's romantic cottage.
Andrew designed a Jacobean interior.

of discussion was Andrew's parents' cottage, despite the fact that it was tucked into the center of the block and barely visible from the street. The board members didn't like anything about it. Why wasn't the squarish plan long and narrow like most Charleston houses, the board members asked, and why wasn't it taller like its neighbors? They particularly didn't like the timber-framed verandas. Too rustic, they said—timber framing belonged in the Appalachian Mountains, not the city. The BAR rarely turns down a project, and in this case it "deferred" the cottage proposal. That meant that Andrew would have to resubmit the plans with the suggested changes.

"The board's decision made me nervous because I had designed the house to my parents' specific wishes and I didn't know how I could change it," Andrew said. To counter the criticisms of the timber verandas, he took pictures of Victorian porches in Charleston that had mortise-and-tenon peg details. He showed these to the BAR and explained that his timber frames would not be rough-hewn and rustic, but would be smoothly finished and painted. He left the plan as it was and made only one architectural change: he added a small parapet wall that hid the slope of the porch roof and made the entrance appear more formal—and more like a single house. Lastly, he pointed out that the cottage was invisible from the street, except for a partial view that could only be glimpsed from the expressway. His arguments convinced the BAR—barely—and his design was approved in December 2010 by a 3–2 vote.

The heavy timbers (eight by eight inches) that comprised the posts, beams, and braces of the cottage were fabricated and erected by Timber Artisans, a local company. One of the two partners, Bruno Sutter, was an Alsatian-born master craftsman, a product of the French artisans guild Compagnons du Devoir. Sutter was also chair of the carpentry and timber-frame department of Charleston's American College of the Building Arts. This unusual school—unique in the United States—is a four-year liberal arts college that offers a bachelor's degree in applied science in six traditional crafts (timber framing, carpentry, plasterwork, masonry, blacksmithing, and stone carving) and has recently added a course in classical architecture and design. Founded in 1999 as an off-shoot of the Historic Charleston Foundation's building crafts training program, the private college is housed in a renovated nineteenth-century trolley barn that contains large workshops in addition to classrooms and a library. Students and alumni have worked on building restoration projects at Drayton Hall, the U.S. Capitol, and Lincoln Cathedral in England. The hands-on approach and emphasis on traditional crafts appealed to Andrew, who had lectured at the college, conducted student building projects, and served on the advisory board. He employed college students in his work at the I'On meetinghouse.

Most contemporary post-and-beam buildings dramatize the heavy timber frames by distinguishing them from the rest of the architecture. "I wanted to integrate the structural and the nonstructural elements," said Andrew. "All the wood in the cottage is painted and the heavy timbers are blended with the wall paneling, cabinetry, and other details." His mother was partial to the British Arts and Crafts, but Andrew thought that wouldn't suit Charleston. Instead, he suggested a Jacobean aesthetic, since the seventeenth century was when Charleston was first settled.

The finished cottage is full of quirky details. "Modern kitchens are so aesthetically noisy, with all those materials and details," Andrew observed. He simplified the cabinets, using plain porcelain knobs, as well as brass drawer pulls that reminded me of old wooden filing cabinets. He personally made a metal chandelier for the living room and carved a bluestone panel—two swans and a Tree of Life—for the fireplace. He designed a winding stair with heavy newel posts and flat-sawn balusters. "I think that took me longer than any other part of the house." The small, cozy living room contains one extravagance: an alcove with a small pipe organ. Andrew had built the instrument when he was fifteen. He had gotten the parts from a company that salvaged old organs— the main mechanical components came from an 1890s Massachusetts church. It took him two years to put it in working order. For a long time the organ stood in the foyer of his parents' Victorian house in Brookline. When they sold the house, Andrew disassembled the organ, stored it in Charleston, and reassembled it when the cottage was complete. He is an accomplished musician and often plays at family gatherings.

When Andrew's parents bought the lot from Jerry, they planned to build two houses; the sale of the second would help to finance the construction of their own home. Andrew designed a large masonry house for the front of the lot. But when their cottage was complete, his parents changed their minds—building the house would be expensive, and anyway they wanted to use the space in front for a garden. Andrew had been sharing an office with George in Bob Holt's square Palladian building at the back of the Cannon Street lot. Holt decided that he wanted to convert the building into apartments, which meant that George and Andrew had to move. George had a home office in his house, but this left Andrew at loose ends. He suggested to his father that he build a small outbuilding at the foot of the garden, which Andrew would then rent. His father liked the idea, and Andrew approached the city architect about getting a waiver, since the site was zoned for exclusively residential use. The city architect said he would prefer if the outbuilding were part of the cottage property, but he would have no objection if Andrew, who was after all part of the family, used it as a home office. Andrew designed a small building with a guest room below and a second-floor studio reached by an exterior spiral stair. He included a bathroom and a kitchenette so that the space could be converted into a small apartment. The area between the outbuilding and the cottage became a walled garden, which Andrew laid out in a formal Jacobean manner, with raised beds and gravel pathways.

The little outbuilding was overlooked by the old house that Jerry had bought from the elderly couple. He had not yet gotten around to renovating it, and the vacant structure was a gloomy presence, with boarded-up windows, peeling paint, and rotted siding. Bare studs and a hastily patched door marked the location of the recently demolished rear addition. Andrew's father complained about the eyesore at the foot of his garden, which was only partly screened by the outbuilding and dominated the view from his upper veranda. That view would soon improve— a new player was about to join the Monopoly game.

Reid's Dream

"The Smallest Palladian Villa in the World"

eid Burgess fell in love with Charleston when he was fifteen. "I
first saw the city on a vacation trip with my parents," he says.
"Later, when I was in college, I didn't spend spring break in
Fort Lauderdale. Instead, my girlfriend, Sally, and I would
drive down to Charleston. We slept in her old Honda and didn't eat out;
I remember a lot of Doritos and canned tuna. But the place was so beautiful, like being transported to some European city." I can't imagine Reid
sleeping in a compact car—he is six foot four, an affable young man with
dark curly hair and a contagious enthusiasm.

Reid was born in Hartford, Connecticut. His father was a business
executive with Kraft Foods and Miller Brewing, and the family moved
around. "We lived in a series of large homes in Chicago, Milwaukee, and
other midwestern cities," says Reid. "There's no doubt that my family was
house-obsessed. My parents subscribed to *Architectural Digest, House
& Garden,* and *Country Life.* My mother is from Virginia, and we had
prints of colonial Tidewater mansions such as Westover, Mount Airy,
and Shirley Plantation on the walls. I recall the family taking long Sunday drives in our station wagon around Chicagoland to gawk at houses.
That bored me when I was little, but later I came to enjoy it." Reid was
also exposed to houses in more exotic locales. His father's work took the
family to Europe, Asia, and the Pacific. They looked at houses there, too.

"I was always sketching floor plans of idealized villas and country houses in high school—extremely crude, I could never draw very well. But it was a real compulsion, and I often got so frustrated that they would consume weeks upon weeks, even if we were on vacation and supposed to be enjoying ourselves."

Reid's compulsive nature may have been hereditary. His great-great-grandfather was Webb C. Ball, a nineteenth-century Cleveland watchmaker. Following a head-on train collision caused by a faulty timepiece, the Lake Shore and Michigan Southern Railway appointed Ball "Time Inspector," a position he would eventually hold at more than half of railroads in the United States. His demanding standards for reliable and accurate railroad chronometers were adopted nationally, and his own watchmaking business prospered. Webb C. Ball railroad watches and station clocks became widely known; the company's slogan was "Get on the Ball."

Reid's boyhood interest seemed to be steering him toward architecture. He looked into several college programs, but was not encouraged. "I didn't have confidence in my drawing skills. I also remembered my father telling me that architects had to do what their clients wanted. Better to make money somewhere else, he advised me, and then build what *you* want. Or be a developer. So I thought a liberal arts school was a better place for me." Reid enrolled in Kenyon College in Ohio, where he majored in history and minored in music.

Music replaced architecture as his consuming passion. Not just any music, traditional bluegrass. Bluegrass, which has its roots in Appalachia, was popularized in the 1940s by the Kentuckian mandolinist Bill Monroe, whose band, the Blue Grass Boys, included such musicians as Lester Flatt, Earl Scruggs, and Vassar Clements. Monroe described his music as "Scottish bagpipes and ole-time fiddlin'. It's Methodist and Holiness and Baptist. It's blues and jazz, and it has a high lonesome sound." Reid taught himself mandolin, and after attending a bluegrass festival he and a classmate, Ted Pitney, started a band. Following graduation, in 2003 they established themselves in Charlottesville, Virginia, which was well situated for touring in the Northeast and the South. They formed a group of six musicians, all in their early twenties—mandolin, violin, banjo, bass, and two guitars—and named it King Wilkie, after

Bill Monroe's favorite Tennessee walking horse. King Wilkie took a purist's approach to the music: traditional acoustic instruments playing the old songs; onstage, the musicians dressed in suits and ties. "Bluegrass appealed to me for many of the same reasons traditional architecture appeals to me," Reid tells me. "It was something *real*, something not connected to machines or cell-phones or synthetic processes. It had its own language and it gave me a sense of connection to history. It could be added to or simply carried forward as another link in the chain."

A year later King Wilkie made its recording debut. The album, *Broke*, reached number one on the bluegrass charts. "We played bluegrass festivals almost every single weekend and different events throughout the week all through the year," says Reid. The group performed at the Grand Ole Opry in Nashville and Town Hall in New York. Despite the success, Reid wasn't satisfied. "It's hard writing about stuff that has never happened to you, ever," he told an interviewer. "You're forced to be creative, because there are these little limits and rules for working the genre. But for us, at least for me, it wasn't really personal enough." King Wilkie moved away from its bluegrass origins. The second album featured new acoustic music and strayed outside the usual bluegrass limits. "*Low Country Suite* had a larger budget for production and marketing, and it got played more on mainstream radio, but it was rejected by many true bluegrass fans, so that hurt us," Reid reflects. Without the discipline of the traditional music, King Wilkie drifted. Eventually, the band broke up. Reid recruited new musicians and released King Wilkie's third, and as it turned out its final, album, *King Wilkie Presents: The Wilkie Family Singers*, a Beatles-esque concept album that, to my ears at least, sounds less compelling than their original bluegrass re-creations. "The band just fizzled out," Reid told me.

Reid and Sally Eisenberg—"my longtime sweetheart"—were now living in Brooklyn. Sally, an accountant, worked for a family trust in Manhattan; Reid was at loose ends. "I had just finished a year of touring in connection with our last recording, so I was ready to get involved in something else." He disliked one aspect of a musician's life. "With King Wilkie it seems like we were always waiting for things to happen, with chunks of downtime between tours, performances, and recordings. It wasn't enough to keep me busy and psychologically satisfied. I remember reading Thomas Jefferson's diary in which he recorded the number of nails he used when building Monticello. I started to think that building things might be more fulfilling."

Reid was drawn back to his interest in architecture, especially old architecture. In New York, he enrolled in an intensive course on classical architecture—the only non-architect in the class—and joined an online discussion group on traditional architecture. That was where he came across an article about George Holt and the Palladian house that he had built for his sister.* Reid, who had acquired a copy of *The Four Books on Architecture* while at Kenyon, dreamed of building a Palladian villa, and here was someone who had actually done it! He contacted George and they started an e-mail correspondence, mostly about their mutual love of traditional building. A year later—in May 2009—George and Jerry were in New York on their annual outing to celebrate coincident birthdays. It was an opportunity for Reid and George to meet. Despite the difference in their ages—George was fifty, Reid was thirty—they hit it off.

Later that summer, Reid and Sally drove to Charleston for a week-long visit. They stayed in Jerry's guest apartment. "I was amazed by George's own house, and the little village that he and Jerry had created on Tully Alley and Charles Street," says Reid. "I loved how it had evolved, where drive-under arches had been filled in, entrances had been reoriented, George's brother's house as a walled-off paradise, and the web of little apartments that seemed to subsidize the whole venture. That's what really fascinated me; not only the artistic spirit and quality architecture, but the economic basis for it all. They were having fun making art *and* making a profit."

George introduced Reid to Andrew, and showed him their latest projects on Ashley Avenue. Reid wasn't impressed by the Blue House, but he loved the solid construction of Andrew's house. He told George and Andrew about his dream of building a Palladian villa. There was a vacant lot behind Andrew's house—only thirty by thirty-six feet. It was "landlocked" with no direct access to the street, so it wasn't expensive. "I didn't consider buying it immediately," says Reid. "I was financially a

---

* I was the author of the article, "Palladio in the Rough," which I wrote shortly after Shirley and I first met George. It was originally intended for *Vanity Fair,* but appeared in *American Scholar.*

bit stressed at the time—that year I actually worked door-to-door for the U.S. Census. But I started to think about building a house in Charleston. I didn't need a lot of pushing as it was already in my mind, and much closer to the front than to the back. The fact that this was the city I had always gravitated toward sealed the deal."

Over the next year, Reid revisited Charleston, and he and George e-mailed back and forth. Reid learned about the costs of financing and building a small house. He also corresponded with the owner of the landlocked lot, who turned out to be willing to sell. Reid made some rough sketches of a house. They were based on a building he had seen in Charleston, the parish house of the Circular Congregational Church, designed by Robert Mills in 1806. The parish house was a little Palladian temple with four tall Doric columns and curved exterior stairs leading up to the main floor. Reid's project seemed to be moving ahead nicely, until he ran into a major snag. The zoning board ruled that the land-locked lot was too small to build on and turned down his application for a building permit. "I was devastated," he says.

George and Jerry felt bad about Reid's setback. The land across from the Blue House was zoned for three small lots, and Jerry offered to sell Reid the center lot, as well as a tandem parking space, for the same price as the landlocked lot—$65,000. The new lot was even smaller, only six hundred square feet, which would require a redesign, and it was also more challenging because the house would be sandwiched between two buildings. Was it possible to design a Palladian villa in the form of a row house? Earlier that year, Reid had accompanied George to an exhibit on Palladio at the Morgan Library in New York. The show featured many of the master's original drawings as well as plaster models of selected build-ings. One of these was the Villa Saraceno, Palladio's smallest villa, only four rooms and a central hall. Its dominant architectural feature was an extremely simple entrance loggia—three arches at the top of a broad exterior stair. Reid was intrigued by the possibility of adapting the Villa Saraceno to the Ashley Avenue site. The entire villa itself was much too large, but the loggia alone could serve as a model.

Reid had imagined his house as a small, one-story building, a sort of garden pavilion. "In my mind that would have been cheaper and sweeter. But in an urban context it made no sense." George, who was

Andrea Palladio's Villa Saraceno in Finale de Agugliaro, c. 1548.

helping Reid with the design, convinced him that having extra rooms to rent would help pay for the construction. The usual practice in Charleston was to locate rental rooms on the first floor, beneath the main house, but because there was insufficient room for a grand Palladian stair, the three-arch facade would occupy the first floor, and any additional rooms would have to be on the second floor. The resulting plan was dictated by the tight dimensions of the site, only thirty-four feet wide and seventeen feet deep. The first floor contained a single large room, its small size offset by a fourteen-foot ceiling. The second floor had two connected guest rooms, each with a bathroom and kitchenette; their windows faced the rear so as not to disturb the main facade. It was Reid who had the idea for two staircases, one on each side of the house. Two staircases in a house this small sounds excessive, but it meant that each bedroom could have its own front door and be used separately or together. The arrangement also allowed the building to be converted into a two-bedroom house if the need arose. When the design was finished, Andrew drew up the construction drawings. The BAR review was uneventful. "Everyone likes a Palladian villa," Reid joked.

Reid Burgess's miniature Palladian villa was modeled
on the loggia of the Villa Saraceno.

By this time, Reid was living in Charleston full-time. He had rented
a room and was regularly driving up to New York to see Sally, or she
would fly down to visit him. Reid's first task was to secure a construction loan. This was right after the recession, and lenders were leery of an
unemployed mandolin player—he was turned down by twenty different
banks. It was only thanks to Sally, who was employed and able to qualify
for a loan, that they secured a construction loan that converted to a five-
year adjustable-rate mortgage once the house was built. Not ideal, but it
meant construction could start. In June 2011, they broke ground.

Reid liked the solidity of Andrew's house, and he wanted similar reinforced cement–block walls. The structure of the second floor was framed in wood: exposed four-by-six pine joists supported on ten-by-ten beams. A second-floor structure of wooden joists reduced noise transmission from the rooms above. The interior of the main room was finished in poplar boards; the exterior of the house was stuccoed and painted gray. After much experimentation, Reid decided on a mixture of white, mushroom, and a color called Elephant. Andrew came up with an ingenious detail, using century-old bricks to create keystones over the arches and stringcourses. The pediment and the cornice were made of bricks laid in dogtooth courses, which gave the impression of rustic classical dentils.

George helped Reid with the planning, and Andrew prepared the drawings and refined the details. The presence of three designers inevitably produced frictions. "Sometimes George and Andrew effectively overruled me," says Reid. The most dramatic difference of opinion concerned the size of the frieze. In classical buildings, the frieze is the middle portion of the entablature. George and Andrew wanted a wide frieze; Reid thought it should be narrow. This was an occasion when he was overruled. Visiting the building site the following day, he saw the wide frieze going up and was very unhappy with the result. "I had a meltdown," he says. "I waited until the workers left at the end of the day, and I went up on the scaffolding and attacked a course of block with a sledgehammer." The next day he calmed down, the damage was repaired, and the wide frieze stayed. "It made George and Andrew happy, so I went along with it," says Reid.

For Reid the stakes were high: this was not simply a building project, it was his dream house. "Since I was fifteen or sixteen I had the idea of creating personalized beauty in the world, maybe even creating my own world," he said. "I think this came from a deep dissatisfaction with reality. That said, I'm not one of those people who feels oppressed and has a self-righteous need to heal the world. I just want to achieve my dream and see it through." Perhaps he didn't want to heal the world, but he was interested in sharing his dream. While the villa was being designed, Reid posted a short animated video on YouTube showing his project; the soundtrack was a 1932 British music-hall tune, "Underneath the Arches." He also started a blog that followed the day-to-day construction of the house. The blog, which he called "The Smallest Palladian Villa in the World," included this heartfelt declaration.

> Every town needs a castle.
> Every castle should be built by that same spirit that pulls kids into the woods to put up a tree fort. It doesn't need to be elaborate, ornate, or expensive. It should be richly built from things that were scraped together and sparks of creativity nourished by sweaty work.

A year later, Reid's castle was complete. Although it was less tall than either Andrew's house or the Blue House, it had an undeniably monumental presence, like a Roman triumphal arch. Modern architects stress originality, so copying a facade by a long-dead master might seem odd. Yet architects across the ages have found inspiration in Palladio: Inigo Jones in the seventeenth century, Colen Campbell and William Kent in the eighteenth, Stanford White in the nineteenth, Robert A. M. Stern in the twentieth. We have seen that Jefferson and Mills both looked to Palladio, as did the Irish architect James Hoban when he designed the White House. In most cases, what they made were not literal copies but evocations, similar to the way that musical composers might take an earlier theme as inspiration, or jazz musicians might rework an old standard. When Chet Baker and Gerry Mulligan play "My Funny Valentine" we first recognize Richard Rodgers's melody, but soon it is just Baker and Mulligan we hear.

Once completed, the tall room accommodated a double bed, a café-size dining table with two chairs, an easy chair, and a velvet-covered chaise longue, the last a gift from George. Folding doors in the back wall concealed a miniature kitchen whose nine-foot counter included sink, stove, oven, and refrigerator and freezer drawers. A door on the opposite side led to the bathroom with a shower tucked under the stair. Reid was influenced by George's practice of reusing found materials. The old bricks of the fireplace mantelpiece were recovered from the site when the foundation was excavated; the battered-looking doors at each end of the room were rescued from the trash; the worn Persian rugs were from the attic of an old Charleston mansion. The atmosphere was both homey and grand. The three arched openings, the beamed ceiling, and the proportions of the tall room were Palladian; the rest was Reid's dream world. With a little help from his friends.

While Reid's house was being built, another house was under construction next door. It was for Mary Turner, Jerry's sister. She no longer lived on Tully Alley. A decade earlier, she and her husband had moved to Ireland. Seven years later, divorced, she returned to Charleston and was now living in the Blue House. She was not in the best of health. Years earlier, she had been diagnosed with HIV. Long-term AIDS survivors are often afflicted with disabling neurocognitive disorders that can be accompanied by memory loss and mental slowness, as well as motor dysfunctions characterized by clumsiness and poor balance. Jerry and George decided that Mary needed a home that would better accommodate her disabilities.

They chose the lot immediately next to Reid's villa. George and Andrew built both houses at the same time, which meant that operations such as excavation, pouring concrete, and building masonry walls could be combined. Mary's house was for a single person, but it was still a tight fit on the tiny twenty-by-twenty-four-foot lot. The first floor was occupied by a carport—a zoning requirement—and a guest room. George estimated that the rental income would cover Mary's taxes and insurance. A stair led up to the second floor. A stair is not ideal for someone with physical challenges and it was designed to accommodate an electric lift, although Mary didn't want it installed until it was absolutely necessary. Her living accommodations were on the second floor. The third floor contained a bedroom and bathroom intended for a live-in caregiver, if—or rather when—that became necessary.

George paid a lot of attention to the interior. His elderly father lived in an assisted-care facility. "These places are so remarkably unergonomic that I get the impression the designers didn't bother to talk to or even observe an older person before putting their drawings on paper," George said. "It's not a money problem, just lack of interest in the people for whom the buildings are designed." He was determined to do bet-

ter. He observed Mary performing various household chores. He kept a
notebook and a tape measure handy. He noticed that she had problems
handling pots and pans, occasionally involuntarily releasing her grip.
"A drop of even two inches can cause quite a mess when frying bacon,"
he said. To allow Mary's bent elbow to remain at a comfortable ninety
degrees, he lowered the kitchen cooktop. For the same reason, the sink
and the countertop were two inches higher than normal. Because she
had trouble keeping her balance when bending over, he installed refrigerator and freezer drawers at waist height; a cabinet-like wine refrigerator was at eye level. Crouching down nearly always resulted in falling
over, so he eliminated low cabinets and made the dishwasher a drawer
that could be loaded without bending over. "Designing for aging in place
and for folks with special physical needs is not difficult," said George.
"The trick is to not call attention to the unusual features."

Mary's bathroom was designed to her specifications, with a walk-in,
sit-down tub and a bidet. The immediately adjacent space, which served
as a dressing room, included a washer-dryer opposite the closet to min-
imize carrying laundry through the house. The bedroom was separated from the living room by seven-foot-wide sliding panels. "It's very
depressing to be stuck in bed in a small room," says George. "If Mary
becomes bedridden, the main floor can visually be transformed into one
large space by opening the panels." The bedroom above had similar sliding panels that gave a measure of privacy, but would allow a caregiver to
see—and hear—what was going on below.

Hospitals and retirement homes seem too often to be designed
for the convenience of the medical personnel—or the janitorial staff.
George's thoughtful modifications underline the need for the designer to
put himself in the shoes of the user and imagine life from that different
perspective. Designing for the elderly—or the handicapped—involves
more than just accommodating wheelchairs. The experience of light and
space and materials, which is the foundation of architecture, may be
even more important when a person is confined, let alone bedridden.

Mary was delighted with her new home. By the time the house
was finished she was no longer able to drive and so used the carport as a
shaded sitting area. Her balance and motor coordination improved, but
her dementia worsened, and eventually she had to be hospitalized. "She

The interior of Mary Turner's house was an exercise in special-needs design.
The carport resembles a medieval undercroft.

had been close to death on at least four previous occasions and always
bounced back from the brink," said George, "but no such luck this time."
She died two years later.

Mary's house is one of George and Andrew's most accomplished
projects. The two-story living room provides a feeling of expansive space
to the small interior. A double range of tall windows overlooks the water
oak and the Blue House. The glazed wall includes a striking interior
detail: the windows are separated by half-round Tuscan pilasters, made
from columns that George salvaged years earlier. Their unpainted wood
grain resembles zebra skin. The wooden walls are painted a restful minty
color called Spring Green; the firebox and hearth of the plastered fireplace are made of old bricks. On the exterior, the arched carport looks
like a medieval undercroft, and the tall stepped gable with its large vertical windows reminds me of the house in Johannes Vermeer's *The Little*

Street, although the Charleston house is yellow ochre stucco rather than red brick. The Dutch allusion was more or less accidental. The kitchen was required to cantilever over the alley to allow cars to pass below. "I designed it like an oriel, and since there was no glazing required I added permanently closed shutters, to make sense of it," says Andrew. "That led the house in a Late Gothic style direction, English or Dutch, early seventeenth century. It was a way of framing a narrative to help keep the language of the building internally consistent." The wooden oriel is supported by carved timber brackets and painted blue, and the closed shutters give it a slightly mysterious appearance.

Despite George and Andrew's successful collaboration, New World Byzantine had not worked out quite as they had anticipated. They still worked together on specific projects, but increasingly as independent consultants rather than as partners. There were several reasons. One was their approach to business: George was pretty casual about finances, but Andrew liked things to be organized. This was partly a difference in temperaments, and also a difference in situations. Andrew was a family man with growing responsibilities—he and Julie had just had a second child. Moreover, George and Andrew's interests were diverging. George was starting to think about what he called "semiretirement," while Andrew was devoting more time to his religious projects. He was not only designing churches, but had started a studio that produced liturgical accessories: furniture, candlesticks, vigil lamps, and chandeliers. The work was done by Andrew and his assistant, Tom Podhrazsky, a graduate of the American College of the Building Arts, and by a network of collaborating carvers, woodworkers, and iconographers. One of these commissions was for the Greek Orthodox Cathedral of the Annunciation in Baltimore: three stasidia, or choir stalls, a rotating music stand, and a pair of icon stands. The heavy oak pieces, fabricated by Bruno Sutter, fitted seamlessly into the nineteenth-century Victorian interior.

Reid's stay in his dream house was brief. After a month he moved to an inexpensive rooming house and rented out the ground floor of the villa as well as the two upstairs rooms. Under Jerry and George's influence,

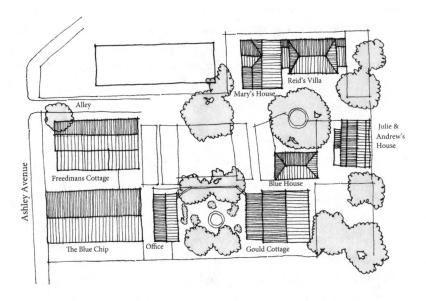

Reid's Villa

Mary's House

Alley

Julie &
Andrew's
House

Ashley Avenue

Freedmans Cottage

Blue House

The Blue Chip

Office

Gould Cottage

The Ashley Avenue compound, which grew piecemeal over eight years,
is an example of organic urbanism.

he was becoming a rentier. "I needed another project that would bring
in more income," he says. The opportunity turned out to be the decrepit
two-story house on Ashley Avenue that Jerry had bought the year before.
Jerry lent Reid the money for the purchase price, and Mark Gould
financed much of the renovation cost because the old house, which overlooked his garden, was such an eyesore. "The loan from Andrew's dad
provided most of the capital needed, and he held the first mortgage," says
Reid. "Jerry had the second mortgage. The rest of the capital came from a
line of credit from my parents, who took an equity line on their house."
    "I thought Reid needed experience in renovation," says Jerry.
"There are a lot more unknowns than in new construction, and there
are always surprises." 264 Ashley Avenue was no exception. The house
had a curious history. It had been built as a freedman's cottage in the
1890s. Sometime in the 1930s, it had been raised up and a lower story
added. The upper piazza had long ago been enclosed, so the building
resembled a simple two-story house. The exterior had been altered in

the 1960s—the second-story walls were covered in yellow vinyl siding, and the cement block had acquired a faux-stone veneer. The first floor, which included a front room, a kitchen, and a pantry, was a restaurant and social club. Reid found an old illuminated Coca-Cola sign in one of the back rooms; it read "The Blue Chip." Later he met a longtime resident of the neighborhood who remembered his father and some of the "old guys" getting together at the Blue Chip in the 1960s.

The first step of Reid's renovation was to remove the vinyl siding and faux-stone veneer. Under the siding, the wood clapboard was still in place, much of it in reasonable condition, but the cement block walls and the foundations turned out to be in poor shape and needed to be replaced. This required jacking up the whole second floor ten feet in the air and supporting it on steel beams while new foundation footings and cement block walls were built underneath. George, who was helping Reid with the planning, restored the side piazzas, which effectively turned the cottage into a single house. He reconfigured the interior as three rental units, two studio apartments on the first floor, and a three-bedroom apartment—with a bedroom in the attic—on the second floor. Each of the units had a separate entrance.

Reid economized wherever he could. He reused much of the exterior siding. He was able to save many of the old interior doors, and at a salvage yard he found three French doors complete with jalousies that had somehow made their way to Charleston from Cairo, Egypt. He hung old lighting fixtures in the piazzas and gave the floor of the lower piazza a lively pattern by having oyster shells scattered over the fresh cement, a traditional Lowcountry detail. Although this would be a rental building, he didn't want the units to feel generic. The front studio apartment was flooded with light from three sides; the rear apartment had a built-in Jeffersonian bed alcove; the tall ceiling of the upstairs apartment extended to the underside of the roof, the rafters exposed. Andrew, who prepared the construction drawings, designed ogee arches over some of the door openings and a distinctive frame for the front door.

The Blue Chip project, completed in 2013, took slightly less than twelve months. As Jerry had anticipated, Reid learned a great deal. "My contractor had a drug problem and actually disappeared halfway through construction," Reid says. "I was forced to finish the job and pay the subs myself. This turned out to be stressful but a good learning experience." Reid had no difficulty finding tenants, young professionals or graduate students from the nearby medical university. "The upstairs tenants have always been young couples, some expecting a child, who needed the extra space, obviously well-off judging from their fancy cars. Most have been new to Charleston, here for career reasons." A small one-room apartment in Cannonborough rented for as much as $1,000 a month, and Reid was pleasantly surprised by the cash flow. In due course, with a history of successful rental income to show the bank, he was able to refinance the house with a conventional mortgage and repay Mark Gould, Jerry, and his father. At the same time, he refinanced the Palladian villa, too.

"The Blue Chip project brought me a degree of financial stability that, combined with the cash flow from the villa, allowed me to think about other projects," said Reid. He and Sally had discussed settling down in Charleston. She was contemplating a career change, taking a degree in social work at the College of Charleston, with an eye to working with disadvantaged children. Where would they live? Sally wanted a garden, Reid needed space for his grand piano, and they both required a measure of privacy that the tiny Palladian villa could not provide. That meant a larger house, but the two lots remaining on Jerry's Ashley Avenue property were both very small. The vacant lot next to George's house on Charles Street was an option, but that was too expensive, even with the income from one or two rental rooms. Little did Reid and Sally imagine that the answer to their problem lay under their very noses.

THIRTEEN

Urban Ergonomics

"Passing under an arch, through a shared
courtyard, you enter your private cortile"

Lewis Mumford once wrote of a group of buildings that they were like "contending dinner-table opinions taking concrete architectural form in an amusing array of politely incompatible, argumentative, but elegantly phrased buildings." This could well serve as a description of the eccentric houses on Ashley Avenue: the no-nonsense freedman's cottage, the demure Blue House, Andrew's severe gambrel-roofed watchtower, Mark and Diane Gould's romantic cottage, Reid's miniature villa, and Mary's quaint Dutch house with its stepped gable and old-fashioned undercroft. Mumford was alluding to a village in remote North Wales. No flinty hamlet, it is a picturesque assembly of vividly colored buildings on a seaside site and has been compared to Portofino. A very eclectic Portofino: Arts and Crafts and Jacobean houses and a Gothic gatehouse stand cheek by jowl with white-washed Cotswolds cottages, whose clay-tiled roofs are punctuated by a Rococo steeple and a Renaissance campanile. There is no attempt at stylistic consistency.

What Mumford called a "fantastic collection of architectural relics and impish modern fantasies" was constructed between 1925 and 1975 by the architect Clough Williams-Ellis. Williams-Ellis was largely self-taught. He left architecture school after one semester, following complaints that he was using the premises as his private office—like his hero, Edwin Lutyens, he got his first commission when he was still a teenager. His career was interrupted by the Great War, in which he served with distinction. In the interwar years he became a successful designer of country houses. It was the waning days of the Edwardian country-house era, whose weekend rituals Williams-Ellis described: "At large country house parties it would be tails and white ties again for dinner, but after the ladies had retired (picking up their silver candlesticks and lighting them in the hall in the less technologically advanced houses) the men would be apt to change into dinner jackets before settling down to their cigars and whisky in smoking or billiard room." A very different time.

Williams-Ellis was an unconventional sort of society architect. He renovated grand country estates and also championed the use of rammed earth as an inexpensive rural construction material. He built an exuberant Spanish Colonial church in Belfast that would have looked more at home in Southern California, and also edited an influential book on environmental conservation with contributions by John Maynard Keynes and E. M. Forster. He was an early critic of urban sprawl, which he decried acerbically in *England and the Octopus* (1928). "I was always more interested in group architecture than in individual structures," he told an interviewer. He hankered to build an entire village, and because no one commissioned him, he decided to do it for himself. "I resolved to purge my passion somewhere."

"Somewhere" turned out to be North Wales. From a distant relative he acquired a rural property that included a rundown country house on a hillside facing the Dwyryd estuary and the spectacular Snowdonia Mountains. "I wanted to show that one could develop and, indeed, exploit even a very beautiful place without defiling it and that, if you did things with sufficient care and skill, you could even enhance what was given as a backdrop." Because he was not wealthy, his architectural manifesto needed a practical foundation. "If I wanted a village it would have to have an economic basis," he explained, "and the obvious thing seemed to be tourism." To Williams-Ellis in 1925, tourism didn't mean the general public but rather his London friends—Keynes, Forster, Bertrand Russell, H. G. Wells, George Bernard Shaw. He converted the crumbling house into a country hotel, renovated several cottages, added others, and invited a group of chums for a gala weekend. "The party went like a bomb," he recalled—and Portmeirion was born.

Portmeirion—he invented the name—began life as an upper-class holiday retreat, an "exclusive sort of Shangri-la," as Welsh writer Jan Morris called it, a place for "toffs and celebrities of one sort and another, actors and dukes, philosophers and playwrights." Morris was not exaggerating—visitors included Charles Laughton and Elsa Lanchester, the future Edward VIII, Noël Coward, and King Zog of Albania. The clientele changed after the Second World War as holiday travel became increasingly popular among the general public. Williams-Ellis welcomed day-trippers and charged an admissions fee that enabled him to build even more. Visitors appealed to his pedagogical side—demonstrating how architecture could touch the human spirit. For the same reason he had no objection to his village being used as the setting for a popular television series, *The Prisoner,* although he insisted that the location not be identified until the final episode.*

Williams-Ellis spent fifty years enlarging Portmeirion, although the bulk of the village was completed by the early 1960s, when Mumford saw it. Many of the buildings had practical uses—a hotel, rental cottages, shops, staff housing—but every now and then the architect would allow himself a flight of fancy. The result, as he put it, was "calculated naïvetés, eye-traps, forced and faked perspectives, heretical constructions, unorthodox colour mixtures, general architectural levity, and all the rest of it." The village was not what would later be called a theme park—it was too eclectic for that—although as in a theme park the aim was visual delight rather than historical verisimilitude. The buildings were traditional because that was Williams-Ellis's taste, and his inspiration came from far afield—he was an inveterate traveler—which explains the dazzling array of styles. Underlying his whimsy was the conviction that "architectural good manners are also ultimately, good business."

There was another side to Portmeirion. At about the same time as Albert Simons was rescuing architectural fragments in Charleston, Williams-Ellis was doing the same in Wales, creating what he drolly

* A freshly minted graduate in 1967, I was a devotee of Patrick McGoohan's surrealistic spy-thriller, although I had no knowledge at that time of either Portmeirion or its maker.

referred to as "a home for fallen buildings." Jacobean paneling and a
magnificent barrel-vaulted plaster ceiling salvaged from a Welsh country house demolition were incorporated into the so-called Town Hall,
a building used for concerts, dances, and exhibitions. Round iron
grills salvaged from John Soane's demolished Bank of England covered a window; a bomb-damaged eighteenth-century Gothic colonnade
from Bristol was painstakingly rebuilt on the village green. Williams-
Ellis was pragmatic: the upper half of a huge red sandstone chimney
piece, designed by the great Scottish architect Richard Norman Shaw,
was turned into the facade of a Pantheon-like building that had no real
function, other than remedying what its maker called Portmeirion's
"dome-deficiency." Williams-Ellis admired some of the early International Style buildings he had seen in Holland and designed a curvilinear
Moderne dining room for the hotel, but he shared Simons's antipathy
to modernist architecture. "There seems to be so little to it," Sir Clough
Williams-Ellis (he was knighted late in life) told an interviewer in 1973,
only five years before his death at ninety-four. "If only [architects] could
descend from their high abstractions to the level of ordinary human-
ity and give us something to enjoy and to look at, life would be much
pleasanter!"

Reid and Sally visited Portmeirion just before he moved to Charleston to start work on their Palladian villa. Reid remembered, "We spent
two days there. I felt inspired by Williams-Ellis's optimism and deter-
mination to create his own cluster of buildings in that fantastical style. It
made me want to put into action his hypothesis that development needn't
be a stain on the earth, that it could be a positive addition on the landscape." Reid discovered a kindred spirit in the maverick British architect.
Williams-Ellis once described his work at Portmeirion: "I have the great
advantage here of being land-owner, developer, contractor, architect,
clerk-of-works and paymaster and we all get on wonderfully together."
That was precisely Reid's role: he made design decisions, oversaw their
implementation—and paid the bills. After building his Palladian villa,
and renovating the Blue Chip, he felt ready to tackle something bigger.
Not a single building, a group.

Reid and George often talked about doing such a project together.
Having put so much effort into Mixson, George was keen to try out his

medieval planning idea. He and Reid decided to form a partnership whose services would encompass not only architecture and urban design but the entire development process. They called their company Urban Ergonomics. The applied science of ergonomics is concerned with fitting the workplace to its human user—whether it's a computer operator's station or a farmer's tractor cabin. In George and Reid's sense it meant "shaping, sizing and grouping buildings to enhance human interactions and optimize energy use."

The experience of leasing the houses on Ashley Avenue convinced Reid that there was a demand in Cannonborough for very small homes. "This seemed like the right location for me," he says. "The community had walkability, nearby amenities, reasonable real estate prices, and neighbors who were tolerant of development." He and George started making rough sketches of village-like clusters, although without a site their plans remained vague, more like elaborate doodles. Meanwhile, Reid had not given up on building a house for himself and Sally. He estimated that they would need about two thousand square feet of space. "I realized that the only way we could afford a large downtown lot was to make it a part of a commercial development. That would subsidize our house as well as creating a place to our liking—our own Portmeirion." Thus the two projects—a housing group and his own house—came together.

There were few large empty lots in Cannonborough. The obvious choice was the double lot next to the Ashley Avenue compound, immediately behind Andrew's house. Facing adjacent Bogard Street, it was almost twice as large as Jerry's property. The vacant lot was currently rented by a landscape supplier who used it for storing topsoil, peat moss, and other gardening materials. "I had my eye on that property even before buying the small parcel for my Palladian villa," said Reid. "My father visited Charleston while I was planning the villa, and I remember him saying, 'You have to get that land.' But I didn't have a plan at that point; it was only a dream."

The owner of the Bogard Street property was prepared to sell; the asking price was $540,000. "I didn't have the money," said Reid. "I spoke to some investors but it was obvious that they would push me out once we had bought the land." He spent several months looking for financing, but to no avail. Afraid that the lot would be sold to someone else, he dug into his savings and put down $10,000 in return for a six-month option. To raise the purchase money he turned to a close friend and high school classmate, David Coles. They had been neighbors in Brooklyn, and Coles had joined Reid in Charleston and was currently studying marine biology at the College of Charleston; he and Reid lived in the same boarding house. Coles had recently come into an inheritance, and he joined Reid and Sally as a partner in a development company—they called it Reverse Sprawl—and in December 2013 they closed on the Bogard Street property.

"I often dreamt of getting those neighboring lots, but I never thought it would happen," Jerry told me. "When the Bogard Street property came on the market, my sister and mother were declining and I needed all my time and energy to offer them the care and attention they deserved. If the opportunity had presented itself ten years earlier, I would have pursued it. I'm delighted that Reid managed the purchase, and I'm glad to pass the torch to him and George. They'll finish properly what I started."

Reid and George worked on the plan together. Its main feature was a new street running the length of the site. It would be wide enough for a car but basically a pedestrian way, the sort of narrow street that was common in the old Italian towns they both loved. "There is no Orvieto or Pienza in the United States, so why not build one?" said Reid, referring to two Renaissance towns famous for their small-scale urbanism. He had another Italian example in mind: in Rome, he had discovered the Arco degli Acetari in the *centro storico*. The Vinegar Makers' Arch is a medieval courtyard surrounded by picturesque houses with exterior staircases and balconies, and walls painted in vivid tones of red, burnt orange, and ochre. Reid imagined something similar. "You lean out your window and see a building across the lane. . . . Passing under an arch, through a shared courtyard, you enter your private *cortile*." "Leaning out your window" might seem like an odd starting point for a real estate venture, but projects such as the garden cities of North Charleston and Forest Hills Gardens in Queens began with a similarly hazy vision.

Reid and George saw the new street as Sitte-esque, irregular, not quite straight, drawing you into the site. The biggest challenge was to accommodate Reid and Sally's house, whose bulk could easily overwhelm its smaller neighbors. The solution was to conceal the house from view by surrounding it with the other buildings. It would be invisible from the street—a secret place.

The new street and the narrow pedestrian passages that gave access to some of the houses would be defined by the buildings themselves; except for Reid and Sally's house, there were no gardens, only terraces and balconies. The zoning in Cannonborough allowed 50 percent lot coverage and four stories of height. The site was barely a hundred feet wide, so creating variety meant shifting houses a few feet from side to side, or turning them a few degrees. "I did some paper cutouts based on house sizes I knew would work, and played with these for months," George told me. He and Reid discussed views and windows, and such details as the location of electricity meters, trash cans, mechanical equipment, and parked cars. The neighborhood zoning required two parking spaces per unit. "I would have preferred fewer parking spaces," said George, "but asking for a variance was a battle we couldn't win, and in the process we would have lost the goodwill of the neighborhood, and every subsequent step in the approval process would have become more difficult." He accommodated parked cars in a variety of ways—in private garages and carports, beneath terraces, and next to the street. When the plan was complete, there were ten houses in all. The new street angled and narrowed as it went deeper into the site, until it reached a tiny plaza, which connected to the existing alley coming from the Ashley Avenue compound. It was Sally who came up with a name, bringing together her love of felines and Reid's musical avocation: Catfiddle Street.

In 2015, two years after Reid purchased the Bogard Street property, he was ready to embark on the permitting process. The first step was to request that the city planning board rezone the land as a Planned Unit Development, or PUD. A PUD is a regulatory tool that allows a city to designate a selected area as a special zoning district. The advantage of a PUD to the city is that it makes allowances for deserving projects without altering regulations or setting precedents for anyone else. The advantage to the developer is that the house lots are owned individually ("fee sim-

George's plan of Catfiddle Street with the Ashley Avenue
compound on the left.

ple," in common law), which makes them easier to market than properties with joint ownership.*

In addition to Reid's ten lots, the Catfiddle PUD included the seven
houses in the Ashley Avenue compound as well as Jerry's two unbuilt
lots. Jerry, Andrew, and Andrew's parents were happy to join in, because
Catfiddle Street would give them a second means of access from Bogard
Street, and belonging to a PUD meant that they could advantageously
refinance their properties. Since Andrew's parents had not built a second
house on their lot, they were able to transfer the zoning permission to
Reid, in exchange for an easement on Catfiddle Street that would allow
Andrew to enlarge his house to accommodate his growing family, which
now included baby Tryphon. Reid had also convinced three immediate
neighbors to join the PUD. One was Judith Aidoo, an African American
lawyer who owned a vacant house on Bogard Street in which her mother
and grandmother had lived. Joining the PUD meant that her deep lot
could be subdivided into two additional lots. The other two neighbors
owned properties at the north end of the site facing Kennedy Court,
which was important to Reid because the properties provided car access
to the Crosstown Expressway. The entire PUD now encompassed twenty-
four lots on almost one acre.

In a PUD, zoning regulations are tailored to the individual project. "We established our own height limit," Reid said. "The neighborhood restriction at that time was fifty feet, but George and I didn't want
anything taller than the chimney of Andrew's house, which was forty-
two feet." Precisely defined setbacks allowed the buildings to be tightly
grouped. "We designated where there would be streets and passages, and
where we could have encroachments on public areas such as balconies
sticking out over the street. We also made extensive use of surface ease-
ments to allow for things like vehicular access beneath elevated portions
of buildings, and pedestrian tunnels underneath houses." The resulting
plan resembled a jigsaw puzzle. "The Catfiddle layout is the most complicated urbanism I've ever done," said George.

Catfiddle Street was a small project with large ambitions. "Our pri-

---

* In projects such as Tully Alley and Jerry's development on Ashley Avenue, houses were owned
individually, but the land itself was owned in condominium. Lenders are generally stricter with
this type of arrangement, which makes it slightly less desirable to homebuyers.

mary purpose is to create a sociable, beautiful and green urbanism by combining durable buildings with a comfortable density, which we feel results in a harmonious living environment," wrote Reid and George on their Urban Ergonomics website. "Density doesn't need to mean high rises." Housing density is generally measured in dwelling units per acre, although this can be deceptive since a "unit" may be a studio apartment or a four-bedroom house. A typical suburban subdivision with houses on quarter-acre lots has a net density (not including roads and public open space) of four units per acre; I'On, with its smaller lots, increased this to ten units per acre. By comparison, when it is finished, the Catfiddle PUD will have a density of about twenty-six units per acre. Since the Blue Chip and the Blue House include several apartments, and some of the new houses will probably have rented rooms, the effective density will actually be closer to forty units per acre. The homes in Catfiddle will have their own front doors and sense of identity, providing a model for how urban neighborhoods can densify without elevators and expensive construction, while maintaining a comfortable human scale.

The zoning change required to create a PUD involved a series of public reviews by the relevant city boards and the neighborhood association. It was a lengthy and arduous process. "I've been very busy helping Reid withstand the torture being inflicted upon him by the city," George wrote to me in an e-mail. "Reid is young and doesn't understand it when he's treated unfairly by a city official who is using his project to get revenge on a former boss. The creativity of bureaucrats is actually amazing as is their ability to research and locate archaic and inane regulations to bring up at the last minute and create further delays. Sadly, Reid will eventually have to learn how to fight this nonsense since it's part of getting lovely things built in this town."

It took more than a year to get approval for the Catfiddle PUD. Fire protection was a key issue. The normal street width requirement for fire truck access was twenty feet plus space for a turnaround; in some places, Catfiddle Street was only ten feet wide. The fire marshal approved the narrow street as long as the houses were sprinklered. "We also needed to demonstrate that there were existing hydrants within four hundred feet of where fire trucks would be stopped," said Reid, who was obliged to commission flow tests on the fire hydrants. "The project had to be compact enough that fire hoses carried from a parked truck reached all the nooks and crannies of the houses." He regularly recalculated the cash flow of his project to meet such additional costs. A developer's financial obligations are divided into "soft" and "hard" costs. Soft costs include legal, engineering, and architectural fees, city-mandated transportation studies, and soil tests; hard costs include not only the cost of the land but also the cost of building streets, and underground power, water, and sewer infrastructure, the so-called site improvements. The most expensive site improvement on Catfiddle was the storm-water retention system. The low-lying Charleston peninsula was prone to serious flooding during storms, and the city had recently mandated that any project with more than three dwellings retain rainwater on-site, so that it could later be released slowly into the storm sewer, which required giant underground tanks, catch basins, and control boxes. "This was hands down my least favorite frustration of the entire project," said Reid.

While Catfiddle Street was going through the approvals process, Reid and George finished working on the design of Reid and Sally's home; because their house would be surrounded by the other lots, it would have to be built first. The house would be inward-looking, and because Sally wanted a garden, the obvious solution was some sort of courtyard. Courtyard houses were the first urban dwellings. The remains of one of the oldest known human settlements, seventh-millennium BC Jericho, include mudbrick houses consisting of rectangular rooms grouped around a central court. The ancient cities of Egypt, Greece, and Rome consisted primarily of courtyard houses, as did cities in dynastic China. The courtyard type survived in European cities in the form of the Renaissance palazzo and the Parisian *hôtel particulier,* and continues to be the common urban dwelling in Latin America and the Middle East. Now, as in the past, a courtyard house combines privacy and security in a compact form that allows close-packing in tight urban conditions. And there is a modern advantage: because a courtyard house shares walls with its neighbors, it is extremely energy efficient.

It was George who came up with the idea of raising the courtyard.

A ground-level courtyard surrounded by tall houses would be dark, he reasoned, so why not raise it up one story? The first floor under the house could be used for a guest apartment, a garage, and storage; the space immediately beneath the courtyard would be filled with earth, like a huge flowerpot, to allow for tree planting and gardening. The courtyard would be approached by an exterior public stair that would also provide access to neighboring houses. The stair would be located deep inside the block and reached by a covered passage—just as Reid had imagined.

The design of the courtyard was influenced by a visit that Reid had made to Rome with George and Jerry two years earlier. "It seemed like the right time for some inspiration," Reid recalls, "and I wanted to see Rome with George and through the eyes of his many previous visits." George showed Reid one of his favorite buildings, the church of San Clemente al Laterano. This twelfth-century basilica is attached to a cloister that resembles the atrium of a Roman house. "I've always particularly enjoyed the courtyard, and the artful use of spolia really takes it to an emotional level for me," said George. "Spolia" refers to architectural components that are reused from earlier buildings, a common practice in the ancient world. The antique granite columns of the San Clemente courtyard, with their dissimilar capitals, were recycled from older buildings, as was the entablature. The result is unusual because the entablature of the side colonnades contrasts with the arched openings of the church facade, which was restored in the eighteenth century. This combination of classical and Renaissance elements appealed to Reid and George, and they incorporated it into the design of the Catfiddle courtyard, giving the loggia a tripartite arcade, and placing a freestanding colonnade along one side. Reid, taking his cue from Williams-Ellis, slightly angled the walls of the courtyard to create a forced perspective. George designed the colonnade. He used a simple Tuscan order rather than the Ionic of the original. "I thought the design would risk looking pretentious if it were too academic, so I incorporated deliberate 'mistakes' in the moldings of the colonnade entablature to suggest the use of spolia. The concrete fabricator, with whom I've worked before, was a good sport about these oddities. The effect is intended to be casual, with a relaxed, warm aesthetic, as opposed to the intellectually correct designs that many classicist architects favor today."

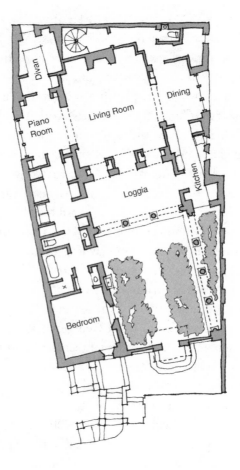

Reid Burgess and Sally Eisenberg's
courtyard house is shoehorned into an
awkwardly shaped site.

Reid and Sally's house was not visible from the street, so the BAR did not require a public review—a staff review was sufficient. The design was approved, and construction began three months later, in September 2016. The cement block walls went up first. As the space below the courtyard was being filled with earth, Reid and Sally buried a time capsule. The various items were carefully labeled and included a jar of local honey (for future archaeologists), a soft-drink can, one of Reid's bluegrass CDs, a chunk of masonry from their Brooklyn brownstone, a

New York Times article about the little Palladian villa, a Hillary Clinton campaign sticker, and locks of Sally's and Reid's hair with the message "Please clone us!"

The courtyard colonnade was complete the day I visited the construction site. It looked like an ancient artifact. Thanks to George's organic street plan, Reid's lot had an unusual shape—no two sides were parallel. Renaissance palazzos were often built on irregular sites, and Reid and George resorted to a similar planning technique: they kept the major rooms rectangular but shoe-horned the secondary rooms such as kitchen, bathrooms, and closets into the wedge-shaped leftover spaces. In some cases, the poché, as architects call the thickness of a wall, made up the difference. "Ironically, some of the secondary spaces, such as the snug divan room for watching television, which seemed like it might be a liability, are shaping up to be my favorite spaces," said Reid. The divan room was reached by going through what he called the piano room, which would house his 1910 Lester Model A grand. He and Sally wanted the piano in a separate room that could be opened up to the living room, or closed off if desired, and which would be acoustically separate from the bedroom, but not be isolated from the life of the house. The living spaces were all on one floor; a guest bedroom was upstairs.

The construction was robust. The cavities of the cement block walls were filled with concrete and reinforced; the ceilings of the main rooms consisted of timber joists resting on heavy beams. Reid had to rent a crane to put the massive beams in place. The floor of the house was a reinforced-concrete slab, to ensure acoustic and fire separation from the rooms below. There were niches and deep recesses to emphasize the thickness and solidity of the walls. Many of these details were Reid's handiwork. After the experience of building the little Palladian villa, he wanted to make design decisions himself, and he engaged Tom Podhrazsky, Andrew's assistant, to make the construction drawings. The pair discussed many of the details together, such as the wood paneling in the dressing room and the courtyard gate canopy. The house was hardly immense by today's standards—about two thousand square feet—and most of the rooms were modest in size, but they had high ceilings and ample proportions.

While the colonnade of the courtyard showed a Roman influence, the loggia had a Renaissance formality. On the other hand, the unadorned arched openings at each end of the living room reminded me of the early California architect Irving Gill. When I asked Reid to describe the style of his house, he called it "a simplified Renaissance courtyard house with elements of Charleston, the West Indies, tropical Central American, Spanish Colonial, New Orleans, Havana, and industrial warehouse, all blended together indiscriminately." This stylistic bouillabaisse was a matter of personal taste. Reid and Sally's furniture was a diverse mix that included a massive antique bookcase and Webb C. Ball's old rolltop desk. "I enjoy nineteenth-century eclecticism, and its attitude of anything beautiful goes," Reid says. "This house embraces that sort of Aesthetic movement spirit, although not necessarily its style." But the interior also reflected a modern sensibility. Media, especially movies, have blurred the distinction between past and present, and most people see no contradiction in talking on a smartphone while sitting on a rocking chair, or blending different cuisines, or combining different styles of dress. So why not mix different architectural styles? Reid and Sally's house incorporated a rich architectural narrative. Not "I am American Colonial," or "I am minimalist," but "I am here to remind you of different times and different places." When I visited the construction site, Reid was in the process of selecting a mantelpiece for the fireplace. He was leaning toward a carved stone Gothic Revival design with a pointed arch and decorative spandrels. "It will look like a piece of art rather than something absolutely architectural," he said.

The design of Reid's house was unusual: an exterior that revealed nothing about the interior; a freestanding colonnade that didn't support anything and incorporated intentional inconsistencies; walls that were thicker than they needed to be; a heavy beamed ceiling that didn't actually support the roof; a narrow, wedge-shaped kitchen that appeared at first glance like an afterthought; a leftover space behind the living room that felt like backstage. There *was* something faintly theatrical about Reid's house—things were not always what they seemed. A Baroque architect would have appreciated this legerdemain, but it flew in the face of the modernist architectural ethos that considered structural honesty and functional expression to be not only an aesthetic but also a moral imperative. Geoffrey Scott, the author of *The Architecture of Humanism,* which his friend Clough Williams-Ellis called "the best book of architectural criticism yet written," referred to this attitude as an "Ethical Fallacy."* In Scott's view, architecture could be beautiful or ugly, but not honest or dishonest. He gave the example of the false window, a common Renaissance device. "If the window, in regard to its utilitarian properties, had been wanted at that point, presumably it would have been made," he wrote. "But, on the contrary, it was—very likely—definitely *not* wanted. But its aesthetic properties—a patch of colour, shape, and position—*were* required in the design, and these I have been given." The courtyard wall that faced Reid's neighbor was blank to ensure privacy, but it was visually enlivened by four false windows.

As Reid's house was well under way, he was able to focus more on the rest of his project. The total hard and soft costs of Catfiddle Street now exceeded $1 million. "We still don't have enough capital to complete the project," he said, "and we'll be relying on some of the initial lot sales to finish the street." He estimated that the individual lots would have to sell for about $200,000, so he would need to sell at least six lots to cover the hard and soft costs; the profit would come from the sale of the last four lots. "Reid doesn't like being called a developer, but he's amazingly good at putting investors and bank loans together for what are considered risky projects," said George. "At his age that's a remarkable achievement."

* Shortly after Scott published *The Architecture of Humanism* (1914), he introduced Williams-Ellis to Portofino, which would have a major influence on the later design of Portmeirion.

FOURTEEN

Building Catfiddle

"The physical construction of the buildings
themselves cannot be separated from
the wholeness of the city"

One of George's jobs was to talk to prospective buyers about Catfiddle Street. "The project is already popular in the neighborhood," he wrote in an e-mail.

Many younger folks are in negotiations with us to buy lots. This demographic seems to value walkability, proximity to urban amenities, and social interaction more than large lots and suburban commuting, and seems very excited about our project. The total money needed will be in the range of 400K to 600K for homes ranging in size from one thousand to two thousand square feet. Many prospective buyers have complained to me that there's nothing "cool" for sale downtown in this price range and that they never thought it would be possible to participate in the design of their own small house without being rich.

The first construction after Reid's house was on two adjacent lots at the north end of the street. These belonged to his friend David Coles, who was building a house for himself and a second house for rent.

George laid out the lots and developed schematic interior plans for both houses, but he and Reid agreed that Catfiddle should not be the result of a single creative imagination, and so they put the project in the hands of Bevan & Liberatos, a small Charleston design firm.

Jenny Bevan and Christopher Liberatos were committed traditionalists, but they had arrived at their convictions by different routes. Bevan was from Virginia and had studied architecture at the University of Virginia, which, like almost all schools, followed a modernist program. "You weren't actually forbidden to design a pitched roof, but they let you know that this was simply not done today," she remembers. Modernism did not appeal to her. "When I graduated in 2005 I was confused. All I knew was that if what I was taught was architecture, then I should probably find something else to do." Her first employer was Peter Moor of Vero Beach, Florida, a traditionalist architect who opened her eyes to contemporary classicism and introduced her to the writing of Léon Krier, an advocate of traditional building. Eventually she moved to New York and got a job with Fairfax & Sammons, a leading classicist firm. That is where she met Christopher Liberatos. He was a fourth-generation Charlestonian; his great-grandfather, a Greek immigrant, had opened a restaurant on Meeting Street, opposite the grand Charleston Hotel. Christopher attended the College of Charleston, and although he was a premed student he minored in studio art, taking several drawing classes with John Michel, a local sculptor. The summer after he graduated, Liberatos had what he described as an epiphany—he realized that what he really wanted to be was an architect. When he looked into graduate programs, he discovered that many had an architecture history requirement, so the following year he enrolled in a history course at the college. Coming across a studio course in architectural design, he took that, too. In due course, he was accepted at Yale and the University of Pennsylvania, but chose the University of Notre Dame instead. Notre Dame is the unique American graduate school that teaches classical architecture. "It was the only school I visited where I saw beautiful drawings," Liberatos says. After graduating in 2001, he worked for Randolph Martz in Charleston, spent several years in Europe working for classicist architects in Paris and London, and returned to join Fairfax & Sammons in New York, where he met Bevan. In 2007, the firm, which was increasingly active in the South, decided to open a small branch office in Charleston; Liberatos and Bevan were sent to manage it. Not long after, thanks to the recession, building commissions dried up and the Charleston office was closed, but the pair decided to stay in the city and strike out on their own. While they were establishing their practice, Bevan enrolled in the University of Notre Dame's graduate program and in 2015 received a master's degree.

Like all young firms, Bevan & Liberatos took on house additions and interior renovations, small projects but thoughtfully designed with sophisticated details that had impressed Reid and George. Bevan & Liberatos's designs for the two houses on Catfiddle Street did not disappoint. They included interesting ironwork railings and cornice details, all described in beautiful hand-drafted drawings. The Coles house was in a pivotal location, bridging a lane that connected Catfiddle Street to Kennedy Court. George had sketched an arcaded entrance loggia facing the little piazza. Bevan & Liberatos expanded this into a double arch supported by a giant Doric column. The single column was a striking presence and looked like the surviving fragment of some old Renaissance palazzo. This was a more theatrical gesture than George and Reid expected, but they accepted the change—after all, a different sensibility was precisely what they wanted. The column was supported by an arch whose keystone was carved in the shape of a human head. "It was sculpted by John Michel, my friend and former drawing professor at the college," said Liberatos. "I like to think of the head as the likeness of a Lowcountry swamp god."

In short order, Reid sold two more lots. The buyer was Donna Gates, a nutritional consultant, lecturer, and author. One house was for herself, and the second was for her son. The designer of the houses was Kenny Craft, a newcomer to Charleston. He had grown up in Atlanta, studied architecture at Auburn University in Alabama, and had worked for a decade for Dover, Kohl—the co-planners of I'On—as the supervising architect of a large New Urbanist community in Colorado. Craft had met Vince Graham at a New Urbanism conference, and when he decided that it was time to open his own office, Vince encouraged him to move to Charleston and helped him get a commission for a house in I'On. He also introduced him to Reid, which is how Craft got involved in the Catfiddle project.

One of Bevan & Liberatos's houses on Catfiddle Street
includes a keystone in a human likeness.

I asked Craft what it was like to work with Reid and George. He
said that when he started, he asked Reid to show him the plans of the
other Catfiddle houses so that he could get an idea of what would be
there. Reid resisted. "I want everyone to come up with their own ideas,"
he said, and instead, he gave him images of Portmeirion as well as the
Arco degli Acetari. He also showed him old black-and-white photographs of the stage set of an early production of *Porgy and Bess:* a dense
courtyard with stairs and balconies and people leaning out of windows.
"I'd like our project to look something like that," Reid told him.

That sounded pretty vague to Craft, but when he started to design
he discovered many specific constraints. George had laid out the PUD

master plan and defined the lots in order to maximize the buildable areas and fulfill the city's parking requirements. He even sketched out plans for the houses. The drawings were crude—George is no drafts-man—but they included precise dimensions. For example, one of the houses that Craft was designing was to be fifteen feet and four inches wide, the other was nineteen feet and four inches. The heights of the eaves and slopes of the roofs were similarly detailed. Craft was also con-strained by Reid's desire for privacy, which mandated that there not be any windows in walls overlooking his courtyard.

At the end of 2015, while George was working with Craft to finalize the layout of the two houses, his own house burned down. George had his hands full dealing with that calamity, which left Craft free to plan the interiors. His client wanted sunny rooms, so he enlarged the win-dows, which made the exterior resemble an Amsterdam canal house, with more glazing than solid wall. He was used to working on house designs for New Urbanist projects, which tend to favor a traditional but rather polite architecture. Reid wanted something rougher, and sug-gested adding a rustic brick cornice, rounding off the stucco corners, and toning down some of the refined exterior moldings to make them appear more crude. Following another of Reid's suggestions, Craft gave the roofline of the smaller Gates house an asymmetrical shape—Reid called it catawampus—that recalled the eighteenth century. The exterior stucco would be finished with a silicate lime paint, a German product that George and Reid liked because it looked like an aged wash.

By 2017, a year after breaking ground, Catfiddle Street was tak-ing shape, although construction of the Coles houses was not going as smoothly as Reid had hoped. The workers tended to be from Central America, and while they were excellent masons, wood framing was new to them and they sometimes made mistakes. Liberatos was demand-ing, but he could be imperious, which irritated the contractor. Or per-haps the contractor was simply overextended. Since the Catfiddle project began, Charleston had experienced a commercial and residential con-struction boom. The activity had brought many new builders to the city, and although prices had gone up, quality and reliability had gone down. Most of the new housing was being built in the suburbs, and contractors were reluctant to take on jobs downtown, with its congested sites and demanding regulations. "It's been challenging just to get people to show up," said George. He and Andrew had done their best to help Reid, but construction has been agonizingly slow. "Everything's behind schedule," said George. Reid had experienced problems with his own house. He discovered water leaking through the wall beneath the courtyard. To find the cause, all the soil had to be removed, and because the courtyard was now completely walled-in, this work had to be done laboriously by hand. It turned out that the waterproofing system specified by the engineer had been improperly installed and needed to be entirely redone. That slipup set the work back three months.

Reid sold one of the lots in front of his house to Vince. Following his setback at Mixson and the ensuing economic recession, Vince had scaled back his development activities and concentrated on completing I'On. Some of his time was taken up with public work. Governor Nikki Haley of South Carolina had appointed him chairman of the South Carolina Transportation Infrastructure Bank, which financed highway construction. It was a controversial appointment because Vince was a proponent of reducing car dependency and building fewer highways.* In 2013, in partnership with a local real estate company, Vince got involved in a small development in Old Village, the historic center of Mount Pleasant. He had bought the property eight years earlier and held onto it during the recession. The project, named Earl's Court after his golden lab, was a small-scale version of George's medieval plan at Mixson: two dozen compact houses and several mixed-use buildings tightly grouped on less than one acre of land. Despite initial vocal opposition from the immediate neighbors, construction began the following year. Vince commissioned Kenny Craft to design one of the mixed-use buildings, and Craft was also building a house in Earl's Court for himself and his family.

"Vince's building on Catfiddle Street is intended as a rental property," said George, who, with Andrew, was designing the house. "The plan is for it to pay for itself for a decade or so and then afterward to be sold at a profit." The lot was tightly wedged in next to Donna Gates's

---

* Vince's tenure lasted only two years. When Governor Haley resigned to join the Trump administration, her replacement appointed a new chairman.

house. Vince's house had exposure on only two sides and the footprint was tiny, less than five hundred square feet, but the four stories would have to accommodate a three-bedroom unit as well as a small guest apartment on the first floor. The construction would be reinforced-cement blocks and included a loft with exposed timber framing, and interesting kitchen and bathroom details. In the present building boom, the construction bids came in very high. "Even with downtown Charleston's steep rents, it isn't easy to make the numbers work for such a high cost," said George. But he wasn't discouraged. "It's been a pet project of mine for years to show investors that quality construction yields more rent per square foot and better resale value, and that additionally annual maintenance costs are lower. Jerry and I showed that this works. It's true that our interiors are far smaller than normal but people really respond to architecture and will accept less space if they feel that a place—even a two-hundred-square-foot place—is special and different."

The house that George and Andrew designed for Vince would definitely be special: it was as small as the Blue House, but the interior was more complex. The sixteen-foot-high living room, overlooked by a loft that connected to one of the bedrooms, had three sets of tall French doors leading to a covered veranda. The first-floor apartment, with its own door off the passageway, had a built-in sleeping platform. Despite the Italian influence on the urban design of Catfiddle Street, George didn't want to re-create a Tuscan town—he wanted this house to reflect Charleston. To that end, Andrew incorporated one of the distinctive features of the city's mid-nineteenth-century domestic architecture: decorative ironwork. The transom in the archway of the pedestrian passage that led to Reid and Sally's house was ornamental wrought iron, as were the iron columns and the ornamental balustrade of the veranda that projected into the street. They reminded me of New Orleans.

Catfiddle Street would not be an architectural set piece like Mixson. The master plan was more like a musical score that the musicians—the individual house designers—would follow. But this was not chamber music; the melody left plenty of room for improvisation, and in that sense it was more like jazz—or perhaps bluegrass. The underlying theme was described by Reid in a set of general architectural principles that he provided to building owners. "Architectural variety will give Catfiddle

Houses along Catfiddle Street, designed (left to right) by Julie O'Connor, George Holt and Andrew Gould, and Kenny Craft. The master plan is like a musical score that leaves plenty of room for individual improvisation.

Street its vitality," one of them read, "but architectural harmony and quality materials will ensure the beauty of the streetscape." The emphasis was on durable construction. Doors and windows had to be wood, bricks should be either reclaimed or handmade, large expanses of brick veneer were prohibited, as was synthetic stucco.

Reid had used Vince's I'On code as a model, but he added his own requirements. Perhaps the most unusual was a demand for roughness. "Unevenness. Looseness. Rounded corners . . . if something is *too* perfect and *too* precise, it becomes precious and can become soulless." The roughness requirement sounds a lot like Christopher Alexander. "Alexander puts into words ideas that are floating around in my subconscious, and which George seems to understand intuitively," Reid told me. His emphasis on construction echoed Alexander's observation in *A New Theory of Urban Design:* "The physical construction of the buildings themselves cannot be separated from the wholeness of the city." This sounds obvious, but urban designers, especially if they are not architects, often emphasize the spatial experience of streets and public spaces as if that can be separated from the design of the buildings themselves. However, the experience of successful urban places cannot be divorced from the detailed design of the surrounding buildings. Replace Raymond Hood's soaring RCA Building with a banal glass box and Rockefeller Center is diminished. Replace the rough plastered walls and the wrought-iron balcony railings of the Arco degli Acetari with vinyl siding and plastic shutters and it's no longer the same place.

What impressed Reid about old places like the Arco was their human qualities and their longevity. These places had endured for centuries largely because of their inhabitants' affection. In Chesterton's words, they were great because people loved them. Reid shared his generation's concern for the environment, and he believed that a "green" building was one that had a long life. That meant not only using materials that aged gracefully, but also building places that people cared about—cared about enough to look after them for years to come. Or, as he put it, "Buildings and cities last a long time, so it's worth taking trouble when we build them."

In December 2017, eleven months after my last visit to the Catfiddle construction site—and five years after Reid had optioned the property on Bogard Street—his and Sally's house was finished, except for the landscaping, which would be completed the following year. "The courtyard will likely look pretty jungly, which is what we like," he said. Even empty, the house felt inviting. Reid had paid a lot of attention to the materials and details, and it showed. The floor of the entrance loggia was covered with hourglass-shaped terra-cotta tiles from Nicaragua. The doors had solid wooden shutters, called weather doors in New Orleans, which is where Reid first saw them. The living room, with its tall, timber-framed ceiling, was as impressive as a Palladian *sala*. The ceiling structure, like much of the wood in the house, was salvaged lumber: massive beams from Florida, joists from Kentucky, heart pine floors from Ohio. The large wood sliding doors that led to the piano room showed old wormholes. The nineteenth-century shutters in the bedroom had been recovered by Reid from a New York building site seven years earlier, and the salvaged transom lights over the bedroom doors were from a demolished dorm of the College of William and Mary. The presence of old materials created a different impression than one usually encountered in a brand-new house. So did the hand-plastered walls. The finished plaster had been given a lime wash and was burnished with Moroccan black olive soap—a traditional technique called *tadelakt*. "The house reeked

Reid and Sally's finished courtyard with new plantings. The colonnade
on the left was inspired by a Roman church.

of olives for a week," said Reid. "The soap seals and toughens the walls.
It also slightly yellows them so that they look almost nicotine-stained,
like a French bistro coated with years of cigarette smoke."

The interior was a combination of extravagance and frugality. The
carved stone mantelpiece for the living room proved too expensive, so
Reid and George designed a cast-concrete substitute. The living room
ceiling was sixteen feet tall, but the compact bedroom was modestly
sized. The kitchen, with a blue ceiling and yellow window frames, was
thoughtfully planned according to Sally's exacting specifications, but it
felt improvised, as if the narrow space had been used for something else
before being converted to a place for cooking. The smooth counters next
to the Bertazzoni stove were not granite or marble but hand-troweled
concrete. "The mason made the drainboard by scribing the wet cement
with a stick," Reid said. He and Sally moved in two days before Christmas. "At first the big room was a little lofty and alien," Reid e-mailed me.

"Since everything isn't unpacked we'll know better in a little while, but as we arrange our belongings it's starting to feel more familiar." They christened their house Highcourt.

Four Catfiddle lots remained unsold. Reid and George decided to finalize the plans for the lot in front of Reid's house, and in 2017 Reid hired Julie O'Connor, a local house designer who had worked on several houses in I'On. She designed a simple but attractive house with a long second-floor veranda overlooking the little piazza. Reid intended to sell the construction drawings together with the lot. "Our original business plan was to market individual lots and let people hire their own architects, which would have provided variety," he said. "The problem is that most people lack the imagination to see what might be done. In hindsight, we should have had the architectural plans prepared in advance for each of the lots." The problem was also that most homebuyers had not experienced working with an architect. I remember early house clients of mine. After many evenings spent sitting around a kitchen table discussing their requirements—and dreams—and exploring different alternatives, the husband said to me, "I had no idea that this is what an architect did."

Reid's vision for Catfiddle Street assumed a variety of houses produced by different designers. But finding architects to work on the remaining houses proved difficult. Not that there weren't talented architects in Charleston, but according to George, talent wasn't enough. "People don't realize that designing on tiny urban lots requires more time supervising the construction work and dealing with the numerous city authorities than it does doing the actual design work," he said.

Being a good designer isn't much use, unless experience with the construction process and a nimble ability to deal with frequent city issues is part of the package. Contractors are not accustomed to such complex projects, which results in frustration and battles when ordinary construction mistakes take on a life of their own. You also need to be able to diplomatically handle city inspectors and officials when they have questions. Frequent on-site availability of a project designer is key to a successful outcome. Andrew is excellent with all of the above, as is Julie O'Connor, although neither are particularly good at making the finances work on investment property design—but then nobody seems to be. Unfortunately, I'm no longer inclined to take somebody under my wing for a few years as I did with Andrew. Looking back, my happiest years professionally were when Cheryl and I had our own construction company and everything was under one roof.

The great American architect Henry Hobson Richardson is supposed to have said that the three principal considerations in the practice of his profession were: "First, get the job; Second, *Get the Job;* Third, GET THE JOB." He might have added, "Fourth, build the job," because for every design that is realized, most architects have a drawerful of stillborn projects. That was certainly true of Andrew; most of his church clients did not have the funds to build immediately, and frequently years elapsed before they were ready to start. "Finally, some of my early designs are getting built," he told me in 2017: a church for an Orthodox monastery in Ohio, and another church in North Carolina. Closer to home, he had just completed his first commercial building, a store selling wine and craft beer in Charleston's Half Mile North district. Andrew approached this project the same way he approached his religious commissions: "One of the main principles I advocate in church architecture is that all materials should be used honestly," he wrote in an article on his website. The owner of the wine store wanted a timber-frame building, and Andrew worked with Bruno Sutter again. "I began this project by saying that the timber frame should be exposed on the interior of the structure, fully expressing its skeletal structural nature, obviously doing its job of supporting the floors and roof. The exterior would be encased in a masonry shell, the perfect material for exposure to weather, a solid and fortress-like envelope around the precious and fragile goods within." The building, in a semi-industrial district on the edge of downtown Charleston, had the sturdy no-nonsense presence of a nineteenth-century pump house.

In addition to collaborating with George on Vince's Catfiddle rental house, Andrew was restoring the Bogard Street house that belonged to Judith Aidoo. In an example of reverse gentrification, joining the Catfiddle PUD allowed her to capitalize her property and renovate the old house, which had stood unoccupied for twenty-five years. "It was almost as bad as a house can get," said Andrew. He was able to save some of the interior woodwork, but the exterior cladding had fallen prey to termite and water damage and had to be completely replaced; he added a new two-story veranda at the rear. The small project was being filmed for public television by *This Old House,* which was preparing a season on historic renovation in Charleston. The film crew visited the site every few months to record the process. Andrew didn't take the filming very seriously—he didn't own a television.

Andrew's third project on Catfiddle Street was an addition to his own house. With a third child, Basil Caedmon, he and Julie needed more space. The easement that his father had negotiated with Reid allowed a raised rear addition to project twelve feet into Catfiddle Street, leaving space for parked cars beneath. The addition, which was the full height of the house, included a dining room on the second floor, a bedroom for Madalene on the third floor together with a bathroom and closet for the master bedroom, and an open attic that could be turned into a nursery or study. Andrew imagined the new wing as an addition of the 1740s, and incorporated more elaborate Baroque elements than the original house: a dining room with a vaulted ceiling and intricate wood paneling. The exterior was modeled on Andrew's favorite house in Brookline, which had beveled thumbnail wood siding with pedimented windows as well as quoins—the corner blocks of traditional masonry buildings. Wood imitating stone is an early American tradition—George Washington used it at Mount Vernon—but it is uncommon in Charleston. After his experience with his parents' house, Andrew was skittish about subjecting his design to what he saw as the vagaries of the BAR. The regulations stipulated that an owner's addition to a non-historic building needed only a simple staff review, and he insisted on that. There was no objection. The small addition, with its gambrel gable, formal details, and wood construction, was a striking departure from the more casual architecture of Catfiddle Street. "Some people aren't sure about Andrew's addition," George told me, "but I like it."

George and Andrew had been working together on another residential project for Vince. After Mixson, Vince felt he needed to econ-
omize by selling Mugdock Castle, which he was renting out while he
looked for a buyer. He moved into town and rented Jerry's old house
on Charles Street. In 2013, Vince bought the house and decided to radi-
cally reconfigure the interior. The footprint of the small house was only
twenty by thirty feet, and George opened up the first floor into a single
room, divided by Tudor arches, with a fireplace at each end. The unconventional kitchen was camouflaged as part of the living room—the sink
and induction range were housed in an island that resembled a Victorian specimen cabinet. Andrew detailed the elaborate Jacobean paneling
and built-in bookshelves. Renée Killian-Dawson, who chose the color
scheme, designed a painted chevron pattern on the ceiling that pulled
the whole thing together. There were guest rooms on the third floor;
Vince's bedroom on the second floor opened up onto a new veranda
that stretched across the entire width of the house and overlooked the
garden.

Between working on Vince's house, helping Reid on Catfiddle
Street, and doing some projects for his brother, George's semiretirement
was proving busy. He had not had time to attend to the rebuilding of
his own home. In any case, it had taken two years to resolve the insurance claim and to square things with his mortgage company. Now he felt
ready to proceed. The walls had fire damage but most were judged struc-
turally sound, so the main outline of the house would remain the same,
he told me. The domed room would be rebuilt. George had considered
filling in the swimming pool but decided to keep it, and since he needed
to replace the mechanical equipment, he turned it into a saltwater pool.
The chief architectural changes were in the wings on either side of the
atrium. What had originally been tall rooms with an attic would be converted into two stories. He was changing the wing that was once Cheryl's
apartment into an apartment for Jerry's sister, Celia. She and her husband, who lived in New York, planned to spend winters in Charleston.
George designed the apartment to accommodate Celia's osteoporosis. "I
want to create an ergonomic situation for her, put all the basic needs on
one floor, get rid of sharp corners, make the doors wider, and so on." He
was currently researching flooring that could cushion impact in case of

falls. The second floor would have guest rooms for the married children and a convertible sleeping loft for the grandkids.

The wing on the other side of the atrium would be his own living quarters—George had decided to not move back into his old apartment. "What do I need all that space for? This has become an expensive town. It seems wasteful for one person." After two years in Jerry's tiny guest apartment, he had become used to living in a small space with less "stuff." George has an ascetic side. For years he had been observing what Jerry called "monastery days"—three days a week George turned off his phone and e-mail and didn't leave the house. His new quarters would be only four hundred and fifty square feet and would include a home office; the floor above would house a small guest apartment. As for the domed room, he was thinking of renting it out as a shared office. "It's a very restful space," he said. "I think people will enjoy working in it."

George being George, there would be innovations. He was thinking of a green roof for the two new wings. A friend of his had been experimenting with soil-cement blocks, and George wanted to use the heavy material for the interior walls, to improve sound separation. "Since I no longer have a construction company, I've been trying to line up subcontractors for some of the highly specialized work," he said. "I met a good craftsman who has been doing carpentry on Reid's house and is interested in doing the wood framework for the main rooms—arches, pendentives, and the dome. I've also had success with an excellent plasterer, a friend of Chris Liberatos, who has done domes and is eager to do mine." In Charleston, a person doing work on their own home is not required to hire a licensed contractor, and after seeing the problems and delays that Vince and Reid had experienced, George was thinking he would be his own contractor. In that way, at least, he had come full circle.

FIFTEEN

Keeping Charleston

Building in a booming historic city

The City of Charleston's approval requirements were as demanding for a small infill project as for a large apartment complex. This was one of George's favorite bugbears. "It took almost two years for Catfiddle to be approved, before we were able to break ground," he said. "Reid and his partners had to shell out a million dollars before they could sell even a single lot." The lengthy and expensive process meant that Catfiddle Street could only proceed because Reid had patient partners and because current buyers were prepared to pay a significant premium for living in downtown Charleston. Bootstrap operations such as Tully Alley were a thing of the past. It was a simple matter of the economies of scale: the number of units required to amortize high regulatory costs favored larger developments—and larger developers.

George was not sanguine about the future. "In downtown areas that are zoned for large buildings, there will be only large buildings built," he said. Just such a project was taking shape only a few blocks away from Tully Alley. Courier Square, which began in 2014, consisted of eight-story apartment buildings, a five-story office block, a six-story parking garage, and storefronts lining Meeting Street. The appearance of the brick complex recalled Charleston's nineteenth-century industrial heritage and was attractively designed in a traditional manner—

Robert A. M. Stern was the architect—but it was *big*, covering half a block. What developers call mixed-use was all the rage in Charleston. An even larger project, not far from Catfiddle Street on a landfill site beside the Ashley River, had broken ground in 2016. At twenty-two acres, WestEdge was the largest real estate development ever undertaken on the peninsula. Situated adjacent to the campus of the Medical University of South Carolina, WestEdge billed itself as the future home of biomedical research labs and technology startups. Although the WestEdge website featured attractive photographs of waterfront mansions along East Battery and shops on Broad Street, traditional Charleston architecture didn't figure in the plans released by the Atlanta-based developer. The block-size multistory buildings and wide streets were in sharp contrast to the diverse and intimate urban fabric of old Charleston; it was like comparing an allotment garden to an industrial farm.

When WestEdge was finished, it would comprise more than a dozen new buildings. The architectural renderings, by a firm based in Atlanta and Washington, D.C., showed undistinguished, generic designs that would be at home in Tyson's Corner or Orange County: large expanses of glass, rows of balconies, repetitive storefronts—not a piazza in sight. The predominant building type was something called a Texas donut. This development model, which originated in Houston, consists of five- to ten-story apartment buildings wrapped around a multilevel parking structure. In WestEdge, the buildings filled the block and the large garages accommodated the cars of not only residents but also commuting office workers, shoppers, and restaurant patrons.

The Birmingham, Alabama–based construction company building WestEdge was a big international operation with offices in Houston, London, and Dubai. Christopher Liberatos pointed out to me that its slogan is "Build Anything, Anywhere." "Could it be more perfect?" he asked sardonically. He and Jenny Bevan were critical of WestEdge. "Instead of building Anyplace USA, Charleston should be building more of Charleston," they wrote on their website. To demonstrate how West-Edge could have been developed in a manner that was more in keeping with local traditions of planning and building, they showed a counter-proposal that included smaller blocks, a hierarchy of streets—some quite narrow—three-story single houses with lower outbuildings in the rear,

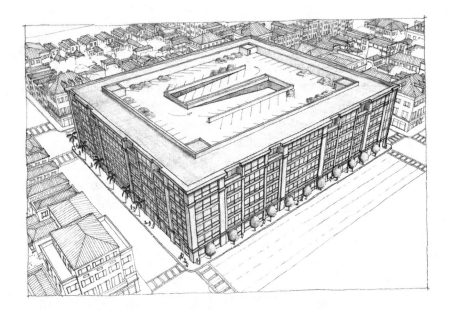

Bevan & Liberatos's study of a city block showing two options for Charleston. Option 1: More Texas donuts, apartments wrapped around a parking garage.

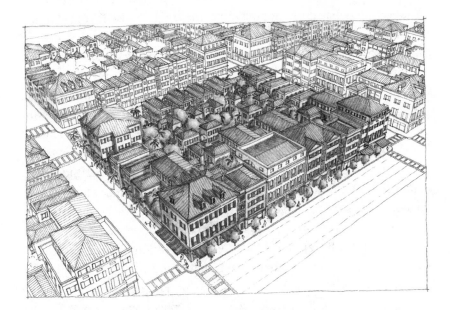

Option 2: Variety, density, and human scale, a traditional urbanism consisting of small apartment buildings and Charleston single houses.

and small four-story apartment buildings. There was even what they called a Charleston donut, a multilevel parking structure surrounded by housing units that resembled single houses. "There is room for more development in Charleston, but only if it is in keeping with the city's DNA," they wrote.

Is there really such a thing as Charleston DNA? "Everyday environments always have been highly thematic," writes the Dutch architect N. John Habraken, who has spent a lifetime studying how occupants create and modify their dwellings. "We immediately recognize a Venetian Gothic palazzo, an Amsterdam canal house, a Georgian London terraced house, or a Pompeiian courtyard house, as members of particular form families, inseparable parts of the urban fabrics that were shaped by them." Habraken's use of "thematic" has nothing to do with themed environments, the staple of so many commercial real estate developments today. He is referring to everyday buildings whose form and internal arrangement have evolved slowly over centuries and been adapted by their inhabitants to their changing needs and conditions. According to Habraken, a successful theme is capable of encompassing many variations. In Charleston, for example, the single-house theme includes grand mansions designed by architects as well as freedman's cottages built by their owners. The side yard can be a lush garden or simply a narrow driveway. On a commercial street a single house may accommodate a shop on the ground floor, or it may be a rooming house with the piazza providing convenient access; if there is insufficient space, the single house may dispense with piazzas altogether. The single-house model has even been adapted to large buildings such as the Mills House Hotel, a 1970s building whose narrow end faces the street and whose "side yard" contains a patio and a swimming pool. Whatever form it takes, the single house consistently shapes the Charleston street with an unmistakable alternating rhythm of facade, piazza, and side yard.

But wasn't Bevan and Liberatos's substitution of two- and three-story houses for seven-story apartment buildings a romantic pipe dream? Not necessarily. Because a Texas donut has single-loaded corridors, and because the parking garage occupies so much space, the net density is deceptively low, fifty to sixty units per acre (compared to forty units per acre in Catfiddle Street). Moreover, the WestEdge project draws heavily on the public purse. The city provided tax-increment financing—public subsidies based on future tax revenue increases—to pay for the expensive foundation piles required when building on landfill and for the construction of the parking structures. In contrast, the inexpensive surface parking in a conventional development such as Catfiddle Street did not require public support. Moreover, since the Catfiddle buildings left a third of the land unbuilt, such projects created a porous urbanism with spaces for trees and greenery.

Another large development project was taking shape on Broad Street, the boundary of the original historic district at the tip of the peninsula. This site had a checkered history. In the eighteenth century, fifty acres of tidal marshland were set aside by the town for public use and designated a common. Over the years, as the low-lying flats were filled in, more than half of the land passed into private hands, until all that remained was a manmade pond, a playground, and a vacant seven-acre plot. In 1949, the city sold the plot to a local developer, who used a federally insured loan to build an apartment building for lower-income tenants. At that time, the site lay outside the historic district and the jurisdiction of the BAR, so there was no oversight of the design. The Sergeant Jasper Apartments, portentously named after a local Revolutionary War hero, were a banal, fourteen-story brick slab lacking architectural refinement, or even balconies. The most that could be said in its favor was that it provided inexpensive housing for downtown workers. To everyone else it was an eyesore.

In 2014, the developer who owned Sergeant Jasper announced that the building had "reached the end of its functional life" and would be demolished. No one objected. The proposed replacement consisted of four-story residential buildings (the central portion of one rose to seven stories) containing twice as many apartments as the previous building, as well as a large supermarket. Neither the lower height nor the traditional appearance did anything to placate the neighborhood and conservation groups, who objected to the increase in numbers, the presence of a twenty-four-hour supermarket, and the resulting increase in car traffic. The public outcry was so intense that the developer withdrew his application for a PUD and instead submitted a project that simply followed current zoning, which reduced the number of apartments but allowed for taller buildings. After two successive proposals were rejected by the BAR on the grounds of incompatible massing and excessive height, the developer sued the city, claiming that the board had exceeded its authority. The judge upheld the suit, and the two sides agreed to a mediated settlement. The result was a twelve-story apartment building, a seven-story office block, and street-level shops, all wrapped around a multi-story parking structure. "It's another Texas donut," observed Liberatos, "but this one has a pool and a terrace over the garage, so perhaps it's a jelly donut."

"What went wrong?" asked the *Post & Courier.* The answer: everything. The groups opposing the PUD counted on the time-tested tactic of stalling a developer until he went away, but because the developer was local and already owned the land—which had become very valuable—he wasn't going anywhere; something was going to get built. The developer did a poor job of explaining the initial proposal and the economic rationale for his choices. The BAR, probably reacting to the public outcry, overstepped its authority. The city, concerned that the judge's ruling might invalidate the BAR altogether (the ruling would be set aside as part of the mediated settlement), was in no position to bargain. The root of the problem was an antiquated zoning regulation that had been passed when Sergeant Jasper was built and allowed extra height if a building was set back from the property line. The city had long since imposed strict height limits elsewhere, but for some reason had neglected to change the zoning on the Sergeant Jasper site. The result, as the *Post & Courier* observed, was "a new building that will be as tall as the unpopular 1950 apartments but will have a much larger footprint."

Sergeant Jasper and WestEdge were both based on the implicit assumption that large sites require large buildings. Tully Alley and Catfiddle Street teach a different lesson. There are certain large buildings, such as hospitals and concert halls, that require large sites, but residential functions can easily be accommodated on small sites. The best way to preserve the scale of a neighborhood street is not to disguise large buildings by making them look like collections of small buildings, but to actually build small buildings. A seven-acre site divided among seven builders will produce a livelier and more vibrant urbanism than a single large project by a single builder. There are special exceptions to this rule,

such as the Royal Crescent in Bath or the Palais-Royal in Paris, but on
the whole the principle holds.

Small-scale residential real estate development has a long history.
Boston's South End was laid out by the city in the early 1800s on filled-in
tidal marshland, following a plan prepared by the architect Charles Bulfinch. A protégé of Jefferson, Bulfinch introduced the first residential
squares to the city, and his plan for the South End included eight small
squares loosely modeled on London's Bloomsbury district. Although
the whole project covered more than a square mile, the building lots
were auctioned off individually or in small groups to speculative builders, who built large houses for the middle class. The new residential district prospered, but then the Panic of 1873 and the subsequent economic
depression stalled new building. In addition, competition from the
newly fashionable Back Bay caused many of the well-off homeowners to
move. Eventually, real estate values fell, the spacious mansions were subdivided into rooming houses, tenements were built, and the neighborhood became home to itinerant workers and immigrants. In due course,
the South End became synonymous with urban poverty and decay. A
hundred years later, thanks largely to historic preservation activists, the
neighborhood experienced a second demographic inversion. In time,
the old houses were renovated and converted into studios and apartments, and the South End became fashionable again. Today, the designated historic district—the largest intact Victorian neighborhood in the
country—has benefited from Boston's real estate boom, and the stalwart
brick houses are undergoing yet another round of renovation.

The South End squares remain the most desirable locations, just as
Bulfinch intended. Union Park, laid out in 1850, is a long, narrow green
surrounded by a decorative cast-iron fence. The central green functions
much the way it did when it was built. The tall houses lining each side
consist of three stories and an attic, above a double basement. A sunken
back alley provides access to the lowest floor and, today, space for parking. Built of red brick with flat and bow-fronts, the architecture is chiefly
Greek Revival, although nearby one finds contemporaneous examples of
Italianate and Renaissance Revival. The theme, in Habraken's sense, is
the result of both building regulations and shared practice: high stoops
close to the sidewalk, a tall main floor, large windows, projecting bays,

brick construction, a uniform building height, and consistent roof shapes. The twenty-four-foot-wide row houses facing Union Park have proven extremely adaptable: most have been subdivided into spacious condominiums; one house serves as a bed and breakfast; and some have even become high-end single-family homes again.*

The South End demonstrates the long-term adaptability of small buildings. Similarly, the houses in the Ashley Avenue compound include small apartments, shared accommodations, and rented rooms, and suit a variety of households: a growing family, a retired couple, young professionals, and graduate students. It is difficult to imagine this heterogeneity in a conventional Texas donut with exclusively one- and two-bedroom apartments. In fifty years, when tap-and-ride, or car-sharing, or hired self-drive cars replace private car ownership, the empty parking spaces on Catfiddle Street will easily be turned into gardens and terraces. But the low-ceilinged, dark, ramped spaces of a multilevel garage will be hard to repurpose. As for the fashionably transparent glass facades of WestEdge, they are ill-adapted to both the climate and the place. Moreover, the lightweight construction is destined for a short life, producing what Jenny Bevan in a TED talk called "disposable architecture."

"One of the reasons we did the counterproposal for WestEdge is because so many of the groups here, in particular the professional preservationists, were campaigning only on No!" Liberatos explained in an e-mail. "We wanted to show a positive vision, provide a model for what preservation ought to be doing, which isn't just saving nice old buildings but advocating for the ongoing extension of those aspects of a place that define it and that make it work. We wanted, too, to provide a method for assessing new projects according to how well they fit in with the local construction culture, the local architectural patterns, and the local urban patterns."

The debate between traditionalists and modernists in Charleston has heated up thanks to the economic resurgence of the city and the accompanying building boom. On the surface, the argument appears to revolve around the question of architectural style: traditionalists main-

---

* When subdivided into condominiums or owner-occupied units with basement rentals, the six-story Union Park houses achieve a net density approaching sixty units per acre.

tain that only certain traditional styles are acceptable, while modernists argue that since the city exhibits a variety of architectural styles, modernism is simply adding one more to the mix. The former position is questionable, for, as George and Andrew have shown, one can build perfectly satisfactory buildings in Charleston in styles that have no historical precedent in the city. On the other hand, the modernist position is somewhat disingenuous, since modernism is based on a rejection of historic architectural styles. The real problem with modernism is not its lack of historical roots, however, but its lack of empathy. Modernist buildings seem to exist in a self-contained aesthetic bubble—perhaps that's why the best examples, Frank Lloyd Wright's Fallingwater or Louis Kahn's Salk Institute, are on isolated sites. Dropped into a city, surrounded by other buildings, modernist buildings all too often appear divorced from their setting, self-contained loners rather than good neighbors.

The traditionalist–modernist debate is playing out in many older cities. The modernist side maintains that architecture is representative "of its time," and therefore that new buildings must be different—as up-to-date as a smartphone or a laptop computer. That sounds simple enough. But does that mean that every decade or two, architecture needs to be stylistically remade, like men and women's fashions? In any case, "of its time" is a slippery concept. Some periods, such as the Jazz Age or the 1960s, have a strong visual identity, but most are less sharply defined, and over time slip into obscurity. Were the 1980s really so different from the 1990s, or are both not simply part of the "late twentieth century"? The traditionalist side argues that a building should represent "its place"—that is, it should belong. I earlier quoted George C. Rogers, Jr., on Charleston: "The people came and went, prospered and went bankrupt; the rivers, beaches, and islands, the marshes, trees, and buildings remained, creating the sights and sounds, the taste, feel, and smell which lingered on for generations to absorb, savor, and love." Are taste, feel, and smell really stronger clues? Perhaps.

Preservationists occupy a somewhat contradictory position in this debate. Their movement began by saving buildings of historical significance (representing a time) but later expanded its vision to include lesser buildings that were simply part of an overall setting (representing a place). Most Charleston preservationists tend to be influenced by the

Venice Charter, which was based on the idea that architecture represents a particular historical moment, so they are ambivalent about new additions to old buildings. This has produced some curious outcomes. The Cathedral of Saint John the Baptist is a 1907 building whose spire was never completed due to lack of funds, but when it was proposed to finish the work—in 2010—the BAR insisted that the new construction had to be differentiated from the existing building, even though drawings for the original spire were available. That same year, when the Charleston County Library, an undistinguished 1960 modernist building, was slated for demolition, the Preservation Society of Charleston, which had originally led the fight *opposing* its construction, now that it was fifty years old considered it "historic" and deserving of conservation.[*]

Charleston preservationists had not had much influence on the anything-anywhere architecture of WestEdge, nor on the height and mass of Sergeant Jasper, but there were other victories. In 2012, Clemson University proposed a new building that would provide an outpost for its architecture program. (The Clemson campus is a four-hour drive from Charleston.) The downtown site was across Meeting Street from Albert Simons's College of Charleston gymnasium, a Depression-era stripped-classical building of restrained simplicity. Clemson commissioned the architect Brad Cloepfil, whose Portland, Oregon–based firm has a national reputation. Cloepfil's proposed design was uncompromisingly modernist: flat roof, glass facade, metal sunscreens, curving white concrete walls. The result was either "sleek" or "glitzy," depending on where you stood in the ensuing controversy. Reid described it as "parasitic"—that is, taking advantage of its location to draw attention to itself. The BAR, with several members abstaining, voted by a slim majority to give preliminary approval to Cloepfil's project. The opposing neighborhood and preservation groups mounted a lawsuit to stop the project on procedural grounds. Faced with such strong community resistance, Clemson backed down and withdrew its proposal. The university's alternative solution was to lease loft space in a renovated nineteenth-century cigar

---

[*] There was no popular support for saving the old library, however, and it was demolished in 2013, to be replaced by a traditional-looking hotel.

factory on the waterfront, surely a more appropriate setting if budding young architects are to learn how to build in a historic city.

Mayor Joe Riley, who was serving the final year of his three-decade-long administration, was known to favor traditional design, but he had stayed out of the Clemson debate. Later, he told an interviewer that he agreed with the outcome. "We watched the phases of design development, and it just got more harsh in its design. So much so that it just didn't work there." Riley was critical of many recent buildings in his city. "Well, they're just not beautiful," he told the *New York Times*. "The materials, the execution—you don't feel excellence there. They're not special. You don't walk by and say, 'I'm glad that got built.'" The recently overhauled Gaillard Center was more to Riley's taste. The original building had been built in 1968. It was a rare example of full-fledged urban renewal in Charleston: the city condemned three blocks of low-income housing and assembled a large site. The new building, which consisted of a civic auditorium and an exhibition space, was said to be modeled on the contemporaneous Kennedy Center in Washington, D.C.—in other words, it was an extremely large, windowless box. Set well back from the street and dwarfing its neighbors, the bulky Gaillard was out of scale and out of place. In 2010, Riley determined that it was time to make a change.

The commission was awarded to David M. Schwarz, who had a reputation for designing buildings that responded to their surroundings. Instead of demolishing the Gaillard, Schwarz set out to civilize it. He reduced its height, and, to create a more sympathetic relationship to the street, added low wings containing new municipal offices that lined the sidewalk in the manner of other Charleston buildings. He gutted the mammoth 2,700-seat auditorium and made it into a more intimate 1,800-seat horseshoe-style concert hall, reminiscent of an old-fashioned opera house. He enlarged the adjacent exhibition space and turned it into a banqueting hall that opened up to an exterior terrace. The most dramatic change was architectural: the mid-century modern concrete frame with brick infill was replaced by a classical facade. The exterior was finished in limestone stucco, a common material in Charleston, with Corinthian porticos signaling the entrances and rows of pedimented windows enlivening the municipal office wings. Schwarz introduced numerous local references: the carved capitals of the giant columns incorporated a crescent moon and palmetto from the state flag, and the interiors included decorative details derived from Lowcountry motifs such as Gullah basket weaving and yellow irises, the state flower.

Some critics found the classical design alien, but classicism has a long, unbroken history in Charleston: the Palladian Old Exchange (1767); James Hoban's County Courthouse (1792), which anticipated his design of the White House; the First Bank of the United States, now City Hall, designed by that talented amateur Gabriel Manigault in 1804; the Charleston Hotel (1838, demolished in 1960), with its imposing colonnade of giant Corinthian columns; the Gibbes Museum of Art, which opened in 1905 and was the work of Frank Pierce Milburn, a prolific architect responsible for many county courthouses and state capitols in the South; and Albert Simons's Memminger Auditorium, designed in 1938 in a stripped classical style reminiscent of his teacher, Paul Philippe Cret. The Gaillard Center was simply the latest version of a tried-and-tested local practice. Or, as Bevan and Liberatos might put it, Gaillard was in keeping with the city's DNA.

The $142 million Gaillard Center was the largest public building project of Mayor Riley's long administration, but in his penultimate year in office he bequeathed the city another legacy. In 2015, he commissioned Duany and Plater-Zyberk's firm to carry out a study of the BAR review process. The board had been established more than eighty years earlier to preserve a small historic district, but its purview now extended over four square miles. The number of projects reviewed had increased accordingly, and their nature and scale had changed over the years; instead of small modifications to historic houses they now included large developments such as WestEdge. Moreover, there was a general feeling that some of the buildings that had recently been approved could have been better, and that the overworked board needed new tools to deal with the new conditions.

Speaking to a public meeting in the packed auditorium of the Charleston Museum, Andrés Duany presented the conclusions of the study. He began with the observation that in the modern world of advertising and media, all successful cities, especially those that depended on tourism, had a particular image—he called it their brand. The brand could be food, music, or a particular natural setting. For Charleston, he said, it was architecture. Duany stressed that it was not only the historic buildings that mattered: "The essence of Charleston is not style but small buildings." Small buildings created the human scale and intimate streets that made the city special. At the same time he emphasized that large buildings such as the Mills House Hotel were also a part of Charleston's heritage. There was nothing wrong with big buildings, he said, it was a question of how they were designed. The problem with WestEdge, he said, was that it ignored the architectural language of the city and imported foreign ideas and foreign forms. Duany was not against new ideas. There was a place for avant-garde architecture, he said, just not in Charleston. That drew a big round of applause.

Duany challenged the audience on several counts. He suggested that current zoning regulations in Charleston were unrealistic and needed to be reconsidered. "If you try to make *everything* better, you inevitably end up making everything mediocre," he said. For example, he proposed that streets should be ranked according to the architectural quality of their frontages: excellent, good, and fair. No effort should be spared to preserve the quality of an "excellent" street, whereas intrusive uses, such as parking garages or long, unrelieved facades, should be located on "fair" streets. He pointed out that Charleston's well-meaning but onerous and time-consuming regulatory process effectively eliminated all but the largest developers, yet people complained when these developers built large projects. He also scolded preservation groups for becoming a "tool of NIMBY-ism," referring to the community opposition to Sergeant Jasper. Historic preservation and neighborhood activism should be kept separate, he said.

Many of Duany and Plater-Zyberk's recommendations were aimed at streamlining the regulatory process. They suggested separating the BAR reviews of large commercial developments from those of small additions and preservation projects, and creating a second board to spread the workload. They proposed more transparency. Currently, the BAR assessed projects on an individual basis, leaving applicants guessing as to exactly what was desired. Duany suggested spelling out specific design guidelines: Do this and you will get an approval quickly; do something else and it will take longer. I asked George what he thought of this proposal. He was skeptical: "My own feeling is that trying to concoct a formulaic rulebook where the outcome will somehow result in 'Charleston' is about as likely as capturing the aesthetic and emotional aspects of the *Mona Lisa* in a paint-by-number set." Andrew, less skeptical, forwarded numerous suggestions and modifications to the guidelines to the city's planning department. I tended to agree with George that architectural rules were unlikely to produce masterpieces; on the other hand, they might help outsiders who had little understanding of the nuances of building in Charleston. And increasingly it was outside developers and architects who were making their presence felt in the city.

The initial driver of Charleston's building boom was the $2.8 billion tourist industry. Ever since the 1980s, when newly elected Mayor Riley had pushed through the construction of Charleston Place, the city's first new downtown hotel in decades, tourism had flourished. The commercial downtown was revived, a cruise-ship port constructed, and a successful music festival drew even more visitors to "America's oldest city." There were now more than forty-five hundred hotel rooms, another five hundred under construction, and a dozen new boutique hotels in the pipeline. Charleston was a small city, but in proportion to its population, it had almost as many hotel rooms as that tourist mecca, San Francisco. And that did not take into account the informal short-term rentals represented by online companies such as Airbnb. Visitors were enchanted by the cobblestone streets and charming houses, the restored mansions and the historic sites. A 2016 survey of its readers by *Travel & Leisure* magazine ranked Charleston number one among "Best Cities of the World" to visit.

With its mild winters, Charleston had always attracted part-time residents, and with the revitalization of downtown their number increased dramatically. Even as the population of the peninsula was shrinking, historic houses in select neighborhoods were being bought and restored by out-of-towners. These part-time residents represented a new challenge. According to the *New York Times*, "The locals call them 'drive-by neighbors'—wealthy outsiders who restore houses to perfection but then shutter them and rarely appear, preferring to spend the bulk of their time in other homes in other cities." Thus, some of the toniest neighborhoods in the city were beautifully preserved—and eerily empty.

Was it possible to discourage part-time residency? South Carolina already levied higher property taxes on non-residents than on locals. The *New York Times* described a city-backed proposal called a Primary Residence Easement. "Under this plan, a homeowner could donate an easement—a legal right attached to the property—to the Historic Charleston Foundation, a preservation group, allowing it to prevent any owner of the house, present or future, from using it as a vacation home. The foundation could take action against any future owner who failed to follow the terms of the easement." I asked my friend Ralph Muldrow, who teaches architecture and historic preservation at the College of Charleston, if after a dozen years this initiative has worked. "I looked into the primary residence easement and was told it has been used only in a single case," he responded.

Like other beautiful old cities—Venice comes to mind—Charleston is discovering the mixed blessings of cultural tourism; unlike Venice, however, Charleston is no longer a one-industry town. In 2009, the Boeing Company announced that it was locating the final assembly and delivery plant for its new 787 Dreamliner passenger jets in North Charleston. The promise of several thousand new jobs had an immediate impact on the local economy and helped it to rebound early from the Great Recession. More recently, Volvo announced that it was building its first American plant—only twenty miles from Charleston. Thanks to such initiatives, the population of the metropolitan area has grown by 11 percent in the last five years. Charleston is experiencing growth in another field: the city is now home to more than 250 small tech companies. This represents a larger percentage of employment in information technology–related businesses than either Austin, Texas, or Raleigh, North Carolina. Part of the attraction to what Richard Florida has called the "creative class" is the city itself—its buildings, its streets, its human scale and walkability, and what Vince called the leisurely pace of Lowcountry life. In 2014, USA *Today* rated Charleston among the top fifteen "twenty-something magnet cities," and indeed between 2000 and 2012, Charleston's millennial population grew by more than 50 percent.

The advent of millennials, winter residents, and retirees, and the constant ebb and flow of downtown workers and students, has produced a rising demand for housing on the peninsula. One result is new residential construction; another is a thriving "gray market" in rented rooms. The oddest by-product is the so-called rocket house. "It's a term people here have been using lately to describe very tall, skinny infill buildings," Andrew explained. "There is no BAR oversight north of the Crosstown Expressway to prevent new houses from maxing out the fifty-foot height limit. These houses are being built by bad developers who hire bottom-of-the-barrel designers, so they look really awful."

Rocket houses have nothing to do with Charleston's architectural heritage, but what about the work of George and his friends? A Byzantine atrium, a Roman terrace, and an Italian *cortile* are not obviously Charlestonian. Yet their connection to the city's past may be more genuine than the "traditional" styles of the big commercial developments. From its beginnings, Charleston has attracted offbeat individuals, and if it really has architectural DNA, it is a quirky mixture of the conventional and the eccentric, of Georgian reticence and Italianate excess, of Palladian windows and Oriental arches. The redoubtable Beatrice St. Julien Ravenel wrote about the self-taught amateurs, contractors, and builder-architects who were responsible for the early buildings of Charleston: "The majority of them were hard-working and conscientious men, and the best were decidedly gifted. As a rule they were young . . . and something of the force of youth went into their buildings." Gifted, conscientious, youthful—all qualities shared by the protagonists of my story.

Charleston's peculiar character is above all a matter of scale. Historically, the peninsula grew in small increments—one house at a time—and the patchwork-quilt result is a major part of its appeal. Building in a manner that is sensitive to local tradition requires local experience and expertise, not likely to be found among national developers and international construction firms. Small local builders are not only more knowledgeable, they are also more flexible, and what they build is more likely to respond to changing needs and conditions, especially over time. It is also more likely to achieve that elusive but recognizable quality: *authenticity*. In a time when so many new places in the United States are resoundingly make-believe—themed restaurants and bars, even themed communities—authenticity has become a rare and prized commodity. It is what attracts the small tech firms to the upper floors of converted industrial buildings on Charleston's waterfront rather than to sterile new offices. An international apartment management company has its headquarters in a restored 1910 office building on Broad Street; a web-based software firm is in a renovated warehouse on upper King Street; and a graphic design studio occupies a refurbished single house around the corner from Catfiddle Street. Similarly, independent shops and restaurants are more likely to be found in old buildings than in the new bland—and expensive—mixed-use projects. In urbanism, small really is beautiful.

Small may be beautiful, but isn't big inevitable? As George observed, large developments seem destined to be a part of Charleston's immediate future. To attract suburban commuters to downtown stores and restaurants, the city administration is subsidizing the construction of costly multistory parking garages, which in turn requires big projects. This may turn out to be a shortsighted strategy. According to Duany, the arrival of the automobile marks a pivotal moment in the history of American cities. "The car changed everything," he told me. "There are the cities built before the automobile, and those built after—they are entirely different." Charleston obviously belongs to the former category, which is why attempts to accommodate parking are having such a disastrous effect. Not only do large parking garages drive up the cost of construction and require public subsidy—and higher rents—they also result in very large buildings whose street frontage is dominated by garage doors, access ramps, truck docks, and service bays. Not what you want in a walker's paradise. The appearance of these projects varies, from the contemporary banalities of WestEdge to the more accomplished architecture of Courier Square, but whatever their appearance, their very size undermines the main attribute of the city: its human scale. Big projects, if there are enough of them, could destroy the very things that drew people to Charleston in the first place.

The current boom is attracting outside money and outside developers and architects to Charleston, but it is the nature of booms that they do not last forever and are eventually followed by busts. When that happens, the Holy City will be thrown back on its own resources. Instead of big new projects, small local investors will turn their attention to repairing and replacing old buildings, filling up vacant lots, and filling in existing backyards. And if they look hard they will find models to follow: Tully Alley, the little compound on Ashley Avenue, and Catfiddle Street. Decades hence, very few will remember Jerry, George, Andrew, Vince, and Reid. But a Charleston guidebook of the year 2100, in addition to mentioning the venerable Joseph Manigault House and Rainbow Row, might draw the visitor's attention to less well-known local sights—a colorful Moorish house on an obscure alleyway in Elliotborough, a tiny Palladian villa hidden in a back mews, a narrow Mediterranean street with an offbeat name. The guidebook might refer to them as part of the Second Charleston Renaissance. It might even include a quote from an unnamed mandolin-playing developer-builder of that long-ago period: "Buildings and cities last a long time, so it's worth taking trouble when we build them."

Notes on Sources

Introduction

The G. K. Chesterton quote is from *Orthodoxy* (John Lane, 1909). The description of early Charleston is quoted in "A Contemporary View of Carolina in 1680," *South Carolina Historical Magazine* 55, no. 3 (July 1954). Beatrice St. Julien Ravenel's *Architects of Charleston* (Carolina Art Association, 1945) is a lively source. Ralph Adams Cram is quoted from his autobiography, *My Life in Architecture* (Little, Brown, 1936).

ONE George's House

The Auguste Perret quote is from Peter Collins's *Concrete: The Vision of a New Architecture* (McGill-Queens, 1959). Marcel Proust mentions a Fortuny gown in *Remembrance of Things Past*, vol. 5, trans. C. K. Scott Moncrieff (Random House, 1932). The Charleston single house is discussed by Gene Waddell in his comprehensive survey, *Charleston Architecture, 1670–1860* (Wyrick, 2003). Addison Mizner's life and work are described by Donald W. Curl in *Mizner's Florida: American Resort Architecture* (MIT Press, 1984); the Addison Mizner quote is from Ida M. Tarbell, "Addison Mizner: Appreciation of a Layman," the introduction to *Florida Architecture of Addison Mizner* (William Helburn, 1928). Ralph Adams Cram is quoted from *My Life in Architecture*.

TWO Tully and Charles

The 1980–2010 Charleston peninsula population change is cited by David Slade in "Racial Shift," *Post & Courier*, March 28, 2011. Alan Ehrenhalt discusses gentrification in *The Great Inversion and the Future of the American City* (Alfred A. Knopf, 2012). The racial makeup of Charleston neighborhoods is described by Robert N. Rosen in *A Short History of Charleston* (Lexikos, 1982). Ernst Hans Gombrich's essay, "The Beauty of Old Towns," appeared in the *Architectural Association Journal* in April 1965 and was republished in *Reflections on the History of Art*, ed. Richard Woodfield (University of California Press, 1987). Christopher Alexander's stimulating study, written with Hajo Neis, Artemis Anninous, and Ingrid King, is *A New Theory of Urban Design* (Oxford University Press, 1987).

THREE   The Unholy City

Samuel Gaillard Stoney was the lead author of *This Is Charleston: A Survey of the Architectural Heritage of a Unique American City Undertaken by the Charleston Civic Services Committee* (Carolina Art Association, 1944). The Stoney quote is from his *Charleston: Azaleas and Old Bricks* (Houghton Mifflin, 1939). One of the best histories of the city is *Charleston in the Age of the Pinckneys* (University of Oklahoma Press, 1969) by George C. Rogers, Jr. The foundation of the Carolina colony is discussed in detail by Thomas D. Wilson in *The Ashley Cooper Plan: The Founding of Carolina and the Origins of Southern Political Culture* (University of North Carolina Press, 2016). John W. Reps describes the Charleston plan in *The Making of Urban America: A History of City Planning in the United States* (Princeton University Press, 1965). A description of colonial Charleston's domestic architecture is contained in Alice Ravenel Huger Smith and Daniel Elliott Huger Smith's classic *The Dwelling Houses of Charleston, South Carolina* (J. B. Lippincott, 1917), whence comes the "for pleasure and for health, for business and for education" quote. Lafayette's letter to his wife is quoted by Phineas Camp Headley in *The Life of General Lafayette* (Miller, Orton & Mulligan, 1854). Richard S. Dunn is quoted on the influence of Barbados on Charles Town from *Sugar and Slaves: The Rise of the English Planter Class in the English West Indies, 1624–1713* (University of North Carolina Press, 1972). Harriet Martineau's impressions of Charleston are contained in her lively memoir, *Retrospect of Western Travel* (Saunders & Otley, 1838). Frederick Law Olmsted described his visit to Charleston in *The Cotton Kingdom: A Traveller's Observations on Cotton and Slavery in the American Slave States* (1861; repr., Alfred A. Knopf, 1970). The description of the antebellum Charleston lifestyle is from Walter J. Fraser, Jr.'s *Charleston! Charleston! The History of a Southern City* (University of South Carolina Press, 1989). I have also relied on Richard C. Wade's excellent *Slavery in the Cities: The South 1820–1860* (Oxford University Press, 1964). Thomas Gunn is quoted in Christopher Dickey's *Our Man in Charleston: Britain's Secret Agent in the Civil War South* (Broadway, 2015). Fanny Kemble's impression of the city is contained in *Fanny Kemble's Journals*, ed. Catherine Clinton (Harvard University Press, 2000). I also consulted *Writings of Hugh Swinton Legaré*, ed. Mary Legaré (Burges & James, 1845). Henry James described his visit to Charleston in *The American Scene* (Harper & Brothers, 1907).

FOUR   Loving Charleston

DuBose Heyward's *Porgy* was reviewed in an unsigned article in the *New York Times*, "A Romance of Negro Life," September 27, 1925. The Albert Simons quote on the pillaging of Charleston's antiquities is contained in Robert R. Weyeneth's interesting history of Charleston preservation, *Historic Preservation for a Living City: Historic Charleston Foundation 1947–97* (University of South Carolina Press, 2000). Alice Ravenel Huger Smith and Daniel Elliott Huger Smith's *The Dwelling Houses of Charleston, South Carolina* (1917) was one of the earliest attempts to document the city's old architecture. See also Albert Simons and Samuel Lapham, Jr., *The Octagon Library of Early American Architecture*, vol. 1, *Charleston, South Carolina* (Press of the American Institute of Architects, 1927). Susan Pringle Frost is quoted in Stephanie E. Yuhl's *A Golden Haze of Memory: The Making of Historic Charleston* (University of North Carolina Press, 2005). A good source on the Charleston Renaissance is James M. Hutchisson and Harlan Greene, eds., *Renaissance in Charleston: Art and Life in the Carolina Low Country, 1900–1940* (University of Georgia Press, 2003). Frederick Law Olmsted is quoted from *The Cotton Kingdom*. V. S. Naipaul was not entirely convinced of historically restored Charleston, which he referred to as "Toytown" in *A Turn in the South* (Alfred A. Knopf, 1989).

FIVE Palladio and Polystyrene

I described the Otranto house in "Palladio in the Rough," which appeared in *American Scholar* 75, no. 1 (Winter 2006). The Jefferson quote is from Jack McLaughlin's *Jefferson and Monticello: The Biography of a Builder* (Henry Holt, 1988).

SIX Turrets and Domes

The origins of Holy Cross Chapel are described in *Sullivan's Island Historical and Architectural Inventory* (Preservation Consultants, 1987). Cheryl Roberts's obituary was in the *Post & Courier*, November 8, 2006. Ralph Adams Cram is quoted on Rice University from *My Life in Architecture*. The interview with Andrew Gould is contained in "Reflecting the Heavenly Jerusalem: Building New Churches with Dignity and Grace," *Road to Emmaus* 17, no. 1 (Winter 2016). He describes the choros in "The Holy Ascension Choros," *Orthodox Arts Journal*, June 14, 2012, www.orthodoxartsjournal.org.

SEVEN Andrew's World

The Christopher Wren quote on Tom Tower is in Adrian Tinniswood's *His Invention So Fertile: A Life of Christopher Wren* (Jonathan Cape, 2001). The question of how to add to historical buildings is explored in detail by Steven W. Semes in *The Future of the Past: A Conservation Ethic for Architecture, Urbanism, and Historic Preservation* (W. W. Norton, 2009). Robert Venturi is quoted from "Plain and Fancy Architecture by Cass Gilbert at Oberlin and the Addition to the Museum by Venturi and Rauch," *Allen Memorial Art Museum Bulletin* 34, no. 2 (1976–77). Robert A. M. Stern is quoted from "Forum Discussion," *Harvard Architectural Review* 1 (Spring 1980). The Gertrude Jekyll quote is from *Home and Garden: Notes and Thoughts, Practical and Critical, of a Worker in Both* (Longmans, Green, 1901). George and Andrew's church conversion project is described by Robert Behre, "Former Church Converted to Homes," *Post & Courier,* November 17, 2008. Cram's description of his partner, Bertram Goodhue, is from *My Life in Architecture.* The Andrew Gould quotes are from "Mass Transfigured by Light," an interview in *Road to Emmaus* 16, no. 4 (Fall 2015). The second part of this interesting conversation is contained in "Reflecting the Heavenly Jerusalem: Building New Churches with Dignity and Grace," *Road to Emmaus* 17, no. 1 (Winter 2016).

EIGHT　The Education of a Developer

A revealing interview with Vince Graham can be found in the podcast "Call to Adventure," February 7, 2016. Charles E. Fraser was the subject of a profile in the *New Yorker* by John McPhee: "Encounters with the Archdruid, II—An Island," March 27, 1971, later published as *Encounters with the Archdruid* (Farrar, Straus & Giroux, 1971).

NINE　New Urbanism in Old Charleston

The description of Kentlands is in "Best of 1991," *Time,* January 6, 1992. The vicissitudes of the I'On project are described by David Quick in "The Jordan Tract," *Post & Courier,* February 13, 1997. John McPhee discusses Fraser in "Encounters with the Archdruid." Camillo Sitte's *City Planning According to Artistic Principles* is available in a modern reprint as *The Art of Building Cities: City Building According to Its Artistic Fundamentals,* trans. Charles T. Stewart (Hyperion, 1991). I interviewed Charles Fraser for my essay on Celebration, "Tomorrowland," *New Yorker,* July 22, 1996. Vince's observations on developers and community are from the podcast "Call to Adventure."

TEN　Townscapes

The Olmsted Brothers' report on Chicora Park is contained in the *Fifth Annual Report of the Park Commissioners of the City of Charleston, South Carolina* (Walker, Evans & Cogswell, 1901). Frederick Law Olmsted, Jr., is quoted on Forest Hills Gardens by Susan L. Klaus in *A Modern Arcadia: Frederick Law Olmsted, Jr., and the Plan for Forest Hills Gardens* (University of Massachusetts Press, 2002). A description of the planning of North Charleston is contained in Robert A. M. Stern et al., *Paradise Planned: The Garden Suburb and the Modern City* (Monacelli, 2013). The long quote from Andrew Gould about Cashiers is from his unpublished report, "Town of Cashiers" (December 2007).

ELEVEN The Monopoly Game

The history of the freedman's cottage on Ashley Avenue is contained in an unpublished report by Lissa Felzer and Frances Ford, "Analysis of 266 Ashley Avenue: A Study Conducted for Jerry Moran and George Holt" (September 2006). Felzer is the author of an interesting study: *The Charleston Freedman's Cottage: An Architectural Tradition* (History, 2008). George and Andrew's website can be found at www.newworldbyzantine .com. The American College of the Building Arts is described by Logan Ward in "A Class by Itself," *Garden & Gun*, December 2017/January 2018.

TWELVE Reid's Dream

Reid Burgess's bluegrass career is described by Barry Mazor in "King Wilkie—Monroe's Horse, Just a Different Color," *No Depression: The Journal of Roots Music*, May 31, 2007, www.nodepression.com. The article on the Otranto house that led Reid to George Holt was my "Palladio in the Rough." I describe the Villa Saraceno in detail in *The Perfect House: A Journey with the Renaissance Master Andrea Palladio* (Scribner, 2002). Reid's blog, "The Smallest Palladian Villa in the World," can be found at www.charlestonvilla .tumblr.com. For more about Reid's house, see Brooke Hauser, "In Charleston, a Palladian Villa, Preshrunk," *New York Times*, August 30, 2012.

THIRTEEN Urban Ergonomics

Lewis Mumford's article on Portmeirion, "From Crotchet Castle to Arthur's Seat," appeared in the *New Yorker*, January 6, 1962, and was republished in *The Highway and the City* (Harcourt, Brace & World, 1963). Clough Williams-Ellis's quote about country house customs is in his spirited autobiography, *Architect Errant* (Constable, 1971). Clough Williams-Ellis, ed., *Britain and the Beast* (Readers' Union, 1938), is his work on environmental conservation. Williams-Ellis described the creation of his village in *Portmeirion: The Place and Its Meaning* (Faber & Faber, 1963). Jan Morris's essay "Clough's Shangri-la" is contained in Jan Morris et al., *Portmeirion* (Antique Collectors' Club, 2006). The 1973 Williams-Ellis quote is from an interview with Peter Davey in *A Continuing Experiment: Learning and Teaching at the Architectural Association*, ed. James Gowan (Architectural Press, 1975). George and Reid's website can be found at www.urbanergonomics.com. Geoffrey Scott is quoted from *The Architecture of Humanism: A Study in the History of Taste* (Houghton Mifflin, 1914), and his visit with Williams-Ellis to Portofino is described by the latter in *Architect Errant*.

FOURTEEN Building Catfiddle

The H. H. Richardson quote is from Neal Bascomb's *Higher: A Historic Race to the Sky and the Making of a City* (Doubleday, 2003). Andrew Gould describes his design of the beer and wine store, Edmund's Oast Exchange, in "The Principles of Orthodox Architecture Expressed in a Secular Building," *Orthodox Arts Journal,* November 2, 2017, www.orthodoxartsjournal.org.

FIFTEEN Keeping Charleston

The Bevan & Liberatos counterproposal for WestEdge is described on their website, www.civicconservation.org. N. John Habraken is quoted from his website, www .thematicdesign.org. Habraken is the author of the classic *Variations: The Systematic Design of Supports* (MIT Press, 1976) and more recently *Palladio's Children: Essays on Everyday Environment and the Architect* (Taylor & Francis, 2005). Robert Behre's analysis, "Sergeant Jasper: What Went Wrong?" is in the *Post & Courier,* December 24, 2016. The history of Boston's South End is recounted by Phebe S. Goodman in *The Garden Squares of Boston* (University Press of New England, 2003). The George C. Rogers, Jr., quote is from *Charleston in the Age of the Pinckneys.* The debate about architectural styles in Charleston is described by Richard Fausset, "Stately Old Charleston, the New Buildings on the Block Are Struggling to Fit In," *New York Times,* January 23, 2015. The BAR review of the Clemson architecture building is reported by Robert Behre in "Clemson Dropping Modern Plan for Building," *Post & Courier,* November 18, 2014. Mayor Joe Riley is quoted by Wayne Curtis on the Clemson building in "How Mayor Joe Riley Shaped Charleston," *Architect* (November 3, 2015). Reid Burgess's comment about the Clemson building and the mayor's quote about recent buildings in Charleston are recorded by Fausset in "Stately Old Charleston." The creation of the Gaillard Center in 1968 is described by Weyeneth in *Historic Preservation for a Living City.* The histories of the Gaillard Center and the Charleston County Library are described in detail by David Payne in his unpublished doctoral dissertation, "Charleston Contradictions: A Case Study of Historic Preservation Theories and Policies" (Clemson University, 2013). The DPZ study of BAR is an unpublished report, "The Board of Architectural Review, City of Charleston" (October 16, 2016). Andrés Duany's March 13, 2015, presentation at the Charleston Museum is on YouTube. Charleston's hotel boom is discussed by Stephanie Hunt in "Room on the Peninsula," *Charleston Magazine,* January 2017. Charleston was ranked first in "The World's Best Cities in 2016," *Travel & Leisure,* July 6, 2016. The issue of part-time residents is described by Fred Bernstein in "Charleston: The Case of the Missing Neighbors," *New York Times,* October 22, 2004. Greg Toppo and Paul Overberg discuss Charleston's attraction for millennials in "'Post-College' Towns Brim with Youth, Jobs," *USA Today,* April 27, 2014. The admirable Beatrice St. Julien Ravenel is quoted from her *Architects of Charleston.*

Acknowledgments

One balmy Charleston evening five years ago, Vince Graham, George Holt, and I were sitting around a raised fire pit in the garden of Vince's house on Charles Street. We were drinking wine, and George, in a reminiscing mood, was telling us about the early days of building Tully Alley. "You really should write a book about this," Vince told me. Well, I have. One of the pleasures of this undertaking has been my conversations with this group of remarkable builders, hearing their stories and following their various endeavors. All were unfailingly generous with their time. Vince, whom I have known for more than two decades, not only described the ins and outs of development in Charleston and elsewhere, but also introduced Shirley and me to Frogmore stew. George was patient with my persistent questions, and detailed in his explanations, both in person and via many late-night e-mails. Jerry Moran took me through some of the intricacies of the "Monopoly game" and explained the genesis of his project on Ashley Avenue. I introduced George to Andrew Gould and watched their collaboration blossom and evolve, as all real architectural partnerships do. I am grateful to Andrew for his thoughtful and frank observations on architecture and allied subjects, and for his assistance in assembling illustrations. I was unknowingly instrumental in bringing George together with Reid Burgess, whose admirable Catfiddle Street project serves as the capstone to my story. Reid was patient with my questions and liberal with his time. I blush to mention that he christened the little Palladian house on Ashley Avenue, Villa Witold.

Several people in Charleston helped in ways small and large. Ralph Muldrow of the College of Charleston offered his personal assistance on numerous occasions, guided me around town, introduced me to the American College of the Building Arts, and kindly provided the delightful drawing that graces the jacket of this book. Jenny Bevan and Christopher Liberatos discussed their practice and provided information about their work on Catfiddle Street and about their interesting alternative to "Texas donuts." Kenny Craft took me through his construction site and took time to make a drawing of Catfiddle Street. Retired Army Lieutenant General Colby Broadwater III, president of the American College of the Building Arts, showed me around that admirable institution. Stella French organized a memorable evening at George's house not long after the fire: "Let's come together to celebrate the Byzantine phoenix rising from the ashes" read the invitation. Thanks also to Renée Killian-Dawson for her observations on Mugdock Castle and Vince's renovated house on Charles Street. My appreciation to LeGrand Elebash for his insightful comments about Mixson, and to Diane Roberts Taylor, Geoff Graham, and Jacob Lindsey.

Andrés Duany, whom I met in Seaside in 1990 and whose subsequent career I have followed with admiration, kindly provided a draft of his BAR report and discussed his general impressions. Thanks to Richard Economakis for information about his early involvement with the Holy Ascension Church. Jeremiah Eck introduced me to Boston's South End and provided useful information on Union Park. I am appreciative to Anthony Alofsin, David De Long, and Hugh Hartwell for their friendly comments on parts of the manuscript. My wife, Shirley Hallam, put up with my periodic absences and read the manuscript aloud to me, not once but twice. I offer my appreciation to my agent, Andrew Wylie, for his support throughout the ups and downs of this unusual project. It has been a pleasure to work with Katherine Boller and the people at Yale University Press.

Illustration Credits

Pages x, 37, 84,92, 127, 179, 189: Witold Rybczynski

Pages 8, 20, 35, 77, 101, 137, 138, 145, 155, 156, 158, 177: New World Byzantine

Page 13: ProfReader. File is licensed under the Creative Commons Attribution-Share Alike 4.0 International license.

Pages 29, 93, 142, 162: Andrew Gould

Page 44: From Henry Popple's *Map of the British Empire*. Library of Congress.

Page 54: Historic American Building Survey. Public Domain.

Page 55: Vernon Howe Bailey. Public Domain.

Page 61: Alice Ravenel Huger Smith drawing of Miles Brewton House, 1914. Conté crayon and pencil on paperboard. Courtesy of Gibbes Museum of Art/Carolina Art Association.

Page 73: Goingstuckey. File made available under the Creative Commons CCo 1.0 Universal Public Domain Dedication.

Page 75: Courtesy of the Virginia Department of Historic Resources.

Pages 83, 115: I'On Group

Page 114: Cdamgen at English Wikipedia. Public Domain.

Page 171: Hans A. Rosbach. Licensed under the Creative Commons Attribution-Share Alike 2.5 Generic license.

Page 172: Urban Ergonomics

Page 201: John Michel

Page 205: Witold Rybczynski, based on a drawing by Kenny Craft

Page 207: Reid Burgess

Page 215: Bevan & Liberatos

Index